Enacting Disability Critical Race Theory

This edited volume foregrounds Disability Critical Race Theory (DisCrit) as an intersectional framework that has informed scholarly analyses of racism and ableism from the personal to the global—offering important interventions into theory, practice, policy, and research. The authors offer deep personal explorations; innovative interventions aimed at transforming schools, communities, and research practices; and expansive engagements and global conversations around what it means for theory to travel beyond its original borders or concerns. The chapters in this book use DisCrit as a springboard for further thinking, illustrating its role in fostering transgressive, equity-based, and action-oriented scholarship. This book was originally published as a special issue of the journal *Race Ethnicity and Education*.

Beth A. Ferri, Ph.D., is Professor and Associate Dean for Research in the School of Education at Syracuse University. She has published widely on the intersections of race, gender, and disability, including her 2022 co-edited book (with Annamma and Connor) *DisCrit Expanded: Reverberations, Ruptures, and Inquiries (Teachers College Press)*.

David J. Connor, Ed.D, is Professor Emeritus of Hunter College (Learning Disabilities Masters Program & Instructional Leadership Doctoral Program) and the Graduate Center (Urban Education Doctoral Program) of The City University of New York, USA. He has published numerous articles, books, and book chapters.

Subini A. Annamma, Ph.D., is Associate Professor in the Graduate School of Education at Stanford University, USA. Her research critically examines the mutually constitutive nature of racism and ableism as it impacts the educational trajectories of youth in urban schools and youth prisons. She has won numerous awards and honors for her scholarship.

Enacting Disability Critical Race Theory

From the Personal to the Global

Edited by
Beth A. Ferri, David J. Connor, and Subini A. Annamma

LONDON AND NEW YORK

First published 2023
by Routledge
4 Park Square, Milton Park, Abingdon, Oxon, OX14 4RN

and by Routledge
605 Third Avenue, New York, NY 10158

Routledge is an imprint of the Taylor & Francis Group, an informa business

Introduction, Chapters 1–8 © 2023 Taylor & Francis

All rights reserved. No part of this book may be reprinted or reproduced or utilised in any form or by any electronic, mechanical, or other means, now known or hereafter invented, including photocopying and recording, or in any information storage or retrieval system, without permission in writing from the publishers.

Trademark notice: Product or corporate names may be trademarks or registered trademarks, and are used only for identification and explanation without intent to infringe.

British Library Cataloguing in Publication Data
A catalogue record for this book is available from the British Library

ISBN13: 978-1-032-46159-5 (hbk)
ISBN13: 978-1-032-46160-1 (pbk)
ISBN13: 978-1-003-38031-3 (ebk)

DOI: 10.4324/9781003380313

Typeset in Minion Pro
by codeMantra

Publisher's Note
The publisher accepts responsibility for any inconsistencies that may have arisen during the conversion of this book from journal articles to book chapters, namely the inclusion of journal terminology.

Disclaimer
Every effort has been made to contact copyright holders for their permission to reprint material in this book. The publishers would be grateful to hear from any copyright holder who is not here acknowledged and will undertake to rectify any errors or omissions in future editions of this book.

Contents

Citation information	vii
Notes on contributors	ix

Introduction 1
David J. Connor, Beth A. Ferri and Subini A. Annamma

1 Becoming, belonging, and the fear of everything Black: Autoethnography of
a Black-mother-scholar-advocate and the movement toward justice 11
Lydia Ocasio-Stoutenburg

2 *Sobreviviendo Sin Sacrificando* (Surviving without Sacrificing)—An
intersectional DisCrit *Testimonio* from a tired mother-scholar of color 27
Lisette E. Torres

3 Black families' resistance to deficit positioning: Addressing the paradox of
black parent involvement 41
Hailey R. Love, Sylvia N. Nyegenye, Courtney L. Wilt and Subini A. Annamma

4 DisCrit at the margins of teacher education: Informing curriculum,
visibilization, and disciplinary integration 58
Saili Kulkarni, Emily Nusbaum and Phillip Boda

5 Extending DisCrit: A case of universal design for learning and equity in a
rural teacher residency 75
Beth S. Fornauf and Bryan Mascio

6 *Traerás tus Documentos* (*you will bring your documents*): Navigating the
intersections of disability and citizenship status in special education 91
Lilly B. Padía and Rachel Elizabeth Traxler

7 Bringing DisCrit theory to practice in the development of an action for
equity collaborative network: Passion projects 107
Tammy Ellis-Robinson

CONTENTS

8   Global conversations: Recovery and detection of Global South multiply-marginalized bodies   123
Shehreen Iqtadar, David I. Hernández-Saca, Bradley S. Ellison and Danielle M. Cowley

Index   141

Citation Information

The chapters in this book were originally published in the journal *Race Ethnicity and Education*, volume 24, issue 5 (2021). When citing this material, please use the original page numbering for each article, as follows:

Introduction

From the Personal to the Global: Engaging with and Enacting DisCrit Theory Across Multiple Spaces
David J. Connor, Beth A. Ferri and Subini A. Annamma
Race Ethnicity and Education, volume 24, issue 5 (2021) pp. 597–606

Chapter 1

Becoming, belonging, and the fear of everything Black: Autoethnography of a Black-mother-scholar-advocate and the movement toward justice
Lydia Ocasio-Stoutenburg
Race Ethnicity and Education, volume 24, issue 5 (2021) pp. 607–622

Chapter 2

Sobreviviendo Sin Sacrificando *(Surviving without Sacrificing)—An intersectional Dis-Crit* Testimonio *from a tired mother-scholar of color*
Lisette E. Torres
Race Ethnicity and Education, volume 24, issue 5 (2021) pp. 623–636

Chapter 3

Black families' resistance to deficit positioning: Addressing the paradox of black parent involvement
Hailey R. Love, Sylvia N. Nyegenye, Courtney L. Wilt and Subini A. Annamma
Race Ethnicity and Education, volume 24, issue 5 (2021) pp. 637–653

Chapter 4

DisCrit at the margins of teacher education: Informing curriculum, visibilization, and disciplinary integration
Saili Kulkarni, Emily Nusbaum and Phillip Boda
Race Ethnicity and Education, volume 24, issue 5 (2021) pp. 654–670

viii   CITATION INFORMATION

Chapter 5

Extending DisCrit: A case of universal design for learning and equity in a rural teacher residency
Beth S. Fornauf and Bryan Mascio
Race Ethnicity and Education, volume 24, issue 5 (2021) pp. 671–686

Chapter 6

Traerás tus Documentos (you will bring your documents): *Navigating the intersections of disability and citizenship status in special education*
Lilly B. Padía and Rachel Elizabeth Traxler
Race Ethnicity and Education, volume 24, issue 5 (2021) pp. 687–702

Chapter 7

Bringing DisCrit theory to practice in the development of an action for equity collaborative network: Passion projects
Tammy Ellis-Robinson
Race Ethnicity and Education, volume 24, issue 5 (2021) pp. 703–718

Chapter 8

Global conversations: Recovery and detection of Global South multiply-marginalized bodies
Shehreen Iqtadar, David I. Hernández-Saca, Bradley S. Ellison and Danielle M. Cowley
Race Ethnicity and Education, volume 24, issue 5 (2021) pp. 719–736

For any permission-related enquiries please visit:
http://www.tandfonline.com/page/help/permissions

Notes on Contributors

Subini A. Annamma, Graduate School of Education, Stanford University, USA.

Phillip Boda, Independent Educational Researcher, Chicago, USA.

David J. Connor, Department of Special Education, Hunter College, City University of New York, USA.

Danielle M. Cowley, Department of Special Education, Department of Educational Psychology, Foundations & Leadership Studies, University of Northern Iowa, Cedar Falls, USA.

Tammy Ellis-Robinson, Department of Educational and Counseling Psychology, University at Albany, USA.

Bradley S. Ellison, Department of Special Education, Department of Educational Psychology, Foundations & Leadership Studies, University of Northern Iowa, Cedar Falls, USA.

Beth A. Ferri, School of Education Syracuse University, USA.

Beth S. Fornauf, Special Education Program, Plymouth State University, USA.

David I. Hernández-Saca, Department of Special Education, Department of Educational Psychology, Foundations & Leadership Studies, University of Northern Iowa, Cedar Falls, USA.

Shehreen Iqtadar, Assistant Professor Rowan University, College of Education, USA.

Saili Kulkarni, Department of Special Education, San José State University, USA.

Hailey R. Love, Department of Rehabilitation Psychology and Special Education, University of Wisconsin, Madison, USA.

Bryan Mascio, Department of Education, University of New Hampshire, Durham, USA.

Emily Nusbaum, Department of Education, Mills College, Oakland, USA.

Sylvia N. Nyegenye, Department of Special Education, University of Kansas, Lawrence, USA.

Lydia Ocasio-Stoutenburg, Department of Teaching and Learning, University of Miami, USA.

Lilly B. Padía, Teaching and Learning, New York University, USA.

Lisette E. Torres, Department of Academic Affairs – Cooper Foundation Center for Academic Resources, Nebraska Wesleyan University, Lincoln, USA.

Rachel Elizabeth Traxler, Teaching and Learning, New York University, USA.

Courtney L. Wilt, Department of Special Education, University of Kansas, Lawrence, USA.

INTRODUCTION

From the Personal to the Global: Engaging with and Enacting DisCrit Theory Across Multiple Spaces

David J. Connor ⓘ, Beth A. Ferri ⓘ and Subini A. Annamma ⓘ

ABSTRACT
This article serves as the introduction to a special edition of the *Journal of Race, Ethnicity, and Education* (REE) dedicated to Disability Critical Race Theory (DisCrit). We begin by sharing the seven tenets of in DisCrit, acknowledging our indebtedness to scholars of color who originally developed theories of intersectionality. Next, we discuss ways in which, from its original publication in *REE* (2013), DisCrit has gained traction as a theoretical tool that is increasingly used in research and practice. Then, we briefly summarize and comment upon the eight featured articles in this special edition. Each article has been purposefully selected to reflect a broad scope of interests – from empirical research to theoretical papers seeking changes within schools, communities, teacher education programs, research practices, and global connections. All contributions are from the USA as a way to consider ways in which DisCrit is being utilized in one country, while encouraging further intra-disciplinary, interdisciplinary, and global conversations.

We are indebted to the *Race, Ethnicity & Education* for publishing our original article *Dis/Ability Critical Race Studies (DisCrit): Theorizing at the Intersections of Race and Dis/Ability* almost a decade ago (Annamma, Connor, and Ferri 2013).[1] Dave Gillborn as editor, and the incredibly thoughtful reviewers he found, were willing to envision a theoretical framing that had not yet existed. With their support, we articulated the value of using a framework grounded in the assumption that racism and ableism are mutually constitutive and collusive – always circulating across time and context in interconnected ways. By racializing ability, and debilitating race, we sought to add a shared sibling that connected Critical Race Theory (CRT) and Disability Studies (DS), fields in which we simultaneously located our own interests, work, and scholarship. In initially articulating DisCrit, we were seeking a theoretical framework that would help to surface the interdependent nature of race and disability, particularly in (but not limited to) educational contexts. We decided to craft this framework in a series of tenets that we believed would prove useful in advancing this necessary and intersectional work. Those seven original tenets are as follows:

(1) DisCrit focuses on ways that the forces of racism and ableism circulate interdependently, often in neutralized and invisible ways, to uphold notions of normalcy.
(2) DisCrit values multidimensional identities and troubles singular notions of identity such as race or dis/ability or class or gender or sexuality, and so on.
(3) DisCrit emphasizes the social constructions of race and ability and yet recognizes the material and psychological impacts of being labeled as raced or dis/abled, which sets one outside of the western cultural norms.
(4) DisCrit privileges voices of marginalized populations, traditionally not acknowledged within research.
(5) DisCrit considers legal and historical aspects of dis/ability and race and how both have been used separately and together to deny the rights of some citizens.
(6) DisCrit recognizes whiteness and Ability as Property and that gains for people labeled with dis/abilities have largely been made as the result of interest convergence of white, middle-class citizens.
(7) DisCrit requires activism and supports all forms of resistance (Annamma et al. 2013, 11)

Within each of these tenets, we acknowledge DisCrit's intellectual lineage as one that stretches back over a century from the work of Anna Julia Cooper ([1892]2017) and W.E. B. DuBois (1920), to the litany of black feminist scholars, particularly Kimberlè Crenshaw (1989), Patricia Hill Collins (2002) and Audre Lorde ([[1980] 2020]), to more recent theorizing connecting racism and ableism in education by scholars such as Theresa Glennon (1995), Alfredo Artiles (2013), Leonardo and Broderick (2011) who influenced our thinking in profound ways. Aware of the longstanding concern about the intersection of race and ability/disability, we also saw its potential to illuminate longstanding inequities within education in the USA and, by extension, society at large (see, for example, Ferri and Connor 2005; Annamma et al. 2013). However, we were also mindful of the critiques about the absence of race and disability in both DS (Bell 2006) and CRT (Delgado and Stefancic 2001), prompting us to foreground these markers of identity particularly, but not necessarily exclusive of other forms of oppression and marginalization.

The encouraging response to that initial article in REE motivated us to publish an edited book (Connor, Ferri, and Annamma 2016), along with several journal articles and books that either individually or collectively extended our first articulation of DisCrit (Annamma 2018; Annamma and Handy 2019; Annamma, Ferri, and Connor 2018a; Connor et al. 2019). In addition, our original DisCrit article was reprinted in the canonical collection, *Critical Race Theory in Education: Major Themes in Education* (Dixson et al. 2017). As part of our own work, we have continued to document how DisCrit has traversed numerous spaces, crossing disciplinary boundaries and geographic borders (Annamma, Ferri, and Connor 2018a), broadening inquiries, expanding interdisciplinary work, to rupture the forces of racism and ableism in schools and society (Annamma, Ferri, and Connor 2018b; forthcoming).

DisCrit also developed far beyond our own work and in ways we originally could not have imagined. In a recent critical literature review, we discovered, for example, DisCrit has increasingly been used in doctoral dissertations and interdisciplinary journals that cross disciplinary boundaries and geographic borders (Migliarini 2017); critically analyze

Positive Behavioral Intervention and Supports (PBIS) in classrooms (Adams 2015); integrate simultaneous issues of race and ability into teacher education for White teachers (Beneke 2017) and teachers of color (Kulkarni 2015), and; that center the voices of disabled scholars of Color (Cannon 2019; Hernández-Saca 2017). Moreover, it has been used as a tool to better understand, and address concurrent issues of racism and ableism in early childhood education (Love and Beneke 2021) and k-12 schools (Friedman, Hallaran, and Locke 2020; DeMatthews 2020). In tracing this growth, we are struck by the ways DisCrit has been taken up, expanded upon, and used as a starting point for further creative articulations and investigations in ways race and ethnicity impact education. The ongoing expansion prompted us to propose this special issue of REE to capture some of the ways in which DisCrit is evolving.

A note on our theme

For this special issue, we wanted to feature various ways DisCrit is currently being used and adapted by scholars in critical fields of educational inquiry around issues of race, ethnicity, and disability (along with other markers of identity). In sending out a Call for Proposals, we reviewed and selected submissions with an eye toward *scope*, ultimately selecting from deeply personal pieces to projects seeking changes within schools, communities, teacher education programs, research practices, and global connections. Hence, our title *From the Personal to the Global: Engaging with and Enacting Disability Critical Race Theory Across Multiple Space*s. Having all contributions hail from the USA is a purposeful choice. Our intention is not to limit a US-centric approach to this work, but rather consider the ways in which DisCrit is being used in one country that is undoubtedly shaped by its history of racial and disability divisions that are still manifested in all aspects of society. That said, the last article titled *Global Conversations: Recovery and Detection of Multiply-Marginalized Bodies* by Iqtadar, Hernandez-Saca, Ellison and Cowley can be seen as an invitation for further dialogue and exploration of the complexities of using an intersectional approach from the Global North to address issues of race, ethnicity, and disability in the Global south. This important context has begun to be addressed by several scholars from the Global South, including Padilla's original LatDisCrit (In Press) and Sarkar, Mueller, and Forber-Pratt (In Press) cautious, thoughtful approach about the dangers of countries around the world uncritically importing Western theory without sufficiently considering their own cultural, social, historical, philosophical, and legal contexts. In sum, while we are pleased and humbled by seeing the growth of DisCrit, we are also mindful of its limitations.

In this special edition, we selected eight articles that highlight ways in which DisCrit has been taken up, expanded upon, and used as a springboard for further creative articulation, reflecting its role in fostering transgressive spaces that generate critical questions. These spaces range from the microintrapersonal, to the mesointeractional, to the macrosociopolitical, purposefully reflecting a range of authors, from established academics to emerging scholars, all of whom demonstrate ways that DisCrit has been engaged with via multiple perspectives and various positionalities. In the remainder of this introduction, we briefly comment upon each contribution, highlighting a selection of issues they raise, before ending with a series of questions designed to stimulate thinking about further possibilities of expanding DisCrit.

From the personal to the global

We begin this special edition with two highly personalized articles. In the first, *Becoming, Belonging and the Fear of Everything Black: Autoethnography of a Minority-Mother-Advocate and the Movement Toward Collective Justice*, Lydia Ocasio-Stoutenburg describes why it is impossible to compartmentalize race, ethnicity, disability, gender, and social class, within her lived experiences, and how specific intersectional viewpoints can be summoned to provide penetrating insights into our culture. Her autoethnography is that of a parent advocate, serving to counter-narrate the dominant, deficit-based discourses on race and disability she experienced in medical and educational settings as a Black mother of a child with a disability. Using 'A Black Story' to tell the 'A Back Story' of 'The Birth Story,' the author reveals how having her son led her to question a host of educational, professional, and societal norms. The centerpiece of her narrative traces her transition from being an astute observer of societal norms to becoming a fierce parent advocate. Her transformation is fueled by knowing how valuing her son – a Black male with a disability – ran contrary to widespread fears of him not fitting into prescribed norms. In rendering this self-portrait, Ocasio-Stoutenburg reveals the complex, challenging reality of being a multiply marginalized parent, spotlighting the adversarial forces that ultimately serve to galvanize her role as a parental activist, a role she also embraces in her scholarship (Harry and Ocasio-Stoutenberg 2020; Ocasio-Stoutenberg and Harry 2021).

In a second deeply personal article titled, *Sobreviviendo sin Sacrificando (Surviving Without Sacrificing)–A Intersectional DisCrit Testimonio from a Tired Mother-Scholar of Color*, Lisette Torres invites us into her world. By exploring Torres's location at the intersections of race, disability, and gender in the context of the neoliberal academy, she describes fears of how having a non-visible disability plays into stereotypic notions casting scholars of color as lazy and incompetent. She reveals how stereotype threat, imposter syndrome, and racial microaggressions are daily challenges that exacerbate the symptoms of her chronic impairment. Torres writes a powerful critique of the 'baby penalty' that continues to disadvantage females in the workforce, the culturally based and family-related expectations of Latinas, and the labor-intensive neoliberal expectations for scholarly productivity of academic institutions. Interestingly, she also writes of the difficulty in embracing the social model of disability, with its primary emphasis on disabling attitudes and barriers, when her chronic condition involves ongoing pain that requires, at least in part, a medical response. Torres's use of *testimonio* allows her to step outside of the expectations of traditional research, providing an opportunity to address both the concept of *sacrificio* (sacrificing self-interest as a female), while simultaneously identifying multiple, powerful forces that actively disable her, including standard practices within educational institutions.

Maintaining the theme of race, disability, and parents, in *Black Families' Resistance to Deficit Positioning: Addressing the Paradox of Black Parent Involvement*, authors Hailey Love, Courtney Wilt, Sylvia Nyegenye, and Subini Annamma call attention to how Black parents and their children experience marginalization within normed expectations of school-parent dynamics. They do this by problematizing traditional conceptualizations of parent involvement, illustrating ways in which school expectations and practices are based on White, middle-class norms that actively marginalize Black families. In discussing experiences of the Black parents of daughters with disabilities participating in their research, Love et al. reveal ways in which these parents resist school practices that position them and their children in deficit ways. Advocating that schools provide meaningful support rather than harsh and inappropriate discipline practices is a key priority that arises from school personnel misunderstanding or ignoring disability-related considerations, thereby unnecessarily exacerbating their child's struggles. By emphasizing support-centered versus disciplinary-centered approaches to resolving commonplace occurrences – such as a student being absent or late due to diabetes-related considerations – Black parents reframe deficit-based perceptions of their daughters with disabilities to include varying cultural considerations, including behavioral norms.

In *DisCrit at the Margins of Teacher Education: Informing Curriculum, Disciplinary Integration, and Visibilization*, Saili Kulkarni, Emily Nusbaum, and Phillip Boda take on the polarized nature of teacher education. Whereas traditionalists tend to center core practices, they illustrate how justice-oriented scholars center ideologies that become embedded within their practices. They assert that both 'positions' must consider how ideologies and practices can operate interdependently to disrupt inequities and cultivate agency among all students. Using DisCrit, they argue that practices (and the ideologies they embody) can be problematized by examining ways in which racism and ableism operate to support the normative center of schooling. In brief, the authors unpack what DisCrit's theory affords critical teacher education in general, while specifically looking at individuals with complex support needs, and the application of DisCrit in the disciplinary case of science education. In pushing the current boundaries of DisCrit, the authors initiate a critical conversation about the relationship between DisCrit, silenced perspectives of populations unaddressed in equity-focused teacher education, and new disciplinary possibilities of what they mean by justice-oriented applications of theory and practice.

In *Extending DisCrit: A Case for Universal Design for Learning and Equity in a Rural Teacher Residency*, Beth Fornauf and Bryan Mascio focus on a program that prepares teachers to work in 'high need' rural schools in the United States. The authors specifically offer a counter-narrative to the commonly held deficit lens applied to schools in rural communities. Framing work using theory and research on DisCrit and Universal Design for Learning (UDL), they share their experiences as rural teacher educators foregrounding UDL to help preservice teachers disrupt assumptions about rurality, socioeconomics, race, ability, gender identity, and privilege. Troubling aspects of UDL, the authors show how the effects of teacher influence can either sustain or challenge norms that are harmful to so many children. The authors describe how their gradual incorporation of the tenets of DisCrit helped re-think UDL and improved their own ability to support preservice teachers' critical examination of structural inequities within school practices, including norms associated with race, ability, and rurality. The authors end by offering insights into their ongoing use of DisCrit as a model, admittedly a work-in-progress, for how teachers can cultivate a transformative and liberatory framework.

In *Traerás tus Documentos (You Will Bring Your Documents): Navigating the Intersections of Disability and Citizenship Status in Special Education*, Rachel Traxler, and Lilly Padia focus on undocumented youth within special education programs. They investigate the experiences of two high school students – Fernanda and Daniel – at the intersection of disability, ethnicity, and immigration status, as the students and their families negotiate the interplay of fear, schooling, and language in their desire to pursue higher education. The authors use DisCrit to help locate historical patterns of citizenship to trace the ways in which racism and ableism, coupled with documentation status, continue to shape which bodies – verified and authenticated by which papers – are rendered deserving of access to educational opportunities. In their research, Padia and Traxler reveal ways in which students at the intersection of immigration status and disability are met with care by teachers and schools while remaining unsupported in other domains. To complicate matters, when graduating from K-12 public school systems, the support and services students were entitled to under the law cease, leave them 'eligible' for similar support and services in college, but without any guarantees of service. The authors note how even well-intended mechanisms to provide students with information about re-acquiring support at the college level for their disability can have the opposite effect when 'documents' to prove disability are confounded with documents proving citizenship.

The aforementioned articles focused on using DisCrit to capture individual disability-related experiences of scholar-authors of color, parents of children with disabilities, current limitations, and possibilities for focusing on race and disability within teacher education, creative classroom practices to engage all students, and supports for undocumented students to transition to college. The following two papers incorporate DisCrit in ways that directly resonate with these communities, albeit in very different ways.

In *Bringing DisCrit Theory to Practice in the Development of an Action for Equity Collaborative Network: Passion Projects*, Tammy Ellis-Robinson shares how she, as an academic activist, took DisCrit into her local community as 'a tool and lens' to ground critical conversations about race and disability within an interprofessional collaborative network comprising educators, community providers, and community stakeholders. The author describes building a series of collective inquiry sessions with a diverse constituency to examine issues of (in)equity. By sharing their experiences in the context of institutionalized practices in educational and community settings, participants discussed aspects of their minoritized identities including disability, race, ethnicity, language, immigrant status, gender, sexual orientation, and socioeconomic status. This collective knowledge of multiple aspects that constituted each other's identity was then used to inform planning for working with pre-service teachers' and supporting their practicum experiences. At its center, Ellis-Robinson's action-research disrupts and reduces inequities while building opportunities for expanding cultural competence and culturally responsive teaching as informed by larger and more inclusive communities of practice. Describing various community-based 'passion projects' developed by the group, all interconnected by a driving interest in cultivating equity within schools, the author exemplifies how to utilize a DisCrit approach for practical purposes to impact the lives of students, practitioners, and community members.

Finally, in *Global Conversations: Recovery and Detection of Multiply-Marginalized Bodies*, Shehreen Iqtadar, David Hernandez-Saca, Bradley Scott Ellison, and Danielle Cowley invite us to contemplate, in the form of a loving critique, the virtual absence of global intersectional disability politics in both fields of Disability Studies and Critical Race Theory. To counter this paucity, the authors advance a more global and humane, liberatory theoretical positioning of DisCrit by analyzing the human rights discourses employed by the United Nations Convention on the Rights of People with Disabilities

(UNCRPD). In citing DisCrit's emphasis on 'the social construction of race and ability . . . which sets one outside of the western cultural norms' (Annamma, Connor, and Ferri 2013, 11), Iqtadar et al. seek to push DisCrit further as a theoretical framework to account for the impact of western cultural norms and ideals as applied to non-western contexts and, in turn, local contexts within those contexts. Additionally, the authors call attention to the problematic binary between the Global South/Global North becoming further reified, generating the global racist and ableist hierarchy of western cultural norms that dominate international discourse, neglectful of the pervasive violence identified within human rights discourses.

Some concluding thoughts and questions

We would like to thank all authors in this special edition of REE who were able to contribute to this project during the challenging conditions of a global pandemic. Each article represents diverse ways in which DisCrit is being utilized in one or more areas of practice, theory, policy, and research. We close our Introduction by posing some open questions to readers, in the hope that the featured articles are not only are finite works in and of themselves but can also serve as springboards to help us think creatively about centering race and disability in our teaching and scholarship. For example, how might the irrefutable power of personal experience and the insights of life at the intersections of race, disability, and parenthood, as demonstrated by Ocasio-Stoutenberg, be included in all teacher education programs? What insights of Torres about the intersectional realities of being a Woman of Color, disabled, with the cultural demands of *sacrificio* can inform hiring practices and support offered within coveted and still overwhelmingly White academic spaces? How can Love et al.'s observations of the dissonance between school and community cultural norms be brought to the attention of school leaders and Parent Teacher Associations (PTAs) in ways that require an honest sharing of perspectives and experiences with a view to supporting multiply marginalized students, parents, and teachers? We suggest Ellis-Robinson's approach, a form of academic activism at the grass roots level, offers one compelling way forward. Culling from Ellis-Robinson's community-based collaborative experiences to date, what are other ways to connect our commitments to research, community service, and teaching? In teacher education, Kulkarni et al. raise important issues about a DisCrit grounding in the content of Science, prompting speculation about what it might look like in Math, English Language Arts, Social Studies, Art, Physical Education, and so on. It might also prompt us to ask about the relative absence of critical disability scholarship in our content- and curriculum-focused journals and publications. By critiquing a lack of attention paid to disabled students of color with complex needs, Kulkarni et al., prompt us to ask in what ways can DisCrit be leveraged to expand and improve multiply marginalized students' educational futures? Likewise, Traxler and Padila's focus on another underrepresented group in the literature – undocumented immigrant students at the interstices of disability, ethnicity, and language – asking us to consider ways in which some of the most vulnerable children and youth can be supported in maximizing their educational opportunities? At the classroom level, Fornauf and Mascio remind us of 'universals' we must be mindful of, including considering DisCrit's applicability to all spaces, including rural ones, and the importance of Universal Design for Learning (UDL) to craft learning experiences in all settings. Their article also prompts us to ask: What might a closer look at UDL, particularly from a DisCrit perspective, look like? Likewise, what happens if we apply DisCrit to other familiar concepts? Finally, Iqtadar et al. call attention to the lack of intersectional politics of race and disability in global educational contexts. They remind us of the need to critically evaluate Western ideas that are often uncritically 'imported' to global contexts in ways that can possibly hinder more than help (see, for example, Possi and Milinga 2017). Scholars who draw on DisCrit in their international work, such as Elder and Migliarini (2020), have taken up this sensitive task by sharing inclusive pedagogical methods used in the West while actively attempting to resist new forms of ideological colonialism. Prompted by Iqtadar et al., we therefore ask, how can we jointly create more shared and dialogic spaces between the Global North and South, concepts that by their very existence reify hierarchies? And how can DisCrit can be placed in service of addressing existing inequities without enacting an imperialist gaze?

In closing, we hope readers of REE will find this collection of articles to be engaging and generative. Likewise, we hope this brief constellation of questions serves as stepping stones leading to DisCrits' future growth, whether that growth is marked by depth or breadth, complexity or refinement.

Note

1. We acknowledge that Critical Deaf Theory – DeafCrit – was originated by Eugenie Geertz (2003), calling attention to audism, that is, discrimination against people who are Deaf or hard of hearing by people who are hearing. Research has been published on living at the intersections of race and Deafness (along with other markers of identity) and the complexities that involve (see, for example, Stapleton 2015). We note this distinction as in the family of 'Crit' theorizing and scholarship, DeafCrit and DisCrit evolved separately, and with different foci. While a discussion to compare both fields of study is merited, it is beyond the scope of this article.

Disclosure statement

No potential conflict of interest was reported by the author(s).

ORCID

David J. Connor http://orcid.org/0000-0002-2886-8149
Beth A. Ferri http://orcid.org/0000-0002-6789-8826
Subini A. Annamma http://orcid.org/0000-0002-8744-6456

References

Adams, D. 2015. "Implementation of School-wide Positive Behavior Supports in the Neoliberal Context in an Urban Elementary School." Doctoral Dissertation.

Annamma, S., B. Ferri, and D. J. Connor, Eds. forthcoming. *DisCrit Expanded: Inquiries, Reverberations & Ruptures*. New York: Teachers College Press.

Annamma, S., D. J. Connor, and B. A. Ferri. 2013. "Dis/ability Critical Race Studies (Discrit): Theorizing at the Intersections of Race and Dis/ability." *Race Ethnicity and Education* 16 (1): 1–31. doi:10.1080/13613324.2012.730511.

Annamma, S. A. 2018. *The Pedagogy of Pathologization: Dis/abled Girls of Color in the School-Prison-nexus*. New York: Routledge.

Annamma, S. A., B. A. Ferri, and D. J. Connor. 2018a. "Cultivating and Expanding DisCrit (Disability Critical Race Theory)." In *Manifestos for the Future of Critical Disability Studies*, edited by R. Garland Thomson, K. Ellis, M. Kent, and R. Robertson, 230–238. New York: Routledge.

Annamma, S. A., A. L. Boelé, B. A. Moore, and J. Klingner. 2013. "Challenging the Ideology of Normal in Schools." *International Journal of Inclusive Education* 17 (12): 1278–1294. doi:10.1080/13603116.2013.802379.

Annamma, S. A., B. A. Ferri, and D. J. Connor. 2018b. "Disability Critical Race Theory: Exploring the Intersectional Lineage, Emergence, and Potential Futures of DisCrit in Education." *Review of Educational Research* 42: 46–71. doi:10.3102/0091732X18759041.

Annamma, S. A., and T. Handy. 2019. "DisCrit Solidarity as Curriculum Studies and Transformative Praxis." *Curriculum Inquiry* 49 (4): 442–463. doi:10.1080/03626784.2019.1665456.

Artiles, A. J. 2013. "Untangling the Racialization of Disabilities: An Intersectionality Critique across Disability Models." *Du Bois Review: Social Science Research on Race* 10 (2): 329–347. doi:10.1017/S1742058X13000271.

Bell, C. 2006. "Introducing White Disability Studies: A Modest Proposal." In *A Disability Studies Reader*, edited by L. Davis, 275–282. Psychology Press.

Beneke, M. R. 2017. "Race and Ability Talk in Early Childhood: Critical Inquiry into Shared Book Reading Practices with Pre-service Teachers." Doctoral dissertation, ProQuest LLC.

Cannon, M. A. 2019. "Because I Am Human: Centering Black Women with Dis/abilities in Transition Planning from High School to College." Doctoral dissertation.

Collins, P. H. 2002. *Black Feminist Thought: Knowledge, Consciousness, and the Politics of Empowerment*. New York: Routledge.

Connor, D., W. Cavendish, T. Gonzalez, and P. Jean-Pierre. 2019. "Is A Bridge Even Possible over Troubled Waters? The Field of Special Education Negates the Overrepresentation of Minority Students: A DisCrit Analysis." *Journal of Race, Ethnicity & Education* 22 (6): 723–745. doi:10.1080/13613324.2019.1599343.

Connor, D. J., B. A. Ferri, and S. Annamma, Eds. 2016. *DisCrit: Disability Studies & Critical Race Theory in Education*. New York: Teachers College Press.

Cooper, A. J. [1892] 2017. *A Voice from the South: By A Black Woman of the South*. Chapel Hill: University of North Carolina Press. Retrieved June 14, 2019. Project MUSE database.

Crenshaw, K. 1989. "Demarginalizing the Intersection of Race and Sex: A Black Feminist Critique of Antidiscrimination Doctrine, Feminist Theory and Antiracist Politics." *University of Chicago Legal Forum*, 1: 139–167. https://chicagounbound.uchicago.edu/cgi/viewcontent.cgi?article=1052&context=uclf

Delgado, R., and J. Stefancic. 2001. *Critical Race Theory: An Introduction*. New York: University Press.

DeMatthews, D. 2020. "Addressing Racism and Ableism in Schools: A DisCrit Leadership Framework for Principals." *The Clearing House: A Journal for Educational Strategies, Issues and Ideas* 93 (1): 27–34. doi:10.1080/00098655.2019.1690419.

Dixson, A. D., D. Gillborn, G. Ladson-Billings, L. Parker, N. Rollock, and P. Warmingon, Eds. 2017. *Critical Race Theory in Education: Major Themes in Education*. New York: Routledge.

DuBois, W. E. B. 1920. "Race Intelligence." *The Crisis* 20 (3): 327.

Elder, B., and V. Migliarini. 2020. "Decolonizing Inclusive Education: A Collection of Practical Inclusive CDS-and DisCrit-informed Teaching Practices Implemented in the Global South." *Disability and the Global South* 7 (1): 1852–1872.

Ferri, B. A., and D. J. Connor. 2005. "Tools of Exclusion: Race, Disability, and (Re)segregated Education." *Teachers College Record* 107 (3): 453–474. doi:10.1111/j.1467-9620.2005.00483.x.

Friedman, T., A. E. Hallaran, and M. A. Locke. 2020. "Rubberbanding in a Liminal Space: Teachers Contemplate the Intersections of Dis/ability and Race in Inclusive Classrooms." *Race, Ethnicity, & Education* 1–21. doi:10.1080/13613324.2020.1753677.

Geertz, E. (2003). "Dysconscious Audism and Critical Deaf Studies: DeafCrit's Analysis of Unconscious Internalization of Hegemony within the Deaf Community." Doctoral Dissertation.

Glennon, T. 1995. "Race, Education, and the Construction of a Disabled Class." *Wisconsin Law Review* 6: 1237–1338.

Harry, B., and L. Ocasio-Stoutenberg. 2020. *Meeting Families Where They Are: Building Equity through Advocacy with Diverse Schools and Communities*. New York: Teachers College Press.

Hernández-Saca, D. I. 2017. "Reframing the Master Narratives of Dis/ability at My Intersections: An Outline of an Educational Equity Research Agenda." *Critical Disability Discourses/Discourse Critiques dans le champ du Handicap* 8: 1–30. https://cdd.journals.yorku.ca/index.php/cdd/issue/view/2267

Kulkarni, S. S. 2015. "Beliefs about Disability, Race, and Culture of Urban Special Education Teachers and Their Retention Decisions." Doctoral dissertation.

Leonardo, Z., and A. Broderick. 2011. "Smartness as Property: A Critical Exploration of Intersections between Whiteness and Disability Studies." *Teachers College Record* 113 (10): 2206–2232.

Lorde, A. [1980] 2020. *The Cancer Journals*. New York: Penguin Classics.

Love, H., and M. Beneke. 2021. Pursuing Justice-Driven Inclusive Education Research: Disability Critical Race Theory (DisCrit) in Early Childhood. *Topics in Early Childhood Special Education*, 41(1): 31–44.

Migliarini, V. 2017. "Subjectivation, Agency and the Schooling of Raced and Dis/abled Asylum-seeking Children in the Italian Context." *Intercultural Education* 28 (2): 182–195. doi:10.1080/14675986.2017.1297091.

Ocasio-Stoutenberg, L., and B. Harry. 2021. *Case Studies in Building Equity through Family Advocacy in Special Education: A Companion Volume to Meeting Families Where They Are*. New York: Teachers College Press.

Padilla, A. In Press. "LatDisCrit: Exploring Latinx Global South DisCrit Reverberations as Spaces toward Emancipatory Learning and Radical Solidarity." In *DisCrit Expanded: Inquiries, Reverberations & Ruptures*, edited by S. Annamma, B. Ferri, and D. J. Connor. New York: Teachers College Press.

Possi, M. K., and J. R. Milinga. 2017. "Special and Inclusive Education in Tanzania: Reminiscing the Past, Building the Future." *Educational Process International Journal* 6 (4): 55–73. doi:10.22521/edupij.2017.64.4.

Sarkar, T., C. Mueller, and A. Forber-Pratt. In Press. "Does DisCrit Travel? Global South and Excess Theoretical Baggage Fees." In *DisCrit Expanded: Inquiries, Reverberations & Ruptures*, edited by S. Annamma, B. Ferri, and D. Connor. New York: Teachers College Press.

Stapleton, L. 2015. "When Being Deaf Is Centered: D/Deaf Women of Color's Experiences with Racial/ethnic and D/deaf Identities in College." *Journal of College Student Development* 56 (6): 570–586. doi:10.1353/csd.2015.0061.

Becoming, belonging, and the fear of everything Black: autoethnography of a Black-mother-scholar-advocate and the movement toward justice

Lydia Ocasio-Stoutenburg (iD)

ABSTRACT

The compartmentalization of (dis)ability from race and ethnicity, and other identity descriptors serves to maintain these constructs at a safe distance from one another. Beyond these broader socially constructed categories, there are also the subtler messages about normativity that manifest in gradients of ability, color, behavior, capital, expression and power. Even more restrictive is the creation of a narrow space for parent advocacy that is culturally-subtractive and bureaucratic, serving to privilege the already privileged while silencing the marginalized. In this paper, I use autoethnography with DisCrit as a framework in order to to trace my journey to becoming a Black mother-scholar-advocate, un/belonging within community and academic forums. The center-piece of my counternarrative is the transition of my own advocacy from valuing my son to addressing others' fears of him as a Black male whose visible (dis)ability does not fit neatly into prescribed norms. A reframing of parent advocacy is imperative, moving beyond the individualistic, unintentionally exclusive aims toward one of collective justice.

The year was 2016. My son Isaiah's school created a partnership with a local community center in order to provide swimming lessons for the children in the two 'IND' classes. These classes were designated for the children who were labeled by the professionally/clinically decided upon (dis)ability label of intellectual (dis)ability. The 'IND kids' as they were referred to, were the kids who sat at the table in the cafeteria away from everyone else, the kids who had recess inside most of the time, the kids tucked away in the back corner of the school who were rarely ever seen.

The school was located in a neighborhood, which could be described as upper middle-class to affluent and white. Many Black families who lived here either had some economic means or were struggling to stay afloat in order to offer their children something better. This was the myth that many Black caregivers like my own had taught us to believe when we were growing up – that going to better schools meant better resources and better teachers and this translated into better opportunities for our children. Some aspects of this was true, as this was the very road many of us had traversed ourselves. So many of us then turned around and reproduced this pattern in

---

This article has been republished with minor changes. These changes do not impact the academic content of the article.

our own children. We did not realize that this was not a guaranteed path, that we were the lucky ones, having stepped over a great many cracks in the process.

Rowan[1] was one of Isaiah's classmates, who like him, was a Black boy with Down syndrome. He was 5 years old, had a very sweet demeanor and an easy smile. Rowan was also quite tall for his age and muscular, defying the stereotypes of children with Down syndrome as heavyset and short in stature. He had beautiful brown skin and a raspy laugh. He wore these little Coke bottle classes, the type that I had not seen since my own childhood. His mother, though very involved in Rowan's education, often had to miss these school events and outings due to her work responsibilities. She and I were the only two Black mothers in the classroom.

It was during the swimming lesson that something happened that rocked me to my core. As we waited for the swimming instructors to provide individualized attention to each child, the parents who came that day held onto their own children, while the paraprofessionals supported the other children. Two of the paraprofessionals from my child's classroom, one white and the other white Latina were laughing among themselves. Holding onto Isaiah in the water, I moved a bit closer, unable to shake the nudging feeling that something was wrong.

"Look, *tiene miedo*," one of them said, "He's scared."

One of the paras held onto Rowan while the other waited to receive him. They took turns letting go of him as he panicked, his arms flailing, until the other reached over to grab him. The look on Rowan's face was one of terror. He was screaming as they just continued to laugh.

"How are you scared like this? I thought he was a big man! You're not so big now, huh?"

They continued to torment him to their amusement as anger coursed through my veins. Isaiah clung to me, worried about his friend. I could not take it anymore.

"Can I take Rowan?" I asked. "He's scared of the water, obviously. Let me have him, I've got him."

"No, it's okay, Mom. We got him."

But they did not have him. This episode did not last long, but for that brief moment, I could not process what was happening before my eyes. Before today, every time I showed up at school these women seemed to be caring and nurturing, doing their best to support our children in developing independent skills. I wondered to myself what else was happening when I was not around. What was happening to Rowan and to Isaiah when we, their mothers, their Black mothers, were not there?

Toward a new understanding of multiply marginalized parents and children

Using the framework of DisCrit, developed by Annamma, Connor, and Ferri (2016), Rowan's situation is a clear example of racism and ableism working in tandem, in ways that extend beyond his social class experience. DisCrit is now a part of the canon of intersectionality, a concept introduced by critical legal scholar Kimberlé Crenshaw (1991) to understand the confluence of systemic and microlevel forces that have an impact on individuals with historically marginalized identities. I make the distinction between social class experience and race because of the prevailing master narrative of Black families being associated with poverty or working-class conditions, which then are seen as contributing to their negative experiences with schooling, health and community life. This master narrative overlooks the hegemony of racism across systems and domains and places the blame on the victims of oppressive structures and systems. In a study conducted among middle-class parents of children with (dis)abilities in the United Kingdom, for example, Gillborn et al. (2016) reported how these parents' efforts and knowledge about their children were continually dismissed by professionals, despite their level of educational attainment and professional status. Rejecting these caregivers' own expertise about their children, participants described experiences that resulted in clinicians' refusal to identify their children with a learning disability (LD) or autism spectrum disorder (ASD), categories for which Black children have been largely under-identified. As literature has often attributed poverty and lack of education to the negative experiences among families of color, this illustrated the profound impact of racism and ableism regardless of wealth, educational status or other social descriptor.

In the previous section and the opening narrative, I intentionally introduced (dis)ability as a term. The parenthetical convention is intentional, a reframing of (dis)ability beyond individual limitations or deficits toward an expression of human variation. This is one of the key tensions between the medical and social models of (dis)ability, the latter emphasizing the constructed nature of what it means to be (dis)abled and whether it is a consequence of innate challenges or environmentally imposed challenges. Many individuals self-describe as disabled as a reclamation of identity and empowerment while others use the term neurodiverse to represent the human diversity of ability and presentation. Accounting for this range of preferences in language, I make no claim that my choice in terminology speaks for everyone. Rather, I emphasize the purposefulness behind the language that we choose that counter the deficit descriptor.

Traumatizing and tormenting Rowan went beyond entertainment at his expense. Instead, their abuse of Rowan was very much driven by the paraprofessional's own implicit biases, exerting their control over his body, his emotions, his mind. Their 'big man' comments and neglect of his fears were an example of how Black children are so often adultified by practitioners. Epstein, Blake and Gonzalez (2017) reported on professionals' perceptions of Black children as young as preschool age being perceived as significantly older, compared to their white peers, resulting in punitive treatments. Indeed, the third tenet of DisCrit[2] helps to illuminate how something as socially constructed as (dis) ability labeling has manifested in a focus on deficits, rather than looking at individuals holistically – a person, having feelings, opinions and rights. In addition to racist ideologies, these women denied Rowan his right to feel safe, not despite of but rather because of his inability to express himself through speech. In Ong-Dean's (2009) historical analysis of parent advocacy for children with (dis)abilities, he noted the persistent stigma towards (dis)ability labels associated with intellectual (dis)ability as compared with other (dis)ability categories. Although racist ideologies have resulted in disproportionate referrals, labeling, and tracking of Black and Brown children, as well children experiencing socioeconomic challenges into these categories, it has also been accompanied by the desire among white and affluent parents to avoid having their own children associated with these categories (Artiles 2011; Artiles and Trent 1994; Blanchett, Mumford, and Beacham 2005; Harry and Klinger 2014; Ong-Dean 2009). Rather than considering all of these practices independently, DisCrit's fifth tenet[3] calls us to explore the historically pervasive manifestations of the constructs of racism and ableism, working together to marginalize children. Consider the impact of 'That Black boy with Down syndrome whose working Black mother isn't here' and the historically, societally-sanctioned pass these women were given to torture him.

In this chapter, I sketch my journey toward advocacy as the Black mother of a Black son with Down syndrome. I emphasize the word value and what I recognize as a battle for our children to have a sense of belonging in this world beyond any other consideration of what society might define as normal. Yet, however socially constructed the parameters of normalcy are, DisCrit emphasizes how they manifest in the othering and exclusion of people who by virtue of birth cannot attain it.

There are several reasons for me choosing to present this as an autoethnography and I'll describe these very simply as voice and choice. At one level the voices of Black parent advocates of children with (dis)abilities are sparse in the literature on parent advocacy. Instead, the testimonies of White, middle class parents dominate the research, policy and community forums on parent advocacy (Groce 1999). The fact that DisCrit seeks to privilege voices like mine,[4] certainly carved out a space for me to write this paper. My advocacy is informed by our unique and rich experiences as Black mothers/parents, in contrast to the neutral, context-free voice of traditional (dis)ability advocacy, which tends to be, 'color-evasive,' a term described by Annamma, Jackson, and Morrison (2016).

At the same time, I recognize my position and privilege as a Black and Puerto Rican mother, advocate and academic, having navigated an exclusionary path though rough waters and still ones. Being heard is a coveted experience, especially within worlds that uphold norms of race and disability, worlds that are not exclusive. This is a role that I do not take for granted; I use this piece to share my voice though knowing I also stand beside my sisters, Black and Latina othered mothers of children with (dis)abilities, advocating for their children, whose voices are dismissed, unheard, left out of research, politics and community agendas. I carry Rowan's mother with me throughout this story.

On another level, autoethnography is a methodological choice which breaks the traditional bounds of academic writing. I am intentionally weaving in storytelling with scholarship, blurring the researcher-writer boundaries, which is disruptive to the rules. However, this is not separated from my identity as a Black woman and the introspection of what that means in a racialized world. During my first year of my doctoral program, a white female professor, whose microaggressions and outright disrespect tore at me the entire semester, told me, 'You need to get the writer out of you. That prose, that poetry. You aren't gonna make it in academia with it.' I learned a great deal from her, on how to remove my voice, my passion, my personal narrative, my culture. How much of my thoughts at the time echoed the words of Carolyn Ellis, who wrote, "If I deviate from this pattern, I'll be risking the scorn of my advisors or rejection from journal referees. I better master and follow the conventions' (2016, 76). Although since then, I have used ethno-graphic approaches in my research with my participants, I had not turned my lens inward. During the last year of my doctoral program, I was sharing some of the testimonials of some of my participants, who were parent advocates, in a session with Dr. David Connor for doctoral students. Thought I did not share my personal story, he could somehow see the invisible thread woven throughout it. He called for me to embrace autoethnography. I realized how much of an injustice it would be not use the opportunity to explore my own advocacy, through autoethnography, as an act of liberation. Hughes and Pennington (2017) pose a reflective question that I use to self-examine my own experiences, asking, 'What can my writing represent about a communal sense of what is real and how might it resemble a provocative weaving of story and theory?' (99).

Therefore, on a deeper level, this autoethnography on parent advocacy is a counternarrative as a Black mother of a child with a (dis)ability. Scholars such as Sherick Hughes and Pennington (2017) have brought to light the critical reflexivity that is afforded by autoethnography, a reckoning that only comes from interrogating one's own broad and microlevel cultural, racial, ethnic, familial, academic and social experiences, rather than removing them from the conversation. The autoethnographer, as Ellis and Bochner (2000) describe, is 'focusing outward on social and cultural aspects of their personal experience; then, they look inward, exposing a vulnerable self that is moved by and may move through, refract, and resist cultural interpretations' (739). In the following sections of this paper, I explore the ways in which I have subscribed to and reproduced the very ideologies that have oppressed me, my family, my community. I begin with peeling back layers of protective countenance that characterize our survival as people of color to find a story of strength and emergence, but not without first encountering some uncomfortable feelings of complicity. Throughout this testimony are pieces of my spoken word, another freedom afforded from the autoethnography, which unfolds my becoming a Black-Puerto Rican-mother-scholar-advocate. We get to tell our stories. We are the vanguard. Our story is resistance.

Becoming

> They want my backstory
> But they don't want my Black story
> They want the birth story
> But they don't want the first story

The first story

I identify as a Black woman and a Puerto Rican woman, with Native heritage. My mother is Black a descendent of a woman by the name of Katherine. Before her capture and enslavement, Katherine's homeland was Johannesburg, South Africa. Her family and companions were from the Bantu tribe. Through my family's oral stories, we learned how the skilled Bantu artisans could flawlessly take down the tallest of trees and construct a home in no time. We learned of Katherine's capture from her white Irish slaveowner by a leader from the Cherokee Nation. She lived among this indigenous community bearing a child by the tribal chief. Although some details of this history have been lost, they involved the recapturing and re-enslavement of Katherine, along with her son. Recaptured, despite her old blood lines, her new blood ties. Katherine's body was property and so was her son. My paternal ancestors had a similar experience.

My father's family could be described as a mostly white Latino/a family with some Black, Brown, and Indigenous heritage. His grandfather, a white man, emigrated to Puerto Rico from Castile, Spain. There he met my *bisabuela*, my great-grandmother,

Carmen, who was the blend of African and Indigenous Taino that represented her local culture. In pursuit of greater opportunities, they moved to Spanish Harlem, New York. At the time, this was a booming explosion of culture, a place where Spanish-speaking immigrants were no longer strangers in a strange land. Yet, discrimination was not limited to the southern United States. In the north, Puerto Ricans became, as Sandoval-Sánchez (1999) describes, the 'Latin domestic ethnic and racial *other*' (63).

By the 1960's, my mother's family had migrated north to the suburbs of New York City while my father's family remained in the urban sector. During the height of the Civil Rights Movement, my parents met in their place of employment, a factory that bound and assembled books. The year that Dr. Martin Luther King was assassinated, they married. Their very union, at that time, was resistance. That was the sociopolitical current they were navigating, those were my introductions into the world, a world that was shaped around identity and race. My mother's stance was to remain invisible and she had tried her best to impart that into me.

My first encounter with (dis)ability was with my cousin, Malcolm. Malcolm was Puerto Rican and his disability was what I now know to be Cerebral Palsy. At the time, the deinstitutionalization process had just begun in the United States. The Education for All Handicapped Children Act (EHA, 1975), the legislation mandating a free and appropriate public education for all children just been passed. Yet similar to the actions of schools after the passage *Brown vs. Board of Education of 1954*, which would outlaw school segregation and the exclusion of children of color, schools were slow to respond. The community was slow to respond to EHA, especially in urban communities where people were living in extreme economic hardships, like the one in which my family lived. There were no supports, there was no respite care. According to my family, Malcolm's (dis)ability *was* an illness and professionals concurred. In the family setting, we were not allowed to even play with him; Malcolm was off limits, he was 'sick' they said. But all of the other indicators, the fact that he would see me, even if it had been some time since we had last seen one another, made eye contact, smiled, remembered me, reached for me, clapped for me, led me to question whether or not this was true. I thought, 'What if I took this tray away? What if we got on the floor?' 'No!' they said. 'Leave him alone.' As we got older, Malcolm's smile began to fade away. He had gotten used to being disconnected from the rest of us and remained in his chair in the corner, watching television during family get togethers. When someone died, it was extra hard for Malcolm and for some odd reason, this always shocked my family members. It was as if they thought that he could not feel the same emotions everyone else was feeling. That was how I remembered (dis)ability in my family, no one made it 'normal' for Malcolm or for us. They made us afraid of him, afraid of hurting him, afraid he would hurt us, afraid of knowing and loving him.

A Black story

Being labeled as gifted was important for my family – they felt it was my ticket to better schools. 'To be young, gifted and Black – that's where it's at,' Donny Hathaway used to sing. I went from attending a middle school close to my neighborhood where most of the students were Black to a school where I needed to take two, sometimes three buses. Although the first school was located in a Black community whose residents had lived there for several generations, the second community, who were mainly second-generation Americans (e.g. Greek, Korean, Italian, Jewish families), had acquired a piece of American culture that the former still had not. Zoning restrictions maintained the non-Black constituency of the school neighborhood. Therefore the response to the mandates to desegregate New York City Public Schools was slow, and inevitably resulted in within-school resegregation. The cafeteria told the tale as it always does, as Tatum (2003) inquired, why all the Black kids are sitting together? Certainly, she added, though all rising adolescents will question their identity, 'not all children think of themselves in racial terms' (Tatum 2003, 56). Only an hour in the morning and an hour in the afternoon was spent with peers from my own neighborhood, with the majority of the school day in a silent disconnect from kids whose searing snickers about my skin color and 'puffy' hair led to my exclusion from their 'American Princess' groups. I recognized the 'opportunity gaps' between the two schools, as so powerfully described by Gloria Ladson-Billings (2007). Though the resources were better, something was lost. I went from having a choral director who made us examine meaning of the lyrics to 'God Bless the Child' before we even sang it to singing show tunes from *Grease* emotionlessly. There was something about my identity being nurtured, appreciating culture, my own culture, a shared microculture with my peers that I lost in the transition. There was a moral and cultural debt that the new white, middle class, suburban schools could never repay (Ladson-Billings 2007). These learning environments emphasized the ideals of meritocracy, which meant you earned the right to acquire status, as defined by education, ability, money and whiteness. My peer experiences also had an impact on me. After a birthday party one evening in my seventh-grade year, the father of one of my classmates offered to give me a ride home, though I insisted on taking the bus. In his strong Greek accent, he emphasized every word so that their meaning would not be lost upon me. I can still hear his words, '*this neighborhood*,' '*these people*,' '*unsafe*,' '*hoodlums*,' '*upbringing*.' I wanted to get out and walk, but I was stuck in this man's car, allowing him to shame me, my family, my community and my culture. '*How did you get to go to school here?*' he asked, without a thought to how that would impact me. I never imagined that I would be asked the same question years later, as a doctoral student, by a white female professor. '*How did you get into this program? Being who you are, with your five kids?*'

My friend did not make eye contact with me at all, in fact she never spoke to me again after that day. When I saw her again in college, she pretended she did not know me. By the time I became a young adult I had already learned the rubric that was not-so-hidden, the societally valued cultural capital that was at a dissonance from my own (Yosso 2005). Part of my lived experience became keeping a carefully crafted story, keeping my vulnerabilities and my emotions hidden and guarded while I navigated a world that did not welcome or understand me. I strongly resonate with the description by Doharty (2020) on developing a *strategic emotionality*, constructing a role, a manner of speaking that tamps down 'angry Black woman' perceptions:

> This is because Black women are aware that despite how they might perceive themselves to be managing their emotions, that is, no matter how softly spoken, articulate, educated, light-footed or introvert she is, she may still possess features that are a little too angry, a voice that is a little too loud and a demeanour that is a little too Black for others (554).

The backstory

The literature on parent advocacy describes a pattern of advocacy development, as an internal process that is sparked very early on. Parents are suddenly confronted with their child's diagnosis (as found in cases for parents with Down syndrome) or perhaps they seek out one by their own initiative (as in the case of parents seeking an autism or a learning disability diagnosis). Quite often, as so well-described by Hess, Molina, and Kozleski (2006), this first encounter with professionals is fraught with tension, with parents experiencing negative, deficit-laden dialogues from the professionals who they may view as expert. However, what makes the experience of parents of children with Down syndrome even more challenging is that these confrontations occur so early on, often disrupting the pregnancy of mothers. Studies have described, for instance, how stigmatization occurs even before the child is born, with an impact on how professionals deliver the diagnosis, the quality of prenatal and postnatal care and prognosis offered to parents (Skotko 2005a, 2005b). The work of Priya Lalvani (2008, 2011) called attention to the phenomenon of the 'othering' of mothers of children with Down syndrome by professionals and community members. A contextualized concept of associative or courtesy stigma, described by Erving Goffman (1963), is a stigma that is assigned to mothers of children with (dis)ability on behalf of their children. Though there are a limited number of studies on minority parents of children with Down syndrome, a few studies suggest even greater stigmatization of minoritized mothers, based on race, ethnicity, language and immigrant status (Martorell and Martorell 2006; Sheets et al. 2012). In my own study of nine parents and caregivers of children with Down syndrome across a range of intersecting social identities, I found that Black and Latina mothers were particularly isolated and pressured into terminating their children with a suspected diagnosis of Down syndrome, with microaggressions, classism, dismissiveness and delays in receiving accurate information (Ocasio-Stoutenburg 2020). My own story was also quite similar.

The birth story

From the moment of my first prenatal visit, I encountered an issue by which I found myself resisting. I overlooked, as we often do, interrogations about my age, how many children I had, and what I did for a living. As I mentioned, you are always trying to balance the perception of being angry and confrontational, so much so that you sometimes let the everyday, nuanced microaggressions go (Solorzano, Ceja, and Yosso 2000). At the time I had a master's degree in biology and was teaching at a local community college. They were shocked that I knew so much of the medical and scientific jargon but also rejected the idea. Despite my insistence that they didn't need to define every single term, they would continue to speak to me very slowly, "So, Down syndrome is a genetic condition … " I'd reply, purposely, in jargon-heavy language. That was how I resisted, but it was to no avail.

I will never forget the phone call from the geneticist, who told me that there was a 1 in 14 chance of my child having Down syndrome. Before I could even process what she was saying, she began talking about scheduling an amniocentesis to confirm the diagnosis and the window for termination. I told her to let the doctor know that I was not interested in the amniocentesis because of my high-risk pregnancy, nor was I interested in abortion.

As a result of that phone call, the climate changed in the doctor's office. I began to wait anywhere from 45 minutes to an hour and a half to be seen. The visits were short, lacking any cordiality. On his notes he would scribble, '34 y.o. A.A. female refuses amnio,' across the top of his notes, which would begin every visit. I could not imagine what my racialized identity, age, or my refusal to have the amnio had to do with every visit or why it had to frame these short, tense encounters. Yet, every visit he would remind me of the time I had left to terminate and every visit I would tell him I was keeping my son.

The othering continued up until, within and beyond the delivery room. I knew the delivery would be quick because I was already experiencing contractions and had four children prior to this one. I distinctly remember the nurse letting him know I was already in active labor. He acknowledged her and then turned to walk out of the door. Within minutes, my husband would have to run out of the door to get the nurse in order to bring the doctor back. He barely had time to scrub in. Within just 5 minutes, Isaiah was delivered. The doctor's only words were,

'*It's* a big one.'

It. My child? My son? It was the most silent birth experience I ever had. This was one of the happiest moments of our lives, yet they tried to make it grim, to take away the joy we were deserving of. They had done this to us in that hospital room. They tried to take away the joy of a Black family. During my postpartum checkup, they did the same thing, isolating me, admonishing me, telling me not to have more children, ever. They made me feel as if I had committed the worst crime, to have this Black boy with Down syndrome – admonishing me for putting a 'burden on the world, on society.' They had done this to Isaiah. In their fear, they failed to welcome him into the world and gave us the message that he did not belong.

Yet, this little one, in *his* resistance, made his way into the world. In his isolette, he turned his little head to the side to face me laying on the bed, recovering. Though medical texts would say this is impossible, he made eye contact with me, he *saw* me. It was a look of absolute love and care for me that took my breath away. He let me know, with his eyes, '*Thank you. I'm here. We made it, Mommy.*'

Belonging

Before he even got that label
They told me ways he'd be unable
'You shouldn't have him, he's disabled'
'You shouldn't decide, you're unstable'

Isaiah's entrance into our family was quite contradictory to the hospital experience. He was soft, he was joy. He was strong, he was everything. He grew, he laughed at silly things. We always called him 'Michigan J. Frog,' a reference to an old Warner Brothers cartoon where a frog would speak, sing and dance, yet to the frustration of his owner, he would only do it when they were alone. In the same fashion, when the therapist would visit our home to deliver early intervention services, Isaiah would do precisely what the therapist asked him to do the very moment she walked out of the door! He would babble sounds, start to say words when no one else could hear but us. He sat, he walked when he was ready. At around 4 years of age, his emerging speech almost completely disappeared. I wept, not only at not being able to hear his voice but at the further loss of ability to prove what he knew, what he felt, knowing that this would be constantly required of him. But I learned that he was on his time. I learned not to prescribe for him. He still does more when he isn't being watched or assessed. Every once in a while, there is a whisper, 'Mama.' I suppose in his own way, Isaiah resists.

Membership has its privileges

In the (dis)ability advocacy arena, there was also a hidden rubric, rules of engagement. (Dis)ability was the master status, full inclusion was the agenda across domains and formal advocacy was the means. In the book, *Meeting Families Where They Are* (Harry and Ocasio-Stoutenburg 2020), I provided my account of a session in a (dis)ability advocacy training series, provided by the state. The speaker discussed the dangerous and potentially fatal consequences of encounters between law enforcement officers and young adults with (dis)abilities. The speaker suggested that a way to address this is for families of young adults with (dis)abilities in to introduce themselves at their local precinct. It hit me hard. My thoughts immediately went to recent events surrounding racial injustice and police brutality in the news, as it was the years following the tragic deaths of Trayvon Martin, Eric Garner, Sandra Bland, Philando Castile and others. I felt compelled to speak at that moment, hating to be the spokesperson for things that should be thought of but knowing that it would only be me as the only Black or Brown person in that room. I said very calmly that this would not only be ineffective overall, it would not work, especially for communities where the issues of race had not been addressed. I immediately realized with my mention of the word 'community' that I had uncovered a topic that no one wanted to address. The room fell silent, followed by a response from the speaker that was so utterly dismissive of any mention of racial injustice with (dis) ability injustice, an event that brought abrupt awareness to my being outside of the established norms (Harry and Ocasio-Stoutenburg 2020). He let me know that is was a very 'controversial' topic and moved on. At other times, I spoke with some of the other parents about the barriers to attending these trainings, which would exclude parents who could not do so because of work responsibilities, emergencies, or those who did not always have someone to provide respite care. Voices of parents for whom full inclusion was not feasible or preferred were also muted in the conversations. While they were 'training' us to have a universal voice, they were also training us to use a voice that was racially, ethnically, culturally, contextually and even personally subtractive. Where I expected to find a network of support, I found a 'hierarchy' of (dis)ability. White, middle class parents of children with autism – they were the ones with the most power. They were the invited speakers, those selected to become facilitators. It was the same people every time, as if no other (dis)ability existed. We were being trained to decentralize our own experiences, to use those emotions to fuel our fire, yet to remain focused on 'the' goal, which reflected their goals, not ours. We were the powerless, we needed to be trained. We were not made to feel as if we were experts. It was more of the same, an erasure and a paradox; in their vocality about battling the '-isms' they cared most about, they were sending a clear message about the ones they didn't, the ones that were outside of their norms. As tenet five of DisCrit noted, racism and ableism acts both collaboratively and independently in order to promote exclusion.

Getting that label

Isaiah had a wonderful experience in early intervention and then in an early childhood program. He attended a center that served children with (dis)abilities in a reverse mainstream classroom.[5] At about 13 months of age, Isaiah had learned some basic American sign language (ASL) and was beginning to use assistive technology to communicate his wants and needs, via an application on the iPad. He was using his spoon, saying a few words. He was thriving. We supported him at home. He was always listening to me speaking, reading to him. I didn't know I was supposed to narrate everything, I just did, as I had done for my other children. I took him to the park. I took him to the library. We went to therapy. I was always at the school. It was ideal because everyone was in full communication, the doctors, coordinators, teachers, peer leaders, therapists, staff. Even the receptionists of the therapists office knew our family. I never felt the need to be confrontational, as everyone always asked me how we were doing, was there anything we needed. It was a brief period of bliss.

Problems began, however, when it was time to transition to public school. We selected a reverse-mainstream preschool classroom that we had heard good things about. The school boasted about his teacher being voted 'teacher of the year' in the previous year. However, the issues at this school went far beyond the usual problem of overcrowding, too many students and too few personnel. Instead, the problem was a paradox: Isaiah was not included in activities within a class that promoted inclusion. This 'wonder' teacher refused to use ASL or an assistive technology device to support his nonverbal communication. Within the first two weeks, the Black paraprofessional was moved from our classroom, due to 'irreconcilable differences' with the white teacher. No one ever explained why, but she whispered to us outside one day, 'I'm not in his classroom anymore, but I'm still watching my baby. I'm not gonna let anything happen to him, you hear?' Shortly thereafter, I felt was time to leave the district, following my family prescription of 'better schools, better resources, better opportunities'.

It was in the new school district that I received Isaiah's I.Q. scores, shortly after the incident with Rowan. I had this feeling that I needed to be ready on my end, though no one had told me how to prepare for an Individualized Educational Planning (IEP) meeting. Before the meeting, they sent home a checklist for me to fill out that was so short and restrictive, 'Can your child put together a sentence?' Yes or no. I began to do some work on my own, taking videos and copious notes to answer and expand on these questions, videos of him communicating, singing very quietly to himself, signing, using technology, playing with his siblings, helping at home. I put them on a flash drive and during the parent input section of the meeting, I asked them to open it. His teacher began to tear up. They were shocked. I still don't know if it was because of Isaiah's abilities, my nerve, or both. Still, it was not enough to move all of the power in that dark room, seven humans feeling threatened by my own perspective and informal assessments. The worst thing was being required to look at the big screen with the drop-down menu of limited options of labels and placements for my son. I realized this meeting was merely a formality. They pushed that number at me (his supposed IQ score). We are to accept that this test and its number are accurate and a comprehensive assessment of his ability – an objective measurement, based on normative modes of comprehension and communication and missing the alternative indicators of intelligence and understanding that were so obvious to anyone who knew Isaiah. I had presented the data that contradicted every item on that test, a snapshot of what he could do in his natural settings, yet this was rejected. I knew my child, but I smelled the air of defeat. Afterwards, I sat in my car and I cried. The I.Q. number was their indicator of how they felt, that he was an outlier of normalcy, even when his behaviors clearly defied this measure. The scores they gave me were so low they threw me into a short bout of depression. I had done everything I could do. I had to examine my beliefs about what I was feeling head on. It was the chasm between the obvious knowledge that my son had Down syndrome, while also being forced to drink the poison, to swallow this static, limited portrayal of his ability.

Deciding as resistance

Parents don't speak enough about these tests, which are like receiving the diagnostic news a second time. If it isn't framed with hope, you can spiral down into a pit of constant fear. Then suddenly my thoughts began to shift, just as they did in the hospital room thirty minutes after I received his diagnosis of Down syndrome. I realized that the painful dilemma was not my own but constructed by the perceptions that other people had imposed upon me, my family members, schooling, the world. I recognized what hurt me was, as Hudak and Kihn (2001) described, the 'staying power' of labels (9) and how this label would automatically confer a deficit-based perception of him in school. It exposed the new battleground that was mine, having a child with a (dis) ability in a world that constantly defined and reified norms. But even more daunting was understanding the battle of having a child who is Black male with a (dis)ability in a racialized, stigmatizing, labeling world that chooses not to see past who they think he is/they are. Eventually my body and my soul rejected the poison. I would drink no more. A different mother emerged from this abyss, as I entered the arena of the next school year.

> "So, would you want him to be in a regular Kindergarten, just sitting there, doing nothing?" the special education staffing specialist asked.
>
> "I want him to be in a place where he is valued and where he is supported but challenged, learning," I said.
>
> "The document states, 'Because of Isaiah's intellectual (dis)ability—"
>
> I quickly cut her off. "Because of their determination that he has an intellectual (dis)ability. For all we know he is just delayed in expressing what he knows."

We went back and forth about procedures. My husband stayed silent. She reminded me that I signed that psychoeducational evaluation. I did. She had me. I signed because I thought I had to. I thought they were going to reconsider based on what I had shown them. They told me they would. In all of my education, trainings *no one* had taught me what to do in those meetings. But I tried one more time.

"Yes," I said. "I was uninformed. I didn't know, my rights, I trusted them. I thought they were considering what I was saying. But all they did was label another little Black boy with intellectual (dis)ability. Do you know what that does?"

She paused for a moment and looked at me. Her expression changed, I imagine she was considering the position she was in and the opportunity for justice.

The next thing I knew, she was deleting on the dropdown menu. She began to type: BECAUSE OF ISAIAH'S DEVELOPMENTAL DELAYS . . .

Not every advocacy group would describe this as a win, since I still had to reconcile that evaluation, which was legally binding. I did recognize, however, the change in myself, knowing my rights and pushing past my hesitation to be perceived as angry and aggressive. I didn't let that hold me back because I knew what the label and eligibility meant now. I felt fortunate to have learned something, albeit through trial and error. It was a win, that moment. I was heard.

That was the year I turned it around, that was the year I *became* an advocate. It was also the last year that Isaiah attended a public school. I decided.

Emergence from normal

> Now I let my tears flow
> Never let your dreams go.
> I defied them,
> I still had him,
> And we're still here.

Telling this story in many ways is an exercise in coming full circle. I cannot express how many tears I have shed in this writing process, as it has unearthed memories I had buried so deeply. It is also our choice in how we choose to tell our story, in own voice, our cultural and experiential knowledge. At the same time, as Isaiah's mother, I can only pray to God that I have made the right decisions for him, since he cannot express that to me. I replay the words from Vanessa, a student with learning disabilities in *Urban Narratives* (Connor 2008), regarding her mother's decisions to keep her in special education, 'she just did what she had to do 'coz she thought it was best, my mom' (242).

My first step in my own reflection was to consider all of the efforts I had made to prove my son's value against arbitrary norms, always moving against the swirling currents of ableism and racism. It has been a constant struggle trying to tell people about my child, though 'the power of the professional gaze is such that other, nonprofessional perspectives are deemed irrelevant' (Harry and Ocasio-Stoutenburg 2020, 23). I also recognize the limitations of any instrument to assess my son's intelligence, his capabilities and his worth. As Dudley-Marling and Gurn (2010) expressed, 'the normal curve is a poor model of social reality, and therefore, human diversity cannot be understood with reference to a fictitious average (or normal) person' (20). The facilitators of those former advocacy trainings might have perceived the events I described as losses in the educational foreground. However, I recognize these as battles I won for Isaiah, for my family, for kids with Down syndrome, for humanity. The victory was in the reclamation of his identity, to strike the language beyond deficits and labels, to a child with potential. I can look back on this event through the lens of DisCrit and claim it as success, as this framework values resistance in all of its forms. Advocacy was something I had not learned through schooling, relationships, the community, the (dis)ability trainings, my upbringing nor any other entity. I learned that the true advocacy was not in the erasure of his (dis)ability, nor his race but rather seeing him as he is, emerging from all the tangible (psychoeducational evaluations) and figurative (exclusion and stigma) bondages of normalcy. And the power to do so came from me, his mother.

Coming full circle as an advocate meant also understanding my own shortcomings, past and present. Retelling what I had witnessed those women do to Rowan years ago was a critical point of reflection for me, in understanding how my own role as another Black mother, another 'othered' Black mother, on behalf of other Black mothers, disregarded as having any authority or control. I was struck by the sudden awareness of my own residual deference to teachers as authority figures when my perceptions of healthcare practitioners had already abruptly shifted so early on. What an uncomfortable feeling it was to accept the realities of these culturally ingrained perceptions, perhaps indoctrinated within my own schooling and maintaining some guard over my interactions in the school at that time (Harry, Allen, and McLaughlin 2016). It occurred to me that on some microlevel, that part of my own reckoning, by becoming, was also resisting my own fear of being perceived as the 'angry Black woman,' as confrontational when I needed to advocate for him. Part of this meant examining how my experiences had trained me to think of my own resistance this way and needing to come under control. As Doharty (2020) states, 'the monopoly whiteness has on Black women's emotionality: as only angry or strong' (549) often becomes internalized. Thus, our moments of understanding and empowerment often emerge from such moments of internal conflict and pure agony. I include the powerful words of resistance to this characterization by Black feminist autoethnographer Rachel Griffin, 'I AM an Angry Black Woman. I AM an Angry Black Woman who feels hopeful, sees promise, and desires progress' (2012, 152).

Finally, through these experiences I learned what it meant to be a Black mother-scholar-advocate of a Black child with Down syndrome. There were social identities that we could not hide, not his identity as a Black boy with Down syndrome and not my own identity as a Black mother. But we do not want to be hidden. I learned that not all people in the (dis)ability community think like me. Because of the historical and pervasive stigmatization of (dis)ability, some would desire to make him invisible the way some people would love to make being racialized as Black invisible, to 'pass' for able or to be universally disabled in a way that could exclude Blackness. I know that these are the residuals of the ideologies we unknowingly adopt through societal messages about what normal is. I actively resist this in my life, in my efforts for him and in my work. I know that makes me brazen, bold and different. But I also know that makes me free.

Notes

1. Pseudonym used.
2. DisCrit's third tenet, 'DisCrit emphasizes the social constructions of race and ability and yet recognizes the material and psychological impacts of being labeled as raced or dis/abled, which sets one outside of the western cultural norms' (Annamma, Ferri, and Connor 2018, 46).
3. DisCrit fifth tenet states, 'DisCrit considers legal and historical aspects of dis/ability and race and how both have been used separately and together to deny the rights of some citizens' (Annamma, Ferri, and Connor 2018, 59).

4. DisCrit's fourth tenet states, 'DisCrit privileges voices of marginalized populations, traditionally not acknowledged within research' (Annamma, Ferri, and Connor 2018, 58).
5. A reverse-mainstream classroom model, is described as a classroom with the majority of children with (dis)abilities and a smaller population of their typically-developing peers serving as classroom role models. In this model, the children with (dis)abilities are the 'mainstream' children while their typically-developing peers are the smaller minority.

Disclosure statement

No potential conflict of interest was reported by the author(s).

ORCID

Lydia Ocasio-Stoutenburg ⓘ http://orcid.org/0000-0003-3760-4476

References

Annamma, S. A., B. A. Ferri, and D. J. Connor. 2018. "Disability Critical Race Theory: Exploring the Intersectional Lineage, Emergence, and Potential Futures of DisCrit in Education." *Review of Research in Education* 42 (1): 46–71. doi:10.3102/0091732X18759041.

Annamma, S. A., D. Jackson, and D. Morrison. 2016. "Conceptualizing Color-evasiveness: Using Dis/ability Critical Race Theory to Expand a Color-blind Racial Ideology in Education and Beyond." *Race, Ethnicity and Education* 20 (2): 147–162. doi:10.1080/13613324.2016.1248837.

Annamma, S. A., D. J. Connor, and B. A. Ferri, Eds. 2016. *DisCrit—Disability Studies and Critical Race Theory in Education*. New York: Teachers College Press.

Artiles, A., and S. C. Trent. 1994. "Overrepresentation of Minority Students in Special Education: A Continuing Debate." *Journal of Special Education* 27 (4): 410–437. doi:10.1177/002246699402700404.

Artiles, A. J. 2011. "Toward an Interdisciplinary Understanding of Educational Equity and Difference: The Case of the Racialization of Ability." *Educational Researcher* 40 (9): 431–445. doi:10.3102/0013189X11429391.

Bochner, A., and C. Ellis. 2016. *Evocative Autoethnography: Writing Lives and Telling Stories*. Routledge. doi:10.4324/9781315545417.

Connor, D. J. 2008. *Urban Narratives: Portraits in Progress, Life at the Intersections of Learning Disability, Race, and Social Class*. New York : Peter Lang.

Crenshaw, K. 1991."Mapping the margins: Identity politics, intersectionality, and violence against women." *Stanford Law Review* 43 (6) 1241–1299.

Doharty, N. 2020. "The 'Angry Black Woman' as Intellectual Bondage: Being Strategically Emotional on the Academic Plantation." *Race Ethnicity and Education* 23 (4): 548–562. doi:10.1080/13613324.2019.1679751.

Dudley-Marling, C., and A. Gurn, Eds. 2010. *The Myth of the Normal Curve*. Peter Lang. doi:10.3726/978-1-4539-0039-0.

Ellis, C., and A. Bochner. 2000. "Autoethnography, Personal Narrative, Reflexivity." In *Handbook of Qualitative Research*, edited by N. Denzin and Y. Lincoln, 733–768, New York: SAGE.

Epstein, R., J. Blake, and T. González. 2017. *Girlhood Interrupted: The Erasure of Black Girls' Childhood*. Washington, DC: Center on Poverty and Inequality at Georgetown Law. doi:10.2139/ssrn.3000695.

Gillborn, D., N. Rollock, C. Vincent, and S. Ball. 2016. "The Black Middle Classes, Education, Racism, and Dis/ability: An Intersectional Analysis." In *DisCrit: Critical Conversations across Race, Class, and Dis/ability*, edited by D. Connor, B. Ferri, and S. A. Annamma, 35–54, New York: Teachers College Press.

Goffman, E. 1963. *Stigma: Notes on the Management of Spoiled Identity*. New York: Simon & Schuster.

Griffin, R. "I AM an angry Black woman: Black feminist autoethnography, voice, and resistance." *Women's Studies in Communication* 35 (2): 138–157.

Groce, N. 1999. "Disability in Cross-cultural Perspective: Rethinking Disability." *The Lancet* 354 (9180): 756–757. doi:10.1016/S0140-6736(99)06140-1.

Harry, B., and L. Ocasio-Stoutenburg. 2020. *Meeting Families Where They Are: Building Equity through Advocacy with Diverse Schools and Communities (Disability, Culture, and Equity Series).* New York: Teachers College Press.

Harry, B., N. Allen, and M. McLaughlin. 2016. "Communication versus Compliance: African American Parents' Involvement in Special Education." *Exceptional Children* 61 (4): 364–377. doi:10.1177/001440299506100405.

Hess, R., A. Molina, and E. Kozleski. 2006. "Until Somebody Hears Me: Parent Voice and Advocacy in Special Educational Decision Making." *British Journal of Special Education* 33(3): 148–157. doi:10.1111/j.1467-8578.2006.00430.x.

Hudak, G., and P. Kihn. 2001. *Labeling: Pedagogy and Politics.* New York: Routledge Falmer.

Hughes, S., and J. Pennington. 2017. "Second Guiding Process: Legitimizing Autoethnography with Three Approaches." In *Autoethnography: Process, Product, and Possibility for Critical Social Research*, 88–109. Thousand Oaks, CA: SAGE. doi:10.4135/9781483398594.n4.

Ladson-Billings, G. 2007. "Pushing past the Achievement Gap: An Essay on the Language of Deficit." *The Journal of Negro Education* 76 (3): 316–323.

Lalvani, P. 2008. "Mothers of Children with down Syndrome: Constructing the Sociocultural Meaning of Disability." *Intellectual and Developmental Disabilities* 46 (6): 436–445. doi:10.1352/2008.46.

Lalvani, P. 2011. "Constructing the (M)other: Dominant and Contested Narratives on Mothering a Child with down Syndrome." *Narrative Inquiry* 21 (2): 276–293. doi:10.1075/ni.21.2.06lal.

Martorell, S. J., and G. A. Martorell. 2006. "Bridging Uncharted Waters in Georgia: Down Syndrome Association of Atlanta Outreach to Latino/a Families." *American Journal of Community Psychology* 37 (3–4): 219–225. doi:10.1007/s10464-006-9055-2.

Mumford, B. W., and F. Beachum. 2005. "Urban School Failure and Disproportionality in a post-Brown Era." *Remedial and Special Education* 26 (2): 70–81. doi:10.1177/07419325050260020201.

Ocasio-Stoutenburg, L. L. 2020. "Voices of Diversity in Parent Advocacy for Children with down Syndrome: Intersectional and Contextual Considerations for Special Education and Health Care Practitioners." Doctoral dissertation, University of Miami.

Ong-Dean, C. 2009. *Distinguishing Disability: Parents, Privilege, and Special Education.* University of Chicago Press. doi:10.7208/chicago/9780226630021.001.0001.

Sandoval-Sánchez, A. 1999. *José, Can You See?: Latinos on and off Broadway.* Madison, WI: University of Wisconsin Press.

Sheets, K. M., B. J. Baty, J. C. Vázquez, J. C. Carey, and W. L. Hobson. 2012. "Breaking Difficult News in a Cross-cultural Setting: A Qualitative Study about Latina Mothers of Children with down Syndrome." *Journal of Genetic Counseling* 21 (4): 582–590. doi:10.1007/s10897-011-9425-2.

Skotko, B. 2005a. "Mothers of Children with down Syndrome Reflect on Their Postnatal Support." *Pediatrics* 115 (1): 64–77. doi:10.1542/peds.2004-0928.

Skotko, B. 2005b. "Words Matter: The Importance of Nondirective Language in First-trimester Assessments for down Syndrome." *American Journal of Obstetrics & Gynecology* 195 (2): 625–626. doi:10.1016/j.ajog.2005.11.012.

Skotko, B. G. 2005b. "Communicating the Postnatal Diagnosis of Down's Syndrome: An International Call for Change." *Italian Journal of Pediatrics* 31 (4): 237.

Solorzano, D., M. Ceja, and T. Yosso. 2000. "Critical Race Theory, Racial Microaggressions, and Campus Racial Climate: The Experiences of African American College Students." *Journal of Negro Education* 69 (1–2): 60–73.

Tatum, B. 2003. *"Why are All the Black Kids Sitting Together in the Cafeteria?": And Other Conversations about Race.* Hachette, UK: Basic Books.

Yosso, T. J. 2005. "Whose Culture Has Capital? A Critical Race Theory Discussion of Community Cultural Wealth." *Race, Ethnicity and Education* 8 (1): 69–91. doi:10.1080/1361332052000341006.

Sobreviviendo Sin Sacrificando (Surviving without Sacrificing)– An intersectional DisCrit *Testimonio* from a tired mother-scholar of color

Lisette E. Torres 🆔

ABSTRACT

This paper is my *testimonio* of being a Latina mother-scholar trying to complete a doctorate while managing a chronic condition. I draw on intersectionality and DisCrit to share how my social identities influence my experiences with marginalization and oppression within a neoliberal university context. I highlight the ways in which my impairment was invisibilized and minimized as the normal fatigue associated with motherhood. I note the role Latino communities play in the marginalization of disabled Latinas via disability avoidance and the gendered socialization process that makes Latinas feel obligated to sacrifice for their families and others. This socially constructed narrative of *sacrificio*, when combined with ableism and the neoliberal university's focus on productivity, makes it difficult to reveal and embrace an intersectional disability identity. I encourage scholars to consider the implications of this narrative, discussing how intersectionality and DisCrit can help them to (re)imagine knowledge production in the academy.

Project Entry – October 2016

> *Waiting for my research participant to call into Google Hangout. Just downed a cup of tomato basil soup, which was probably a mistake given my sensitive stomach lately. I feel like shit, but I felt like shit even before the soup. With fall weather finally here, my fibromyalgia is flaring up. Cleaning the house yesterday for my son's third birthday party has left me feeling battered and bruised, and working days and evenings the past couple of weeks has not helped. My back hurts, my hips hurt, my hands hurt, even the bottoms of my feet hurt! I just want to hibernate somewhere, alone. I'm really not in the mood to talk generally, let alone interview someone! I'm secretly hoping my participant will want to reschedule . . . Oh, they called in. Oh, well.*

My first sojourn into the ivory tower left me psychologically and emotionally wounded (Torres 2016a). I had to leave science to save myself and my spirit, but I knew that I could not in good conscience walk away while knowing that other undergraduate and graduate students of color entering science, technology, engineering, and mathematics (STEM) fields would be facing similar challenges. With the support of mentors of color in the academy who I have been blessed to meet and work with, including Mark Giles, Riyad Shahjahan, Nana Osei-Kofi, David O. Stovall, and Lorenzo Baber, I now have my doctorate in the field of higher education, melding my love of science and knowledge production with my passion for racialized gender justice.

However, as my above project entry indicates, I have acquired new social identities that prolonged my degree journey by at least five years and are now causing me to face a slew of challenges to my career. In 2013, I became a mother for the first time to a cautious and precocious boy. Two years later, in the spring of 2015, I was diagnosed with fibromyalgia, a chronic, incurable condition characterized by widespread muscle and joint pain, stiffness, and fatigue. In need of an additional source of income and health insurance, I began working full-time as an administrator at a predominantly White liberal arts institution while trying to complete my doctorate degree. This article is an intersectional *testimonio* documenting my lived experience of being a Latinx[1] with a non-apparent dis/ability,[2] a mother, a graduate student, and an employee within higher education.

Emerging from the field of Latin American Studies, *testimonio* is a method of narration that allows an author to bear witness to an injustice that they have endured and that has significantly impacted their life (Pérez Huber 2009; Brabeck 2001). The literal translation of the word testimonio from Spanish to English means 'testimony' or 'proof,' signifying that the witness is truthfully sharing their account of the occurrence. Unlike narratives or other genres, a *testimonio* 'implies factuality and first-hand experience' (Webb 2019, 4). According to Pérez Huber (2009), *testimonios* are 'usually guided by the will of the narrator to tell events as she sees significant, and is often an expression of a collective experience, rather than the individual' (644). Thus, they are meant to relay the impacts and learnings of the lived experiences of a group of people through the authentic observations, interpretations, and narration provided by an individual from the group. *Testimonios* can be used as a method or a methodology (Delgado Bernal et al. 2009) that allows the subaltern, particularly women of color, to document and theorize their own lived experiences (Pérez Huber 2009; Latina Feminist Group 2001). Though there is no specific definition of *testimonio*, I use a variation of Pérez Huber's (2009) explanation of *testimonio* as a 'journey of a witness who speaks to reveal the racial, ... gendered, and ... [ableist] injustices they have suffered as a means of healing, empowerment, and advocacy for a more humane present and future' (644).

Throughout this work, I use intersectionality and Dis/ability Critical Race Studies (DisCrit) to illustrate how my social identities influence my experiences with marginalization and oppression within the academy. Intersectionality is a term coined in 1989 by Kimberlé Crenshaw (Crenshaw 1989), a leading Critical Race Theory (CRT) scholar, to challenge dominant logics within the legal system and reveal how Black women experience intersecting forms of privilege and marginalization, often times rendering them invisible. As she noted at a 2016 keynote address at the Women of the World Festival, 'Intersectionality is not primarily about identity. It's about how *structures* [emphasis added] make certain identities the consequence of and the vehicle for vulnerability'(Crenshaw 2016). Despite the risk of being additive (Bowleg 2008), I share my distinct lived experience as a Latinx mother-scholar with a dis/ability to reveal how racism, sexism, and ableism are woven into the culture and discourse of higher education institutions, excluding numerous individuals with similarly marginalized identities from knowledge production. I also aim to connect intersectionality with scholarship that explores the 'embodied realities' of working at a neoliberal university (Mountz et al. 2015, 1245).

Naturally, given my discussion of dis/ability, I also interlace the tenets of DisCrit throughout my *testimonio*, placing the tenets throughout the text parenthetically where possible. DisCrit is a theoretical framework that racializes disability while disabling race (Annamma, Connor, and Ferri 2013). It confronts binary notions of normality and simplified conceptions of identity as well as the often-hidden ways in which ableism and racism are simultaneously built into institutional policies and practices (Annamma, Connor, and Ferri 2013; Connor, Ferri, and Annamma 2016). It also recognizes 'the material and psychological impacts of being labelled as raced or dis/abled' (Annamma, Connor, and Ferri 2013, 11), which significantly connects to my lived experiences as a disabled Latinx in the academy. This work specifically touches on DisCrit tenets[3] one, two, three, six, and seven. These tenets serve to highlight the 'evidence' of racism, sexism, and ableism within my *testimonio* as a disabled Latina in the academy in response to Brown and Leigh's (2018) question, 'Where are the disabled and ill academics?'

On being Brown and female in the academy

Being on a predominantly White campus as a graduate student-now-doctorate-degree-holder and as an administrator, I am constantly reminded of the fact that my short, Brown, female body is a rare sight as it engages in 'smartness trespassing' (Carrillo and Rodriguez 2016) in an educational space historically meant for White, abled bodies (DisCrit tenet six). It is evident by my interactions with White faculty, staff, and students that they do not know what to make of me, as I 'interrupt a racialized gaze' that views Latinas as 'intellectually inferior' to Whites (Carrillo and Rodriguez 2016, 241). Racial microaggressions (Sue et al. 2007) like 'You're so articulate!' and 'Where are you *really* from?' escape their lips ... if they even have the courage to speak to me at all. Even my office location serves as a reminder of my status on campus – it is located on the top floor of a building, whereas other staff members have offices on the first floor. Diversity is on campus, just quarantined (pun intended) in a cold, ill-lit corner office!

Oftentimes, I am simultaneously hypervisible and invisible, a situation experienced by many Latinx (Vaquera, Aranda, and Gonzales 2014) and disabled people in the U.S. (e.g., Wong 2020; Leary 2016), where our mere presence and access needs are a threat to 'normalcy' (DisCrit tenet one). All eyes fall on me when I enter a room where I am the only person of color, a 'guest in someone else's house' (Turner 1994, 355). I am always on guard because, as a woman of color, I know that I am vulnerable to violence; as Audre Lorde ([1984] 2000) reminds me, 'those of us who have been forged in the crucibles of difference ... know that *survival is not an academic skill*' (112). As a CRT scholar and a token administrator on campus (Mohamed and Beagan 2019), I am well aware that my 'actions, words, demeanor, dress – virtually everything about [me] – is noticed' (Niemann 2012, 473). Like other Latinx academics, I avoid falling into the 'hot Latina' stereotype (Lugo-Lugo, 2012) by dressing modestly, and I try to remain even-tempered but not submissive, maintaining a balance between the imagined 'hot-blooded Latina' and *la sirvienta* (maid, servant) stereotypes. Similar to the Black women student affairs professionals in Okello (2020), I must essentially assess 'the implications of [my] behavior and visual representation, and mak[e] difficult decisions in favor of the larger end game to affect the linkage between race and public opinion' (11) regarding Latinxs.

In faculty and staff meetings, I am rendered invisible by the disregard of my presence (e.g., no greetings, side conversations), the negation of my experiences, and the repetition and co-optation of my ideas, particularly by White men. These experiences undermine my competence and confidence (Gutiérrez y Muhs et al. 2012). Not including my scholarship and professional activities, my contributions to campus as a staff member/ administrator – training and leading over 25 student employees, conducting numerous writing workshops, setting up completely remote synchronous and asynchronous writing consultations, advising and mentoring students, running a successful STEM program, serving on multiple committees dedicated to diversity and inclusion – often go unacknowledged. I would also argue that I am considered to be even less of a 'legitimate academic' (Mohamed and Beagan 2019) as compared to my racialized faculty counterparts given my professional role as a staff member on campus.

Yet, despite the lack of recognition, as a scholar of color who utilizes CRT in her scholarship, I know that I cannot mess up or slack off even a little bit because I would not get a second chance. I am continuously trying to avoid the cultural taxation (Padilla 1994) placed on faculty of color, being an advocate for students who identify as Black, Indigenous, and people of color (BIPOC) and positively contributing to the campus community while also protecting my time and energy. This self-preservation is necessary not only because of my racialized gender identity, but because I literally need to conserve my energy as a disabled academic (DisCrit tenets two and three). I am also well-aware that these unspoken service expectations are not valued and will not lead to 'the tangible or valued outcomes needed ... [for] career advancement' (Guillaume and Apodaca 2020, 6).

The 'baby penalty' and other *sacrificios*

My life partner and I thought long and hard before trying to start our own family. As a dual career couple and with me starting over in a new doctorate program at the time (see Torres 2016a), we debated if and when to have a child. We knew about the 'baby penalty' (Mason 2013) for women in the academy, as mother-scholars are often viewed as being less committed to their field and to the academy as compared to their male counterparts. They are less likely to find a tenure-track job, receive little to no assistance with childbirth support or childcare services, and do not receive the proper mentoring or career advice to help them manage family and work. We also knew that we wanted to be parents. We wanted to experience childbirth together, to love and parent a little person who could one day make a wonderful contribution to humanity. Having a child was the best decision we have ever made, despite the many *sacrificios* (sacrifices) I have had to make as a mother-scholar of color.

As I navigated motherhood while finishing my dissertation and working full-time in the academy and as I currently fight to keep up my scholarship while mothering and being consigned to a staff/administrator role, I have noticed significant tensions between my racialized gendered identities as a Boricua[4] and mother and my academic identity. I have begun to theorize some of these tensions as being a part of a master narrative I call the narrative of *sacrificio*, which I introduced in *Write Where It Hurts* (Torres 2016b). As I write in my invited blog post, growing up in a Puerto Rican household full of women, we were socialized in the ways of *sacrificio*. My sisters and I were continuously reminded about the sacrifices that family members have had to make, mostly out of love but also for survival.

On the island of Boriquen,[5] my grandmother lived with and raised 12 brothers and sisters in a one-room farmhouse, quitting school after third grade to take care of them. She later came to the mainland United States with my father and aunt in search for a better life, working in a toy factory that would later leave her with arthritic hands (a disability, though many in the Latinx community would not call it that due to the stigma). Through these stories of sacrifice, we were not only taught about the resilience of our people but also about the obligation that we have to work hard for the family, sometimes at the expense of our own wants and needs. Social scientists often refer to this socialization as instilling the values of *familismo*, or one's prioritizing family over one's own needs (e.g., Schwartz 2007), and *marianismo*, the notion of the assumed submissive female gender role of Latinas (e.g., Castillo et al. 2010). I cannot help but to see it as the consequence of patriarchy in a Latinx household and an additional burden for me in the academy.

The pressures of a neoliberal university are countless, but include discourses around the quantity of scholarship, efficiency, entrepreneurship through grant funding, competition, increased reliance on contingent labor, and fewer tenure-track positions. The weight of these expectations often leaves me feeling torn and stretched for time. My racialized gendered identity as a Puerto Rican mother wants to prioritize spending time with my son, daughter, and life partner, cleaning the house, and providing healthy meals. I was eaten away by guilt for putting both children in daycare,[6] though the coronavirus has since forced me to keep them at home while I work full-time remotely. I tend to put aside my goals and needs in order for my son, daughter, and life partner to be happy. Pre-pandemic, I would often have to take the day off to care for my children when they were sick and have never expected my life partner to do the same. Yet, I know that I need to spend 'productive' time on research, teaching, and service to stay in the academy, a neoliberal pressure brought in high relief due to COVID-19 (Torres 2020).

Realizing my physical limitations

After having my son in 2013 via C-section, I knew that it would take my body time to heal and to adjust to its new form. I was told by my obstetrician that I would be feeling 'normal' in 2–3 months and that I should take it easy in the meantime, with minimal lifting. A return to 'normal' never happened. I began to notice aching in my hips when I would sit in the living room recliner with my son, pain that varied from dull to shooting. No matter how I situated myself, I just could not get comfortable. I also felt tired all the time. At first, I wrote it off as a consequence of being a parent and staying up with the baby. However, as the days and months and a year went by, I realized something was wrong. I never felt rested, no matter how much sleep I got the night before. My life partner and I began to joke that 'I'm tired' was going to be engraved on my tombstone, but deep down, I did not think it was funny. I began to worry about my health and about how this unknown condition was going to impact my mothering, my doctoral progress, and my prospects of being able to secure a tenure-track position in the future, knowing that the academy has unarticulated intellectual and physical criteria that need to be met for employment (Brown and Leigh 2018).

Other symptoms began to develop, which included chronic headaches, hypersensitivity to sensory stimuli (e.g., cold, heat, light, sound, smell, and touch), inability to concentrate (known in the disability community as 'fibro fog'), stiffness, restless sleep, mood swings, and depression. However, the generalized pain was the worst! There were (and still are) days when I could not sit at a computer to write. The pain in my hips, elbows, knuckles, wrists, and back would be too much for me to spend more than a few minutes at a time seated or using a keyboard and mouse. I finally gave in and saw my general medical practitioner. I was nervous. There is a tradition within the medical field of minimizing a patient's account of their symptoms, particularly those with chronic pain, forcing them to try to figure out and address their condition on their own through specialists, alternative medicine, the Internet, and dietary supplements (Roth 2009). Thank goodness my doctor believed me and encouraged me to see a rheumatologist, who was then able to give me a diagnosis. This did not eliminate the pain, but it did ease my mind.

Unfortunately, having a diagnosis did not lessen the burden placed on me as a mother-scholar of color. Stereotype threat (Steele and Aronson 1995), imposter syndrome (e.g., Solorzano and Yosso 2001), and racial microaggressions (Sue et al. 2007) are almost daily challenges for me. I know that I already have three strikes against me in a White patriarchal society – I am a woman, I am a person of color, and I am a mother. I am viewed as 'less than' and 'unworthy' of being in higher education, as I do not have the 'right look' that is associated with 'intelligent' people in the academy (Carrillo and Rodriguez 2016). I am presumed 'lazy,' 'inarticulate' and 'incompetent' (Gutiérrez Y Muhs et al. 2012). I sometimes dread that my fibromyalgia adds to those Eurocentric assumptions of my subaltern status (Shahjahan 2015), as racism and ableism are inter-dependent (DisCrit tenet one) and stigma within the academy results in non-apparent disabilities being 'dismissed as a fabrication, malingering and an act of a fundamentally lazy or overwhelmed worker seeking validation' (Brown and Leigh 2018, 987).

I am well-aware that ableism in the academy exists and that it 'renders disability as abject, invisible, disposable, less than human, while able-bodiedness is represented as at once ideal, normal, and the mean or default' (Dolmage 2017, 7). I will admit that I have tried to pass as able-bodied to protect myself; for example, I avoided 'access fatigue' (Konrad 2016) by not disclosing my disability to Human Resources up until the recent COVID-19 pandemic. I used to only share my access needs when I had no other choice because I did not want the looks of pity and the apologetic comments. I especially avoid social interaction on my high-pain, high-fatigue days. I live in fear – fear of confirming racist/sexist/ableist stereotypes, of being a bad mother, of letting my family and community down, of never securing a tenure-track position, of being another sacrifice to the White neoliberal university.

Contesting the racist/sexist/ableist narrative of *sacrificio*

In evaluating our life purpose and the value and purpose of others within a framework of capitalist productivity, we not only shame and isolate bodies that aren't valued as productive we unleash a form of body terrorism that communicates that it is not one's body that should be valued but rather what that body can effectively produce. (Giles 2016, para. 10).

In a neoliberal university, there is no 'work-life balance' and accommodations are viewed as a 'cost' (Dolmage 2017, 53). The unspoken expectation is that one must sacrifice time, energy, mind, body, and soul to the functioning of the university and the production of graduates, grants, endowments, and publications. We give symbolic support to self-care, all the while ignoring the culture shift necessary to confront and change the neoliberal influence on productivity in higher education. The consequence is a narrative of *sacrificio*. Bodies are commodified, objectified, and valued by what they can produce; they are sacrificed in one way or another for the good of the university.

As Moutz et al. (2015) highlight, a '[c]ounting culture [in a neoliberal university] leads to intense, insidious forms of institutional shaming, subject-making, and self-surveillance' (1243). We see this in our discourse and actions, as we judge others based on what we assume about them and the expectations of academia. If someone leaves campus before 5 p.m., we think they are slacking off or cutting corners. Daily conversations revolve around the 'publish or perish' mantra and 'how tired' we are because we 'stayed up until 2 a.m. working on a grant proposal/manuscript/course.' We work more than 40 hours per week and complain about our varied activities, while simultaneously looking down on others who may not appear to be as involved on campus. We are complicit in perpetuating the narrative of *sacrificio*.

And we do this without considering the impact, especially the bearing it has on the lived experiences of women of color, individuals with chronic illness/pain, and others who are marginalized in the institution. For them, the sacrifice is much deeper – fragmentation of the mind, body, and spirit, or the creation and acceptance of multiplicity (Ong 2005). When possible, it is passing as White, masculine, and able-bodied, often as a means of survival, but at the expense of reifying racism/sexism/ableism (Ong 2005; Annamma, Connor, and Ferri 2013). It is forgoing having children and relinquishing the ability to speak the language of our ancestors to conform to and converse in the elitist, colonial jargon of the ivory tower. It is physically moving away from our families and communities in pursuit of job opportunities that are often located in hostile, isolating places (e.g., Henry 2015). It is perpetuating Henryism[7] by working so hard to earn the respect of the academy and society as to result in our own death (Okello 2020).

Implications of lessons learned

I have learned a lot through this difficult journey – things about myself, the academy, and my place in academe. I will continue to research, write, teach, mentor, and advocate on behalf of marginalized communities, but after the birth of my son and my diagnosis, I know that I have a finite amount of daily energy that can be significantly reduced by stress. Being a mother with a chronic condition immersed in an increasingly neoliberal institution has forced me to pick and choose how I spend my time. In order to confront the influence of neoliberalism and the narrative of *sacrificio* on my life, I must embrace and engage in a radical reprioritizing (Grollman 2016) while supporting, in any way I can, various forms of resistance (DisCrit tenet seven).

Self-care

For me, that means making sure that I get at least eight hours of sleep per night and eat better than I might have in the past. It means accomplishing as much work as I can between the hours of 9 a.m. and 5 p.m. and saving evenings and weekends for myself and my family; it also means being okay with these decisions. It means strategically saying 'no' to projects and requests from colleagues, staff, administrators, and students (Guillaume and Apodaca 2020). It also means getting my annual check-ups, listening to my body, and learning when to ask for help or to quit entirely (Patten 2016). I am not ashamed to admit that I now take a nap in the middle of the day when my body tells me that I need rest. To reduce my stress and manage pain, I have started weekly meditation, taking nature walks, and getting a massage every month. I also joined a fibromyalgia support group on Facebook and read wonderful self-care reminders and tips on a blog called Being Lazy and Slowing Down (http://lazyslowdown.com/), written by my colleagues Riyad Shahjahan and Kimine Mayuzumi.

Self-care is more than just exercise, sleep, good nutrition, emotional support, and balance. It is a political act. As one of my all-time favorite writers (who was also a disabled woman of color), Audre Lorde, wrote in a *Burst of Light* (1988), 'Caring for myself is not self-indulgence, it is self-preservation, and that is an act of political warfare' (132). Scholars of color and mothers of color, who must confront structural racism/sexism/ableism/etc. on a daily basis, must remind themselves that self-care is not selfishness. Self-care is the complicated and delicate dance between Henryism and respectability in our decision-making, learning that though one is 'capable of more, survival is a worthy and necessary endeavor' (Okello 2020, 16). It is about being healthy enough to fight for equity and inclusion, to support future generations of scholars of color, and to push for scholarship that works with and for marginalized communities. As Sonya Renee Taylor (2018) reminds us, 'How we value and honor our own bodies impacts how we value and honor the bodies of others' (4). For me, in particular, it is also about watching my children grow up to be a part of the endless struggle for human rights.

With the arrival of the coronavirus in the United States, I have had the opportunity to meditate on my lived experience as a disabled Boricua mother-scholar, my relationship to others, and the purpose of scholarship (Torres 2020). Shahjahan (2019) reminded me that the shame we all feel when we feel pressed for time is produced by the continued emphasis on productivity by the neoliberal university. When we cannot meet the unrealistic expectations of the academy, we blame ourselves for our struggles and 'enact shameful ways of knowing/being as [we] consider [ourselves] incompetent, unworthy, and power-less, while applying the temporal "gaze of Other" inwardly' (Shahjahan 2019, 6). These unrealistic expectations of the neoliberal university result in the kinds of turmoil that scholars of color, mother scholars, and disabled scholars often feel. Their collective experiences should compel us to consider how we can embody and promote collective care and mending in academic research and the academy (Torres 2020).

Collective care, disability justice, and DisCrit

Institutional transformation around the intersecting oppressions of racism, sexism, and ableism will obviously be more complicated than focusing on individual-level change. We need to shift to an academic culture that values and fosters intentionality, reflectivity, and collective care, where everyone is committed to an interdependent existence. We need to embrace each other's full humanity and create a community where '[l]ove in action is ... when we refuse to abandon each other' (Piepzna-Samarasinha 2018, 7, 8). As Akemi Nishida (2016) reminds us, 'community care is critical not only for our wellbeing, but also because it is a tangible way to resist the neoliberal academy's compulsion for individualization by nurturing our capacities for democracy' (155).

This is where the disability activist community has a lot to show us in terms of disability justice and inclusion. Along with finding ways to enact the 10 Principles of Disability Justice (Berne, 2015), higher education institutions can be more mindful and adaptable to the needs and concerns of its students, faculty, and staff through the use of universal design for learning (UDL) (e.g., Rose and Meyer 2006); flexible work hours, leave time, and deadlines; accommodation policies and practices; work style identification, work-speed agreements, and check-ins (Nishida 2016); and financial investment in accessible spaces, assistive technology, and disability services. To resist the narrative of *sacrificio*, we must begin to embrace quality over quantity, value each other's wellbeing (including energy levels and time), and be attuned to each other's access needs, what Mia Mingus calls access intimacy (Mingus 2011).

Whereas disability justice can inform changes in individual and institutional practices and culture, DisCrit can point out and contest the neoliberal norms (tenet one) regarding competition, production, efficiency, and independence. This theoretical framework can also challenge our assumptions around what we consider 'normal' and what we say we value, as it centers the voices and multi-faceted identities of marginalized populations (tenets two and four), including scholars of color with disabilities like me. DisCrit helps to reveal and identify the material and psychological impacts of racism/sexism/ableism (tenet three), as demonstrated by the fact that, in my *testimonio*, I share how I needed to take an administrative job for healthcare and my struggle with expectations of Henryism to stay in the academy. Lastly, DisCrit pushes those of us who are disabled in the academy and dedicated to social justice (tenet seven) to make ourselves visible to others through our *testimonios* in order to make others feel safe to be visible, to serve as a resource, and to challenge what it means to be disabled (Leary 2016). The more of us who speak up, the more pressure there will be for higher education institutions to change.

Ultimo consejo/final advice

To be honest, I am still a work-in-progress as I work on a daily basis to confront my internalized ableism through meditation and following the brilliant work of disabled activists, like Alice Wong, Dior Vargas, Mia Mingus, Sandy Ho, Leah Lakshmi Piepzna-Samarasinha, Leroy Moore, Patty Berne, Keah Brown, Lydia X.Z. Brown, Vilissa Thompson, and many others, for inspiration. I probably will always be a work in progress, but I wanted to especially share my lived experience with other women of color, other Latinxs like me who are suffering with a chronic condition but are fighting and pushing through to become scholars, educators, and mothers. I also wanted to be transparent about my experience for those who do not share my positionality; I want to (re)awaken them to the fact that 'Ableism is Trash'[8] and 'Access is Love.'[9]

What my body has taught me is that I need to reconnect with myself. I need to pay attention to my mind, body, and spirit. Fibromyalgia has compelled me to consider how the dominant neoliberal discourse in higher education has rendered the body invisible, being seen solely as a commodity that enhances production and efficiency (Shahjahan 2015). It has also taught me that I have the power to shape my personal and scholarly identities, and to determine how I want to live my life.

The narrative of *sacrificio* is a complicated consequence of intersectional identities and oppressions, the interconnection of time and capitalism (Walker 2009), the colonization of bodies of color by Eurocentric linear epistemologies that (re)define perceptions of laziness (Shahjahan 2015), and the push for a 'counting culture' in higher education that 'requires real *sacrifice* of personal time' [emphasis added], while discounting scholarship that is viewed as 'unproductive' (Mountz et al. 2015, 1242). By allowing the narrative of *sacrificio* to consume our lives, we reify colonialism, racism, sexism, and ableism within our institutions. Therefore, we need to collectively advocate for embodied practices (Shahjahan 2015) and slow, 'care-full' scholarship, where the research process, relationship building, refinement of ideas, and amplifying our work with and for communities are valued more than the actual final products (Mountz et al. 2015). We need to reflect on how we individually and collectively feed into the narrative of *sacrificio*. Ultimately, for scholars of color, self-care is communal care, knowledge preservation, and survival.

Notes

1. I use 'Latinx' throughout the paper as a gender-neutral term that moves beyond normalized gender binaries. It is a linguistic attempt to recognize and embrace the intersectional identities within our community, particularly those who are trans, queer, gender fluid, and gender non-conforming. I want to honor the collective wounds of my people (Pelaez Lopez 2018). I occasionally use 'Latina' when referencing a stereotype or studies that use that term.
2. To honor the DisCrit framework by Annamma, Connor, and Ferri (2013), I have elected to use 'dis/ability' in this particular work rather than 'disability' as a political stance to disrupt the socially constructed separation of ability and disability. I wanted to recognize how dis/ability changes with age and over time in particular historical and social contexts, which is illustrated in this work. However, I also want to acknowledge the fact that the slash in 'dis/ability' has been questioned by some disabled scholars and activists as erasing disability. They have been encouraging us to #SayTheWord, a Twitter hashtag campaign initiated in 2015 by Lawrence Carter-Long, the Director of Communications for the Disability Rights Education and Defense Fund (DREDF).
3. The DisCrit tenets articulated by Annamma, Connor, and Ferri (2013, 11) are the following: (1) DisCrit focuses on ways that the forces of racism and ableism circulate interdependently, often in neutralized and invisible ways, to uphold notions of normalcy.(2) DisCrit values multidimensional identities and troubles singular notions of identity such as race or dis/ability or class or gender or sexuality, and so on.(3) DisCrit emphasizes the social constructions of race and ability and yet recognizes the material and psychological impacts of being labeled as raced or dis/abled, which sets one outside of the western cultural norms.(4) DisCrit privileges voices of marginalized populations, traditionally not acknowledged within research.(5) DisCrit considers legal and historical aspects of dis/ability and race and how both have been used separately and together to deny the rights of some citizens.(6) DisCrit recognizes whiteness and Ability as Property and that gains for people labeled with dis/abilities have largely been made as the result of interest convergence of white, middle-class citizens.(7) DisCrit requires activism and supports all forms of resistance.'
4. 'Boricua' means a person from Puerto Rico.
5. 'Boriquen' is the original name of the island of Puerto Rico. It means the 'Land of the Brave People' and was given to the island by its original inhabitants, the Taino people.
6. Daycare in the United States refers to the early education of children younger than 5 years old.
7. 'Henryism' is a term derived from the behavior of a U.S. folklore character named John Henry. John Henry was an exceptional Black laborer who was known for his fast and

efficient steel driving, and he was asked to compete against a steam drill. Though he successfully beat the machine, he later died of exhaustion as a consequence of the excessive physical exertion. Thus, anyone with 'Henryism' is characterized by having mental and physical vigor, a strong work ethic, and a focus on success (Okello 2020).

8. 'Ableism is Trash' was a project by the Disability Visibility Project's Alice Wong in collaboration with artist Jee Hei Park and activist-scholar Mia Mingus.

9. 'Access is Love' is a project by the Disability Visibility Project's Alice Wong in collaboration with activist-scholars Mia Mingus and Sandy Ho. For more information, check out https://disabilityvisibilityproject.com/2019/02/01/access-is-love/.

Acknowledgments

I would like to thank Subini Annamma, David Connor, and Beth Ferri for inviting me to contribute to this special issue on DisCrit. I also would like to thank my mentors for their continued support and inspiration.

Disclosure statement

No potential conflict of interest was reported by the author(s).

ORCID

Lisette E. Torres [iD] http://orcid.org/0000-0002-1548-0479

References

Annamma, S. A., D. Connor, and B. Ferri. 2013. "Dis/ability Critical Race Studies (Discrit): Theorizing at the Intersections of Race and Dis/ability." *Race Ethnicity and Education* 16 (1): 1–31. doi:10.1080/13613324.2012.730511.

Berne, P. 2015. "Disability Justice – A Working Draft." *Sins Invalid*, June 10. https://www.sinsinvalid.org/curriculum

Bowleg, L. 2008. "When Black + Lesbian + Woman ≠ Black Lesbian Woman: The Methodological Challenges of Qualitative and Quantitative Intersectionality Research." *Sex Roles* 59: 312–325. doi:10.1007/s11199-008-9400-z.

Brabeck, K. 2001. "*Testimonio*: Bridging Feminist Ethics with Activist Research to Create New Spaces of Collectivity." Paper presented at the Feminisms in Participatory Action Research Conference, Newton, MA, June 22–24.

Brown, N., and J. Leigh. 2018. "Ableism in Academia: Where are the Disabled and Ill Academics?" *Disability & Society* 33 (6): 985–989. doi:10.1080/09687599.2018.1455627.

Carrillo, J. F., and E. Rodriguez. 2016. "She Doesn't Even Act Mexican: Smartness Trespassing in the New South." *Race Ethnicity and Education* 19 (6): 1236–1246. doi:10.1080/13613324.2016.1168547.

Castillo, L. G., F. V. Perez, R. Castillo, and M. R. Ghosheh. 2010. "Construction and Initial Validation of the Marianismo Beliefs Scale." *Counseling Psychology Quarterly* 23 (2): 163–175. doi:10.1080/09515070003776036.

Connor, D. J., B. A. Ferri, and S. A. Annamma. 2016. *DisCrit - Disability Studies and Critical Race Theory in Education*. New York, NY: Teachers College Press.

Crenshaw, K. 1989. "Demarginalizing the Intersection of Race and Sex: A Black Feminist Critique of Antidiscrimination Doctrine, Feminist Theory and Antiracist Politics." *University of Chicago Legal Forum* 1989 (1): 139–167.

Crenshaw, K. 2016. "Kimberlé Crenshaw - on Intersectionality – Keynote – WOW 2016." [Video file], March 14. https://www.youtube.com/watch?v=-DW4HLgYPlA

Delgado Bernal, D., S. A. Alemán, D. Calderon, J. C. Flores, N. M. García, and Y. X. González. 2009. "Writing to Heal: An Anthology of the Mind/body/soul." Paper presented at the annual meeting of MALCS (Mujeres Activas en Letras y Cambio Social), Las Cruces, NM, July.

Dolmage, J. T. 2017. *Academic Ableism: Disability and Higher Education*. Ann Arbor, MI: University of Michigan Press.

Giles, G. 2016. "'You Do Not Exist to Be Used': Dismantling Ideas of Productivity in Life Purpose." *The Body Is Not An Apology Magazine*, August 17. https://thebodyisnotanapology.com/maga zine/you-are-more-than-what-you-do-dismantling-ideas-of-productivity-in-life-purpose/

Grollman, E. A. 2016. "Radical Reprioritizing: Tenure, Self-care, and My Future as an Intellectual Activist [Blog Post]." *Write Where It Hurts*, February 24. http://www.writewhereithurts.net/ radical-reprioritizing-tenure-self-care-and-my-future-as-an-intellectual-activist/

Guillaume, R. O., and E. C. Apodaca. 2020. "Early Career Faculty of Color and Promotion and Tenure: The Intersection of Advancement in the Academy and Cultural Taxation." *Race Ethnicity and Education*: 1–18. Advance online publication. doi:10.1080/13613324.2020.1718084.

Gutiérrez y Muhs, G., Y. F. Niemann, C. G. Gonzàlez, and A. P. Harris, Eds.. 2012. *Presumed Incompetent: The Intersections of Race and Class for Women in Academia*. Boulder, CO: University Press of Colorado.

Henry, A. 2015. "'We Especially Welcome Applications from Members of Visible Minority Groups': Reflections on Race, Gender and Life at Three Universities." *Race Ethnicity and Education* 18 (5): 589–610. doi:10.1080/13613324.2015.1023787.

Konrad, A. 2016. "Access as a Lens for Peer Tutoring." *Another Word*, February 22. https://dept. writing.wisc.edu/blog/access-as-a-lens-for-peer-tutoring/

Latina Feminist Group. 2001. *Telling to Live: Latina Feminist Testimonios*. Durham, NC: Duke University Press.

Leary, A. 2016. "4 Important Reasons Why Disability Visibility Matters [Blog]." *Everyday Feminism*, September 27. https://everydayfeminism.com/2016/09/disability-visibility-matters/

Lorde, A. [1984] 2000. "The Master's Tools Will Never Dismantle the Master's House." In *Sister Outsider: Essays and Speeches by Audre Lorde*, 110–113. Freedom, CA: Crossing Press.

Lorde, A. 1988. *A Burst of Light: Essays*. New York, NY: Sheba Feminist Publishers.

Lugo-Lugo, C. R. 2012. "A Prostitute, a Servant, and a Customer-Service Representative: A Latina in Academia." In *Presumed Incompetent: The Intersections of Race and Class for Women in Academia*, edited by G. Gutiérrez y Muhs, Y.F. Niemann, C.G. González, and A.P. Harris, 40–49. Boulder, CO: University Press of Colorado.

Mason, M. A. 2013. "The Baby Penalty." *The Chronicle of Higher Education*, August 5. http://www. chronicle.com/article/The-Baby-Penalty/140813/

Mingus, M. 2011. "Access Intimacy: The Missing Link [Blog]." *Leaving Evidence*, May 5. https:// leavingevidence.wordpress.com/2011/05/05/access-intimacy-the-missing-link/

Mohamed, T., and B. L. Beagan. 2019. "'Strange Faces' in the Academy: Experiences of Racialized and Indigenous Faculty in Canadian Universities." *Race Ethnicity and Education* 22 (3): 338–354. doi:10.1080/13613324.2018.1511532.

Mountz, A., A. Bonds, B. Mansfield, J. JLoyd, J. Hyndman, M. Walton-Roberts, R. Basu, et al. 2015. "For Slow Scholarship: A Feminist Politics of Resistance through Collective Action in the Neoliberal University." *ACME: An International E-Journal for Critical Geographies* 14 (4): 1235–1259. https://www.acme-journal.org/index.php/acme/article/view/1058

Niemann, Y. F. 2012. "Lessons from the Experiences of Women of Color Working in Academia." In *Presumed Incompetent: The Intersections of Race and Class for Women in Academia*, edited by G. Gutiérrez Y Muhs, Y. F. Niemann, C. G. González, and A. P. Harris, 446–499. Boulder, CO: University Press of Colorado.

Nishida, A. 2016. "Neoliberal Academia and a Critique from Disability Studies." In *Occupying Disability: Critical Approaches to Community, Justice, and Decolonizing Disability*, edited by P. Block, D. Kasnitz, A. Nishida, and N. Pollard, 145–157. New York, NY: Springer. doi:10.1007/ 978-94-017-9984-3.

Okello, W. K. 2020. "Organized Anxiety: Respectability Politics, John Henryism, and the Paradox of Black Achievement." *Race, Ethnicity and Education*: 1–19. Advance online publication. doi:10.1080/13613324.2020.1798916.

Ong, M. 2005. "Body Projects of Young Women of Color in Physics: Intersections of Gender, Race, and Science." *Social Problems* 52 (4): 593–617. doi:10.1525/sp.2005.52.4.593.

Padilla, A. M. 1994. "Ethnic Minority Scholars, Research, and Mentoring: Current and Future Issues." *Educational Researcher* 23 (4): 24–27. doi:10.2307/1176259.

Patten, M. 2016. "What Nobody Tells You about Self-care [Blog]." *The Mighty*, September 9. https://themighty.com/2016/09/self-care-how-to-take-care-of-yourself-when-you-have-depression/

Pelaez Lopez, A. 2018. "The X in Latinx Is a Wound, Not a Trend [Blog]." *Color Bloq*, September 13. https://www.colorbloq.org/the-x-in-latinx-is-a-wound-not-a-trend

Pérez Huber, L. 2009. "Disrupting Apartheid of Knowledge: *Testimonio* as Methodology in Latina/o Critical Race Research in Education." *International Journal of Qualitative Studies in Education* 22 (6): 639–654. doi:10.1080/09518390903333863.

Piepzna-Samarasinha, L. L. 2018. *Care Work: Dreaming Disability Justice*. Vancouver, BC, Canada: Arsenal Pulp Press.

Rose, D. H., and A. Meyer, Eds.. 2006. *A Practical Reader in Universal Design for Learning*. Cambridge, MA: Harvard Education Press.

Roth, W. M. 2009. "Living with Chronic Illness: An Institutional Ethnography of (Medical) Science and Scientific Literacy in Everyday Life." In *Science Education from People for People: Taking a Stand(point)*, edited by W. M. Roth, 146–171, New York, NY: Routledge.

Schwartz, S. J. 2007. "The Applicability of Familism to Diverse Ethnic Groups: A Preliminary Study." *The Journal of Social Psychology* 147 (2): 101–118. doi:10.3200/SOCP.147.2.101-118.

Shahjahan, R. 2019. "On 'Being for Others': Time and Shame in the Neoliberal Academy." *Journal of Educational Polic* 35 (6): 785–811. doi:10.1080/02680939.2019.1629027.

Shahjahan, R. A. 2015. "Being 'Lazy' and Slowing Down: Toward Decolonizing Time, Our Body, and Pedagogy." *Educational Philosophy and Theory: Incorporating ACCESS* 47 (5)): 488–501. doi:10.1080/00131857.2014.880645.

Solorzano, D. G., and T. J. Yosso. 2001. "Critical Race and LatCrit Theory and Method: Counter-storytelling – Chicana and Chicano Graduate School Experiences." *Qualitative Studies in Education* 14 (4): 471–495. doi:10.1080/09518390110063365.

Steele, C. M., and J. Aronson. 1995. "Stereotype Threat and the Intellectual Test Performance of African Americans." *Journal of Personality and Social Psychology* 69 (5): 797–811. doi:10.1037/0022-3514.69.5.797.

Sue, D. W., C. M. Capodilupo, G. C. Torino, J. M. Bucceri, A. M. B. Holder, K. L. Nadal, and M. Esquilin. 2007. "Racial Microaggressions in Everyday Life: Implications for Clinical Practice." *American Psychologist* 62 (4): 271–286. doi:10.1037/0003-066X.62.4.271.

Taylor, S. R. 2018. *The Body Is Not an Apology: The Power of Radical Self-love*. Oakland, CA: Berrett-Koehler Publishers.

Torres, L. E. 2016a. "Tigre Del Mar (Marine Tiger): A Boricua Testimonio of Surviving the Sciences." In *Envisioning Critical Race Praxis in Higher Education through Counter-storytelling*, edited by N. Croom and T. Marsh, 21–42, Charlotte, NC: Information Age Publishing.

Torres, L. E. 2016b. "Sacrificio. [Blog Post]." *Write Where It Hurts*, April 27. http://www.writewhereithurts.net/sacrificio/

Torres, L. E. 2020. "Straddling Death and (Re)birth: A Disabled Latina's Meditation on Collective Care and Mending in Pandemic Times." *Qualitative Inquiry*. doi:10.1177/1077800420960169.

Turner, C. 1994. "Guest in Someone Else's House: Students of Color." *The Review of Higher Education* 17 (4): 350–370. doi:10.1353/rhe.1994.0008.

Vaquera, E., E. Aranda, and R. G. Gonzales. 2014. "Patterns of Incorporation of Latinos in Old and New Destinations: From Invisible to Hypervisible." *American Behavioral Scientist* 58 (14): 1823–1833. doi:10.1177/0002764214550293.

Walker, J. 2009. "Time as the Fourth Dimension in the Globalization of Higher Education." *The Journal of Higher Education* 80: 483–509. doi:10.1080/00221546.2009.11779029.

Webb, L. 2019. „Testimonio, the Assumption of Hybridity and the Issue of Genre." *Studies in Testimony* 2 (1): 3–23.

Wong, A., Ed. 2020. *Disability Visibility: First-person Stories from the Twenty-first Century.* New York: Vintage Books.

Black families' resistance to deficit positioning: addressing the paradox of black parent involvement

Hailey R. Love, Sylvia N. Nyegenye, Courtney L. Wilt and Subini A. Annamma

ABSTRACT
Traditional conceptualizations of parent involvement are applied in paradoxical ways to Black families – schools ostensibly seek families' participation in schooling, while positioning multiply-marginalized Black families as deficient and disregarding their contributions. This article explores the experiences of Black families of Black girls using a Disability Critical Race Theory (DisCrit) framing. Our exploration reveals how Black families experience and resist racism and ableism imbued in traditional conceptualizations of parent involvement grounded in white, middle-class families' norms. We describe ways Black families (1) relocated the problem from Black girls' behavior to schools' expectations and actions; (2) shifted schools' priorities from a focus on disciplining dis/abled Black girls to a focus on their support needs; (3) initiated dialogue to support Black girls; and, (4) assisted Black girls in recognizing, processing, and responding to racism and ableism. Through this discussion, we address ways to reconceptualize parent involvement to center multiply-marginalized Black families' priorities and contributions.

Multiply-marginalized Black families[1] face systemic, intersecting barriers, including racism and ableism, as they navigate school systems. For example, Black families are often perceived by educators to be uninvolved and unconcerned about their children's education (Brown and Brown 2012; Cooper 2009; Puchner and Markowitz 2015), or even threatening (Reynolds, Howard, and Jones 2015), despite their actions and commited support of their children's education. Although schools purport to want families to contribute to their children's education, they position Black families in deficit ways that dismiss and devalue their involvement.

This article examines how traditional parent involvement has been conceptualized in contradictory ways, sedimenting deficit-oriented perspectives of multiply-marginalized Black families, and how Black families resist marginalizing narratives. We first discuss how traditional notions of parent involvement marginalize Black families, explicating the paradox of Black family involvement. We then provide a counternarrative (Solórzano and Yosso 2002), highlighting the ways Black families contribute to their children's education in acts of resistance. We center Black families' experiences, discussing: a) how traditional, contradictory conceptualizations of parent involvement marginalized Black families and b) ways Black families strategically resisted marginalization to support their children's education. This juxtaposition contradicts masternarratives (Gotanda 1995) of uninvolved Black families and contributes to a conceptualization of parent involvement that centers the priorities and strengths of Black families. This exploration aids a reconceptualization of parent involvement by centering Black families' voices and refuting deficit-laden, paradoxical parental involvement narratives.

Problemetizing traditional conceptualizations of parent involvement

The concept of 'parent involvement' has been applied as an overarching term to reflect parents' participation in activities that support their children's education (Goodall and Montgomery 2014; Lai and Vadeboncoeur 2013). Traditional definitions of parent involvement cite similar lists of activities expected of parents, such as: (a) volunteering at school; (b) assisting with homework; (c) attending parent-teacher conferences and student performances; (d) monitoring their children's academic progress; and, (e) communicating with teachers (Bower and Griffin 2011). However, while the broadest definitions of parent involvement include activities at home and school, in practice and in scholarly discourses, traditional notions of parent involvement often revolve around parents' participation in school-based activities (Christianakis 2011; Lai and Vadeboncoeur 2013; Marchand et al. 2019). For example, research has often operationalized parent involvement based on parents' physical presence at school-sanctioned events and meetings (e.g. Nzinga-Johnson, Baker, and Aupperlee 2009; Benner and Yan 2015). As such, traditional conceptualizations of parent involvement are primarily based on white, middle-class family norms (Bower and Griffin 2011; Cooper 2009; Ishimaru, Barajas-López, and Bang 2015). Black families are subject to racism when the norms of white families are used to position Black families in deficit ways. Moreover, the use of narrow socially-constructed behavior norms to marginalize Black families reflects ableism because Black families' divergence from said norms becomes a justification to devalue their contributions and dismiss their needs (Campbell 2008).

Traditional conceptualizations of parent involvement also reinforce a differential power dynamic between schools and families (Van Laere, Van Houtte, and Vandenbroeck 2018). Schools retain control over the types, means, and norms of parent involvement (Bower and Griffin 2011; Ishimaru, Barajas-López, and Bang 2015). Schools' narrow dictates about parent involvement and the ways they use said expectations to invalidate parent concerns and assert control is a form of paternalism, a process of ableism (Nario-Redmond, Kemerling, and Silverman 2019). That is, when individuals do not meet a set of norms, that divergence is used as evidence that they are generally incapable and require intervention or 'help,' without consideration of the individual's desires or priorities. For instance, schools often blame Black families not engaging in traditional parent involvement behaviors for any educational challenges their children experience and assert that Black families require training and intervention (Baquedano-López, Alexander, and Hernández 2013). Blaming families shifts attention from the structures and processes that systematically fail Black students and absolves schools of responsibility for addressing racial inequities that Black families call attention to (Brown and Brown 2012; Kohli, Pizarro, and Nevárez 2017). Moreover, teachers may withhold resources and opportunities to both parents and their children when parents do not meet traditional parent involvement expectations (Ho and Cherng 2018), an act of disablement because it removes supportive opportunities that are important for Black students and families.

The Individuals with Disabilities Education Act (IDEA 2004) and its precursors have bolstered traditional conceptualizations of parent involvement for families of children receiving special education services in ways that marginalize Black families. IDEA identifies parents as partners in disability identification, placement, and service delivery decision-making, and specifies avenues through which they can resolve disputes with schools. However, the law establishes narrow parameters of how parents should engage in special education processes, reinforcing the power differential between schools and families and limiting the legitimized ways families of Color, particularly Black families, can advocate for their children once they are labeled as disabled (Kalyanpur and Harry 2012; Lalvani and Hale 2015). Moreover, white families are more likely to posses the cultural and economic capital that is required for the types of advocacy sanctioned by IDEA (2004; Ong-Dean 2009). Consequently, Black parents are tasked with the responsibility to constantly defend their rights during IDEA-mandated processes, such as individualized education program (IEP) meetings, that keep them in a subordinate position (Buren, Maggin, and Brown 2018). Thus, dictating expectations for parent involvement is one way IDEA (2004) has actually perpetuated racism and ableism and maintained existing structural hierarchies (Beratan 2006; Ong-Dean 2009).

The paradox of black parent involvement

There is a two-fold paradox of Black parent involvement animated by racism and ableism embedded in the ways parent involvement has been traditionally conceptualized by schools. First, while schools purport to want parents to be involved in their children's education, they only accept and respond to certain school-based types of parent involvement that reflect white, middle-class family norms (Christianakis 2011; Cooper 2009; Lai and Vadeboncoeur 2013; Ishimaru, Barajas-López, and Bang 2015). When compared to white, middle-class parent involvement norms, Black families are perceived as uninvolved, even as they engage in home-based school support such as positive academic socialization, providing Black children with positive racial messages, and proffering opportunities for community leadership (Bhargava and Witherspoon 2015; Vincent et al. 2013). Black families' parent involvement activities are often driven by their understanding of the pervasive insidiousness of anti-Black racism (Allen and White-Smith 2018). Black families also engage in communal care that shapes how they support children's education at a community-level (Cooper 2009). In contrast, scholars have noted that traditional notions of parent involvement are largely individualistic in nature (Cucchiara and Horvat 2009; Lalvani and Hale 2015). Positioning Black families as uninvolved even as they engage in home-based school support and collective action is racist because white families are held as the standard by which Black families are judged. Meanwhile, traditional conceptualizations of parent involvement are ableist because they position Black families as deficient based on these narrow behavioral expectations. As Lewis (2021) makes clear in her definition of ableism, one does not have to be disabled to experience ableism because it is a form of systemic oppression entrenched in anti-

Blackness. Multiply-marginalized Black families of dis/abled students are particularly prone to ableist interpretations of their behaviors as deficit perspectives about their children's abilities are generalized to deficit perceptions of the family, a pathologizing process Kirshbaum (2000) referred to as disability 'spread.'

Secondly, while research and practice-oriented endeavors ostensibly seek to get Black families to be 'more involved,' when Black families participate in school-sanctioned parent involvement, they continue to be positioned in deficit ways and dismissed (Allen and White-Smith 2018; Puchner and Markowitz 2015). When participating in school-sanctioned parent involvement activities, Black families are often percieved and treated as intimidating, confrontational, and uninformed, reflecting social stereotypes of Black people (Diamond and Gomez 2004; Reynolds, Howard, and Jones 2015). Schools subsequently justify dismissing the efforts of and excluding Black families from decision-making processes (Gillborn et al. 2016), including formalized special education prodecures (Lalvani 2014). This creates a situation where Black families are dually viewed as obstructing *and* not contributing to their children's education, regardless of the supports they provide. Thus, racism and ableism intersect as schools effectively disable Black families by denying them decision-making power and opportunities. The intersections between racism and ableism in traditional parent involvement expectations has largely been rendered invisible through operationalizations of parent involvement that uncritically apply tranditional expectations to Black families (e.g. Nzinga-Johnson, Baker, and Aupperlee 2009), (re)conceptualizations of parent involvement that do not explicitly account for the needs and priorities of Black families, and federal mandates (i.e. IDEA).

Given the paradox of Black family involvement, the present analysis was guided by the question, *in what ways do multiply-marginalized Black families counter the paradox of parent involvement while contributing to their children's lives and education?* By exploring this question, we can better understand how to (re)conceptualize parent involvement in a way that sustains Black families' decisions and priorities.

Shifting from parent involvement

Scholars have argued for a shift away from parent involvement to notions of parent, or family, engagement and partnership that reflect a more dynamic relationship between parents and schools (e.g. Haines et al. 2015), and recognize the many ways families support children's education (e.g. Ishimaru, Barajas-López, and Bang 2015). However thoughtful, these re-conceptualizations of parent involvement often do not explicitly rectify the positioning of Black families as problems who need to be brought into schools (under specific expectations), and who are responsible for the persistence of achievement inequities (Baquedano-López, Alexander, and Hernández 2013). Even as language has shifted, the actions of families often continue to be viewed as a set of discrete behaviors supporting school-determined goals (e.g. Epstein and Sheldon 2016). Such conceptualization leaves room for multiply-marginalized Black families to be deemed 'not engaged' or to be positioned as the reason for partnership failures and children's challenges in school. In this article, we extend previous calls to reconceptualize parent involvement to explicitly counter deficit views of Black families and focus on Black families' resistance, priorities, and contributions.

Illucidating racism and ableism in parental involvement

We use Disability Critical Race Theory (DisCrit), an intersectional lens, to center the experiences of Black families. Tenet one of DisCrit highlights the ways racism and ableism interdependently uphold notions of normalcy, particularly through processes put forth as race-neutral (Annamma, Ferri, and Connor 2018), and illuminates how the paradox of parent involvement positions the behaviors of White families as normal and desired, and Black families as deficient (Cooper 2009; Ishimaru, Barajas-López, and Bang 2015). By recognizing this process as both racist and ableist, we can better explicate the ways marginalization happens, and identify resistance.

DisCrit tenet two calls attention to the multidimensional nature of identities while explicitly rejecting singular notions of identity (e.g. race or disability or class, etc.; Annamma, Ferri, and Connor 2018; Banks 2017). Race, class, and gender identities intersect in the construction of dis/ability[2] and the ways Black families are positioned as they endeavor to get their children's needs met (Gillborn 2015). Accordingly, tenet three emphasizes that race and ability are social constructions with material realities (Annamma, Ferri, and Connor 2018) that justify discriminatory practices (Mendoza, Paguyo, and Gutiérrez 2016). By narrowly defining acceptable parent involvement in racialized and abled ways, schools dismiss the efforts of Black families and deny them resources (e.g. Lalvani 2014; Lareau and Horvat 1999). We distinguish these interrelated processes as effectively debilitating, wherein foreclosure of access (Puar 2017) to education opportunities and resources occurs because Black families are imagined as undeserving of those resources. Finally, DisCrit's seventh tenent recognizes resistance in all forms (Annamma, Ferri, and Connor 2018). We situated Black families as knowledge generators (Matsuda 1987) and aimed to disrupt power-laden definitions of parent involvement by emphasizing the voices of multiply-marginalized Black families who resist deficit positioning. In sum, DisCrit afforded an intersectional analysis, centering Black families as experts on the education of Black girls and highlighting the subtle ways the paradox of Black parent involvement marginalized Black families, but also how they resisted marginalization.

Methods

This exploration was a part of a larger two-year ethnographic study about experiences and understandings of disciplinary disparities centering the voices of girls of color, their families, and their teachers. The present analysis focuses on the experiences of Black families, drawing on: (a) focus groups and interviews; (b) observations of events and district parent meetings; and, (c) document analyses of district documents and news articles. Within the context of the larger study, we identified unique patterns amongst the Black families we interviewed.

Black families in the study

Families were recruited using critical case purposive sampling (Miles, Huberman, and Saldaña 2014). The sample included one Black father (Adrian) who was also the legal guardian to his niece and three Black mothers (Hazel, Christie, Stacy). Their children were not required to have experienced disciplinary systems in order to participate in the study. Our focus was to account for the many ways families of color engaged with schools and their perceptions about the ways schools may (or may not) have addressed the education and discipline of girls of color.

In addition to interviews and focus groups with Black families, we drew from multiple data sources (observations, district documents, news articles) that reflected the experiences of Black families, specifically, and families of color, in general. Thus, prolonged engagement and the use of multiple data sources deepened our understandings (Lincoln and Guba 1985). Additionally, by identifying unique patterns in Black families' experiences across our data sets, we were able to capture an in-depth exploration of their experiences, despite a small sample size (Onwuegbuzie and Leech 2007).

Data collection and analysis

We conducted three focus groups and two interviews with the four Black parents, totaling 5 hours and 57 minutes (156 pages). Discussion topics included their girls' academic and disciplinary experiences, families' experiences communicating and collaborating with school personnel, and other ways families engaged with the district. After the first set of interviews and focus groups, we asked families to respond to the team's initial ideas about emerging themes and used elicitation techniques as forms of member checking (Birt et al. 2016). Throughout data collection and analysis, we wrote research journals to guide a reflexive component (Rodwell 1998).

We analyzed transcripts through several iterative stages of analysis, including unitizing, categorizing, defining, and applying codes (Rodwell 1998; Saldaña 2013). Once the codes were fairly established, multiple researchers coded the same transcript and then compared codes to check consistent application and potential areas for refinement (Lincoln and Guba 1985). After a final check for consistency, all transcripts were re-coded using the established coding structure. Throughout analysis, team members wrote analytic memos connecting data to literature and drawing potential code connections (Maxwell 2013).

The present exploration also draws on field notes (Saldaña 2013) from 4.5 hours of observations taken during three events, two hosted by the district to address the 'achievement gap' and one organized by a local middle school for families of color to discuss challenges and develop community. Additionally, a district feedback document (67 pages) and equity plan (7 pages) were analyzed. The feedback document contained publicly available responses to questions from the district's community educational equity event. Finally, ten news articles were analyzed that covered the two district events and district racial equity initatives. Document analysis of the feedback document and news articles was conducted between rounds of interviews and focus groups to inform data collection and again after transcript coding to look for patterns that informed thematic analysis, reflecting iterative analysis (Bhattacharya 2017).

Repositioning black girls and black families

There are ways that we can always improve excellence, equity, and engagement of school families and community partners. Tonight is about teamwork, our kids, and their future. Whether you enter the room in an emotional state, and I enter in a thinking state, we should find a middle ground. (Superintendent, District Equity Meeting, Field Notes).

This discussion begins with a quote from the district's equity meeting. The impetus for this meeting was an incident where a white teacher made racist comments during class in the most racially-diverse school in the district; students of color accounted for approximately 42% of enrollment. The encounter, and the way it was handled, triggered a series of protests at school board meetings with families sharing concerns about racial equity. The teacher eventually resigned. The equity event was well-attended by school personnel, students, and parents, particularly Black families.

In the above quote, it is noteworthy that, while the superintendent's stated intention was to work with families in attendance, of which Black families were well-represented, he created a false binary (emotional vs. thinking) and immediately separated himself by situating parents as emotional and himself as rational. By opening the event this way, the superintendent positioned the school as being the rightful arbiters of the families' role. In line with the paradox of Black parent involvement, he invited parents to be involved, but only in accordance with school boundaries, while simultaneously positioning them as subordinate, rather than equal partners. This quote is a clear example of several patterns Black families discussed.

While the paradox of Black parent involvement, as illustrated in the above example, served to limit Black families' contributions to their children's education, Black families worked to counter the deficit positioning of themselves and their girls. Black families did this by: (1) relocating the problem from Black girls' behavior to the schools' expectations and actions; (2) shifting the schools' priorities from a focus on disciplining dis/abled Black girls to a focus on providing supports; (3) initiating dialogue to focus on Black girls' support needs; and, (4) helping Black girls recognize, process, and respond to racism and ableism. As Black families made these strategic moves, they repositioned their girls as being in need of supports and repositioned themselves as accurate interpreters and communicators of their girls' behavior and support needs.

Relocating the problem

Black families recognized how schools positioned their Black girls as problems and, in response, they relocated the problem from one of their girls' behaviors to that of the schools' deficit positioning and subsequent actions. For example, Hazel and Christi described:

Interviewer: Do you feel that that's happened to your girls also . . . once they were having difficulties, they started getting treated differently?

Hazel: Mm hm. Because they're labeled a problem child.

Christi: Yep.

Interviewer: Mm hm. Do you think that that label has like followed them, as far as –

Christi: Yes.

Interviewer: Like, teachers knowing, other teachers knowing, or new teachers knowing –

Christi: I do.

Christi and Hazel believed when their Black girls experienced difficulties, schools located the problem within the girls. This label was particularly problematic because it followed the girls as teachers informed other staff, leading to their Black girls being treated differently. By highlighting the ways this narrative was used against their girls, Black families shifted the source of challenges from within their girls to the schools' actions.

Black families also illuminated the larger context of racism and ableism that contributed to their girls being labeled as a 'problem.' For example, families understood that the way Black girls expressed themselves was juxtaposed against a school culture that set narrow communication expectations. Adrian explained:

> They don't, the culture doesn't accept that, you know that people can be passionate and-and loud, and, um, the, that that's a form of communication, you know ... but the culture says that you need to communicate how serious you are about something in a different way which that's you know some people (people) that's not the culture they grew up in ...

As Adrian described, Black girls' behavior was highly scrutinized based on narrow socially-constructed norms against which they were judged as deficient, resulting in their experiences of ableism. Black families' observations illustrate the processes that contribute to Black girls' experiences of their actions being misinterpreted as aggressive, leading to harsh disciplinary practices (Murphy, Acosta, and Kennedy-Lewis 2013) and hyper-surveillance, contributing to the school-to-prison pipeline (Wun 2016). Their experiences with discipline adds to previous literature that has focused on families' reports of similar processes that lead to greater surveillance and control over Black boys (e.g. Gillborn et al. 2016).

Hazel similarly reported harassment and discipline of Black youth from a security guard.

Interviewer: Do you know, does it seem like there are certain groups, or certain students that he um –

Hazel: Black children.

Interviewer: Black children?

Hazel: And he's Black himself ...

Interviewer: So you think he kind of watches Black children more, like, tries to interact with them more –

Hazel: Yeah.

Christi: He gets them in trouble more.

Hazel: If they're not a certain way, or they don't dress a certain type –

Hazel and Christi reported that Black students were subject to greater surveillance and punishment if they did not meet the security guard's expectations. The fact that Black students were uniquely held to these standards and found deficient again reflects an intersection of racism and ableism where Black girls are positioned as deserving of surveillance and discipline. Hazel also noted that the security guard was Black, pointing to the need to consider the disparate treatment of Black students as systemic racism (i.e. the result of racist institutionalized structures and processes) rather than isolated bias of white school staff (Annamma and Morrison 2018). This is similar to the Black Caribbean families interviewed by Gillborn et al. (2016) in the United Kingdom. By illucidating these processes, Black families consistently shifted the locus of the problem from their girls' behavior to schools' expectations and actions.

During the district-sponsored event addressing racial equity, families also located the problem within schools by charging the district with finding a solution. The district-hired facilitator argued that the event should aim for 'progress, not [a] fix' and even had the attendees repeat that phrase before continuing. In seeking to control the parents' expectations and actions while not leaving space for families' desires or open expression, despite inviting parents for open 'conversation,' the school's actions reflected Black families' experience of paternalistic ableism. However, when the event was opened up for final comments towards the end of the night, a Black mother stood to say, in part, 'Our call to the district is more than simply conversations ... We want a fix.' Thus, the Black parent pushed back on the assertion that families could not expect results from the district. Once the Black mother shifted the focus from general discussion to a call for action, parents, students, and community members began sharing their experiences and desires for change. Even as they operated within paradoxical parent involvement expectations, Black families spoke out to relocate the source of racial inequities, and the responsibility to fix it, to the district.

Shifting from dis/abled black girls need discipline to dis/abled black girls need support

The label of 'problem' student that Christi and Adrian previously referred to, and that is more often applied to Black students, resulted in the surveillance and punishment of Black girls (Annamma 2018). However, Black families rejected the school's positioning of their girls as students who required discipline, particularly their girls with dis/abilities. Christi's daughter with significant depression was punished frequently for absenteeism, but typically missed class to receive support from her counselor. Similarly, Hazel's daughter was punished due to her diabetes.

Christi: Hazel's daughter is diabetic. They've had issues with that. Uh, cause she would be late to class, but she would have to go get some juice or a cracker or something real fast ... and they would give her crap about that.

Interviewer: So then she would get in-school suspension for being late –

Hazel: Yeah

Black girls' absences and lateness served as the focal points of school punishment, while their disability-related needs were ignored. Black families recognized that punishment was administered erroneously based on school personnel not responding to Black dis/abled students' needs.

Accordingly, Black families argued for a shift in discourse and approaches regarding their girls' academic and behavioral supports. Christi and Hazel explained that the school sent automated calls to inform them when their girls missed a class. However, while these calls were ostensibly the school's communication effort, Christ and Hazel recognized that they primarily served as discipline. Christi remarked, 'we wouldn't be notified until 4:30 p.m. that they didn't go to school, or they missed this and that class. I mean, if you're so concerned, why can't you call me when she misses the first class, so I know where is she?' The calls were ineffective as a support process, in part, because they were done at the end of the day, after students had already missed some or all of the school day. This was particularly concerning for Christi's daughter because of her significant depression, which the school knew about; when her daughter missed class, Christi worried for her safety. Additionally, because the calls were automated, families were denied the opportunity to gather further information about students' absences or needs and act accordingly if a student was in danger. This example typified how traditional applications of parent involvement are disabling for multiply-marginalized Black families.

Adrian, whose daughter received special education services primarily for behavioral support needs, expressed similar experiences of delayed and ineffective communication. He reported that there had been multiple instances when he would be notified at a parent-teacher meeting that his daughter had engaged in behaviors that led to disciplinary action weeks prior. He pointed out that the delayed communication meant that he and his wife were not able to address his daughter's needs as they saw fit, saying, 'I know that one way we can handle it is if we know sooner than later.' To Black families, delayed communication demonstrated little regard for the support dis/abled Black girls needed and impeded families' ability to address their girls' needs. Black families continually challenged schools to collaborate with them in order to better meet their children's needs, rather than impose ineffective discipline practices.

Black family-intiated dialogue to focus on black girls' support needs

Schools' disciplinary actions occurred without proactive or effective communication with multiply-marginalized Black families. Such ineffective communication relegated Black families to a subordinate role where they were positioned as passive and unnecessary participants in educational decision-making. Communication as a part of traditional parent involvement has often been enacted in ways that position schools as the sole initators of one-way communication (Saltmarsh and McPherson 2019; Stacey 2016) and the authorities on what students need (Goodall 2018). In contrast, Black families in this study initated communication to push schools to focus on their girls' support needs and reposition themselves as authorities on, and supporters of, their Black girls. In doing so, they moved beyond traditional modes of communication and enacted a dialogue to ensure that Black girls would get necessary and appropriate supports. Dialgoue differs from communication in that both parties actively contribute to the discussion and, intermittedly, take on the role of initiator (Goodall 2018). Christi, for example, began proactively checking on her daughter's attendance at school.

Christi: And it got to where up to the, after a while it was me calling, is [DAUGHTER] in school? Did [DAUGHTER] make it today? Are you at school? Like, and they're like, yeah, and I'm like, yeah, she was, but –

Interviewer: So then, you started taking the initiative of calling to check,

Christi: Right, because then I get scared of, like, because she is probably going to hurt herself, so –

Christi shifted the focus of communication with the school from disciplining her daughter to supporting her and preventing harm. While the school used communication with parents primarily as a form of discipline or to notify them of discipline, Black families initiated dialogue with schools as a means of securing support for their Black girls.

Multiply-marginalized Black families that did initiate dialogue with schools were often dismissed or ignored, as previous research has indicated (e.g. Gillborn et al. 2016; Lareau and Horvat 1999). Consequently, they often had to repeatedly follow-up with multiple school personnel, while continuing to advocate for schools to re-focus their attention on supporting their girls. After Stacy's daughter started experiencing significant academic challenges in a math class, Stacy had to constantly follow-up with the teacher, and eventually, her daughter's school counselor. Stacy questioned, 'like all those times with Ms. [counselor], with certain things, you know, what if I didn't follow up? Why, why do I have to, you know, follow-up with you to get you to – ... I shouldn't have to do that.' Even as Stacy engaged in school-sanctioned means of parent involvement that are generally effective for white, middle-class families (meeting with the teacher, communicating about student's academic achievement; Goodall and Montgomery 2014; Stacey 2016), she was repeatedly dismissed and her daughter's challenges were ignored or viewed as a problem with her academic abilities. Racist application of parent involvement expectations and deficit views of Black girls resulted in the denial of supports to Black girls, as illucidated by DisCrit tenet three, which highlights the intersectional ways that social constructions of race and ability sustain discriminatory practices (Annamma, Ferri, and Connor 2018; Mendoza, Paguyo, and Gutiérrez 2016).

Stacy and Christi's experiences also illustrate how multiply-marginalized Black families initiated dialogue as a form of resistance. Black families initiated dialogue with instructional and administrative staff (e.g. teachers, assistant principals, principals), as well as with support offices (e.g. counselors, front office staff). Attending to their actions as a type of resistance, in line with DisCrit tenet seven (Annamma, Ferri, and Connor 2018), gives different meaning to previous characterizations of Black families' involvement as being community-oriented. Indeed, Black families expressed concern for improving educational supports for all children (Cooper 2009; Cucchiara and Horvat 2009), but they also held the entire school community accountable for ensuring their girls received necessary supports. Thus, their parent involvement behaviors were broader than the traditional focus of parent involvement on parent-teacher interactions.

Helping black girls recognize, process, and respond to racism and ableism

Black families recognize that racism is a common experience in their childen's lives and that it is often rendered invisible through subtle actions and patterns (Vincent et al. 2013). Accordingly, Black parents proactively socialize their children to address racism by defining the many ways it manifests, naming the barriers that racism creates, and teaching children how to respond (Allen 2013; Banerjee, Harrell, and Johnson 2011). Black families in this study reported using proactive socialization to prepare Black girls to address racism *and* ableism. For example, Adrian socialized his children to recognize racism and understand their rights. Adrian was his niece's legal guardian and he explained that he was, 'helping her see like these are the types of flags you look for, red flags that say hey, that's racial, that's injustice and you gotta speak up or do something about it.' Black families described similar examples of proactive socialization and saw this as a central component of their support, thereby repositioning themselves as actively engaged in their children's education, even when schools did not recognize or acknowledge their involvement. In doing so, they also repositioned their girls as active self-advocates rather than passive recipients of racism.

While Adrian described preparing all of his children to understand and deal with racism, he discussed the need to uniquely prepare his daughter, who received special education services. He said,

> And so we just have to help her –I believe, we just gotta help her understand what's acceptable in some cultures or not, and when you get in some situations, like school, you actually have to sit down, and you have to leave their pencils alone or whatever, and you gotta learn that behavior ... I don't see it as much as a disciplinary [issue], as much as it is her learning that culture that she's in ...

Even though Adrian previously acknowledged that schools upheld narrow behavioral standards that marginalized Black girls, he recognized that his dis/abled daughter needed to be explicitly prepared to understand and conform to those behavioral standards because of the way she had been labeled. Thus, while Adrian did not agree with these norms, he recognized how adhereing to them was necessary protection for his dis/abled child. Black families prepared their girls to identify racism while also helping them understand and address ableist behavioral standards that were differentially applied to them as Black children.

In addition to proactive socialization, Black families helped their girls process and respond to racist and ableist experiences. For example, after the 2016 election, Stacy's daughter told her about students supporting Donald Trump at school and saying, 'white America.' Stacy responded by helping her daughter reflect on how she felt and offering to intervene. She explained, 'I was like, "Well how do you feel about that" ... I was like, "you just need to call me ... "' Stacy both prompted her daughter to reflect critically about the experience and ensured that her daughter knew she was available for help. Meanwhile, Christi and Hazel both emphasized that they try to help their girls not internalize others' ableist perspectives. Christi advised her daughter, 'Don't let them, these people, define you or ruin your life. You have to get an education. You have to work through this and keep living.' Christi's encouragement when her daughter experienced racism and ableism based on her depression was grounded in the idea that she needed to care for herself. Black families supported their girls' positive self-image in the face of racism and ableism as they helped them resist internalization of deficit messages. These acts of resistance countered paradoxical parent involvement conceptualizations in which Black families were positioned as passive or detrimental to their girls' education.

Conclusion

We explored how Black families repositioned themselves and their girls in the face of the paradox of Black parent involvement, which was animated by racism and ableism. While schools purported to want parents to be involved in their children's education, they asserted narrow bounds around acceptable behaviors that attempted to dismiss Black families' contributions. Yet, Black families continued to push schools to recognize and address the ways school expectations and actions marginalized their girls and shifted schools' focus from disciplining dis/abled Black girls to supporting them. Additionally, schools employed techniques that treated communication with families as disciplinary action and were not responsive to Black families' concerns. However, Black families attempted to intiate dialogue with schools to facilitate supports for their girls and helped Black girls recognize, process, and respond to both ableism and racism.

Black families' resistance provides important implications for reconceptualizing parent involvement based on the priorities and contributions of Black families. 'Critical parent engagement,' as conceptualized by Marchand et al. (2019), may be useful as future research continues to reconceptualize parent involvement in ways that center Black families. The authors conceptualized critical parent engagement as advocacy that includes the many ways Black families support their children's education in light of a critical consciousness that recognizes the influence of race and racism. The present analysis adds the importance of recognizing how Black families also countered ableism, as a system that is interdependent with racism. Conceptualization of critical parent (or family) enagement that incorporates Black families' consciousness of racism *and* ableism can incorporate Black families' use of dialogue and efforts to engage schools across power structures and support offices. Additionally, such conceptualization can highlight the ways Black families hold schools accountable for supporting, rather than disciplining, dis/abled Black students. Future research should continue to explore how Black families resist racism and ableism as interdependent systems and make strategic decisions as a part of their resistance. Centering the voices of multiply-marginalized Black families can lead to reconceptualizations of parent involvement that account for the many ways it is paradoxically applied.

Notes

1. In acknowledging the many adults who contribute to the development and education of children within Black families, specifically Patricia Hill-Collins (2000) work on other-mothering, we focus on the contributions of the myriad of family and community members caring for Black children, not just biological parents. This language also refuses the heteronormative assumptions on who cares for children. Consequently, we use the language of Black Family.
2. In this paper, we use disability and disabled to connote a political identity. We use dis/ability to foreground the ways conceptions of ability and disability rely on each other and coexist (Annamma, Ferri, and Connor 2018). We believe engaging this distinction allows us to better engage in conversations about the ways both ability and disability operate in social arenas.

Disclosure statement

No potential conflict of interest was reported by the author(s).

ORCID

Subini A. Annamma http://orcid.org/0000-0002-8744-6456

References

Allen, Q. 2013. "'They Think Minority Means Lesser Than': Black Middle-class Sons and Fathers Resisting Microaggressions in the School." *Urban Education* 48 (2): 171–197. doi:10.1177/0042085912450575.

Allen, Q., and K. White-Smith. 2018. "'That's Why I Say Stay in School': Black Mothers' Parental Involvement, Cultural Wealth, and Exclusion in Their Son's Schooling." *Urban Education* 53 (3): 409–435. doi:10.1177/0042085917714516.

Annamma, S., and D. Morrison. 2018. "Identifying Dysfunctional Education Ecologies: A DisCrit Analysis of Bias in the Classroom." *Equity & Excellence in Education* 51 (2): 114–131. doi:10.1080/10665684.2018.1496047.

Annamma, S. A. 2018. "Mapping Consequential Geographies in the Carceral State: Education Journey Mapping as a Qualitative Method with Girls of Color with Dis/abilities." *Qualitative Inquiry* 24 (1): 20–34. doi:10.1177/1077800417728962.

Annamma, S. A., D. Connor, and B. Ferri. 2013. "Dis/ability Critical Race Studies (DisCrit): Theorizing at the Intersections of Race and Dis/ability." *Race Ethnicity and Education* 16 (1): 1–31. doi:10.1080/13613324.2012.730511.

Annamma, S. A., B. A. Ferri, and D. J. Connor. 2018. "Disability Critical Race Theory: Exploring the Intersectional Lineage, Emergence, and Potential Futures of DisCrit in Education." *Review of Research in Education* 42 (1): 46–71. doi:10.3102/0091732X18759041.

Banerjee, M., Z. A. Harrell, and D. J. Johnson. 2011. "Racial/ethnic Socialization and Parental Involvement in Education as Predictors of Cognitive Ability and Achievement in African-American Children." *Journal of Youth and Adolescence* 40 (5): 595–605. doi:10.1007/s10964-010-9559-9.

Banks, J. 2017. "'These People are Never Going to Stop Labeling Me': Educational Experiences of African American Male Students Labeled with Learning Disabilities." *Equity & Excellence in Education* 50 (1): 96–107. doi:10.1080/10665684.2016.1250235.

Baquedano-López, P., R. A. Alexander, and S. J. Hernández. 2013. "Equity Issues in Parental and Community Involvement in Schools: What Teacher Educators Need to Know." *Review of Research in Education* 37 (1): 149–182. doi:10.3102/0091732X12459718.

Benner, A. D., and N. Yan. 2015. "Classroom Race/ethnic Composition, Family-school Connections, and the Transition to School." *Applied Developmental Science* 19 (3): 127–138. doi:10.1080/10888691.2014.983028.

Beratan, G. D. 2006. "Institutionalizing Inequity: Ableism, Racism and IDEA 2004." *Disability Studies Quarterly* 26 (2). doi:10.18061/dsq.v26i2.682.

Bhargava, S., and D. P. Witherspoon. 2015. "Parental Involvement across Middle and High School: Exploring Contributions of Individual and Neighborhood Characteristics." *Journal of Youth and Adolescence* 44 (9): 1702–1719. doi:10.1007/s10964-015-0334-9.

Bhattacharya, K. 2017. *Fundamentals of Qualitative Research: A Practical Guide*. New York, NY: Routledge.

Birt, L., S. Scott, D. Cavers, C. Campbell, and F. Walter. 2016. "Member Checking: A Tool to Enhance Trustworthiness or Merely A Nod to Validation?" *Qualitative Health Research* 26: 1802–1811. doi:10.1177/1049732316654870.

Bower, H. A., and D. Griffin. 2011. "Can the Epstein Model of Parental Involvement Work in A High-minority, High-poverty Elementary School? A Case Study." *Professional School Counseling* 15 (2): 77–87. doi:10.1177/2156759X1101500201.

Brown, K. D., and A. L. Brown. 2012. "Useful and Dangerous Discourse: Deconstructing Racialized Knowledge about African-American Students." *Educational Foundations* 26 (1–2): 11–26.

Buren, M. K., D. M. Maggin, and C. Brown. 2018. "Meta-synthesis on the Experiences of Families from Nondominant Communities and Special Education Collaboration." *Exceptionality*. doi:10.1080/09362835.2018.1480953.

Campbell, F. K. 2008. "Refusing Able(ness): A Preliminary Conversation about Ableism." *M/C Journal: A Journal of Media and Culture* 11 (3). doi:10.5204/mcj.46.

Christianakis, M. 2011. "Parents As" Help Labor": Inner-city Teachers' Narratives of Parent Involvement." *Teacher Education Quarterly* 38 (4): 157–178.

Collins, P. H. 2000. *Black Feminist Thought: Knowledge, Consciousness, and the Politics of Empowerment*. 2nd ed. New York, NY: Routledge.

Cooper, C. W. 2009. "Parent Involvement, African-American Mothers, and the Politics of Educational Care." *Equity & Excellence in Education* 42 (4): 379–394. doi:10.1080/10665680903228389.

Cucchiara, M. B., and E. M. Horvat. 2009. "Perils and Promises: Middle-class Parental Involvement in Urban Schools." *American Educational Research Journal* 46 (4): 974–1004. doi:10.3102/0002831209345791.

Diamond, J. B., and K. Gomez. 2004. "African-American Parents' Educational Orientations: The Importance of Social Class and Parents' Perceptions of Schools." *Education and Urban Society* 36 (4): 383–427. doi:10.1177/0013124504266827.

Epstein, J. L., and S. B. Sheldon. 2016. "Necessary but Not Sufficient: The Role of Policy for Advancing Programs of School, Family, and Community Partnerships." *RSF: The Russell Sage Foundation Journal of the Social Sciences* 2 (5): 202–219. doi:10.7758/RSF.2016.2.5.10.

Gillborn, D. 2015. "Intersectionality, Critical Race Theory, and the Primacy of Racism: Race, Class, Gender, and Disability in Education." *Qualitative Inquiry* 21 (3): 277–287. doi:10.1177/1077800414557827.

Gillborn, D., N. Rollock, C. Vincent, and S. Ball. 2016. "The Black Middle Classes, Education, Racism, and Dis/ability." In *DisCrit: Critical Conversations across Race, Class, & Dis/ability*, edited by D. Connor, B. Ferri, and S. A. Annamma, 35–54, New York, NY: Teachers College Press.

Goodall, J. 2018. "Learning-centered Parental Engagement: Freire Reimagined." *Educational Review* 70 (5): 603–621. doi:10.1080/00131911.2017.1358697.

Goodall, J., and C. Montgomery. 2014. "Parental Involvement to Parental Engagement: A Continuum." *Educational Review* 66 (4): 399–410. doi:10.1080/00131911.2013.781576.

Gotanda, N. 1995. "Critical Legal Studies, Critical Race Theory and Asian-American Studies." *Amerasia Journal* 21 (1–2): 127–136. doi:10.17953/amer.21.1-2.2j46202k85658662.

Haines, S. J., J. M. Gross, M. Blue-Banning, G. L. Francis, and A. P. Turnbull. 2015. "Fostering Family–School and Community–School Partnerships in Inclusive Schools: Using Practice as a Guide." *Research and Practice for Persons with Severe Disabilities* 40 (3): 227–239. doi:10.1177/1540796915594141.

Ho, P., and H. Y. S. Cherng. 2018. "How Far Can the Apple Fall? Differences in Teacher Perceptions of Minority and Immigrant Parents and Their Impact on Academic Outcomes." *Social Science Research* 74: 132–145. doi:10.1016/j.ssresearch.2018.05.001.

Individuals with Disabilities Education Improvement Act. 2004. P.L. 108–446, 20 U.S.C. §§ 1400 et seq.

Ishimaru, A. M., F. Barajas-López, and M. Bang. 2015. "Centering Family Knowledge to Develop Children's Empowered Mathematics Identities." *Journal of Family Diversity in Education* 1 (4): 1–21.

Kalyanpur, M., and B. Harry. 2012. *Culture in Special Education: Building Reciprocal Family Professional Relationships*. Baltimore, MD: Brookes.

Kirshbaum, M. 2000. "A Disability Culture Perspective on Early Intervention with Parents with Physical or Cognitive Disabilities and Their Infants." *Infants and Young Children* 13 (2): 9–20. doi:10.1097/00001163-200013020-00006.

Kohli, R., M. Pizarro, and A. Nevárez. 2017. "The 'New Racism' of K–12 Schools: Centering Critical Research on Racism." *Review of Research in Education* 41 (1): 182–202. doi:10.3102/0091732X16686949.

Lai, Y., and J. A. Vadeboncoeur. 2013. "The Discourse of Parent Involvement in Special Education: A Critical Analysis Linking Policy Documents to the Experiences of Mothers." *Educational Policy* 27 (6): 867–897. doi:10.1177/0895904812440501.

Lalvani, P. 2014. "The Enforcement of Normalcy in Schools and the Disablement of Families: Unpacking Master Narratives on Parental Denial." *Disability & Society* 29 (8): 1221–1233. doi:10.1080/09687599.2014.923748.

Lalvani, P., and C. Hale. 2015. "Squeaky Wheels, Mothers from Hell, and CEOs of the IEP: Parents, Privilege, and the "Fight" for Inclusive Education." *Understanding and Dismantling Privilege* 5 (2): 21–41.

Lareau, A., and E. M. Horvat. 1999. "Moments of Social Inclusion and Exclusion: Race, Class, and Cultural Capital in Family-school Relationships." *Sociology of Education* 72 (1): 37–53. doi:10.2307/2673185.

Lewis, T. L. 2021. "Re: Working Definition of Ableism." https://www.talilalewis.com/blog/january-2021-working-definition-of-ableism

Lincoln, Y. S., and E. G. Guba. 1985. *Naturalistic Inquiry*. Beverly Hills, CA: Sage Publications.

Marchand, A. D., R. R. Vassar, M. A. Diemer, and S. J. Rowley. 2019. "Integrating Race, Racism, and Critical Consciousness in Black Parents' Engagement with Schools." *Journal of Family Theory & Review* 11 (3): 367–384. doi:10.1111/jftr.12344.

Matsuda, M. J. 1987. "Looking to the Bottom: Critical Legal Studies and Reparations." *Harvard Civil Rights–Civil Liberties Law Review* 22 (2): 30–164.

Maxwell, J. A. 2013. *Qualitative Research Design: An Interactive Approach*. Los Angeles, CA: Sage.

Mendoza, E., C. Paguyo, and K. Gutiérrez. 2016. "Understanding the Intersection of Race and Disability: Common Sense Notions of Learning and Culture." In *DisCrit: Critical Conversations across Race, Class, & Disability*, edited by D. Connor, B. Ferri, and S. A. Annamma, 71–86, New York, NY: Teachers College Press.

Miles, M. B., A. M. Huberman, and J. Saldaña. 2014. *Qualitative Data Analysis: A Methods Sourcebook*. Thousand Oaks, CA: Sage Publications.

Murphy, A. S., M. A. Acosta, and B. L. Kennedy-Lewis. 2013. "'I'm Not Running around with My Pants Sagging, so How Am I Not Acting like a Lady?': Intersections of Race and Gender in the Experiences of Female Middle School Troublemakers." *The Urban Review* 45 (5): 586–610. doi:10.1007/s11256-013-0236-7.

Nario-Redmond, M. R., A. A. Kemerling, and A. Silverman. 2019. "Hostile, Benevolent, and Ambivalent Ableism: Contemporary Manifestations." *Journal of Social Issues* 75 (3): 726–756. doi:10.1111/josi.12337.

Nzinga-Johnson, S., J. A. Baker, and J. Aupperlee. 2009. "Teacher-Parent Relationships and School Involvement among Racially and Educationally Diverse Parents of Kindergartners." *The Elementary School Journal* 110 (1): 81–91. doi:10.1086/598844.

Ong-Dean, C. 2009. *Distinguishing Disability: Parents, Privilege, and Special Education*. Chicago, IL: University of Chicago Press.

Onwuegbuzie, A. J., and N. L. Leech. 2007. "A Call for Qualitative Power Analyses." *Quality & Quantity* 41: 105–121. doi:10.1007/s11135-005-1098-1.

Puar, J. K. 2017. *The Right to Maim: Debility, Capacity, Disability*. Thousand Oaks: CA: Duke University Press.

Puchner, L., and L. Markowitz. 2015. "Do Black Families Value Education? White Teachers, Institutional Cultural Narratives, & Beliefs about African Americans." *Multicultural Education* 23 (1): 9–16.

Reynolds, R. E., T. C. Howard, and T. K. Jones. 2015. "Is This What Educators Really Want? Transforming the Discourse on Black Fathers and Their Participation in Schools." *Race Ethnicity and Education* 18 (1): 89–107. doi:10.1080/13613324.2012.759931.

Rodwell, M. K. 1998. *Social Work Constructivist Research*. New York, NY: Garland.

Saldaña, J. 2013. *The Coding Manual for Qualitative Researchers*. London, UK: Sage.

Saltmarsh, S., and A. McPherson. 2019. "Un/satisfactory Encounters: Communication, Conflict and Parent-school Engagement." *Critical Studies in Education* 1–16. doi:10.1080/17508487.2019.1630459.

Solórzano, D. G., and T. J. Yosso. 2002. "Critical Race Methodology: Counter-storytelling as an Analytical Framework for Education Research." *Qualitative Inquiry* 8 (1): 23–44. doi:10.1177/107780040200800103.

Stacey, M. 2016. "Middle-class Parents' Educational Work in an Academically Selective Public High School." *Critical Studies in Education* 57 (2): 209–223. doi:10.1080/17508487.2015.1043312.

Van Laere, K., M. Van Houtte, and M. Vandenbroeck. 2018. "Would It Really Matter? The Democratic and Caring Deficit in 'Parental Involvement'." *European Early Childhood Education Research Journal* 26 (2): 187–200. doi:10.1080/1350293X.2018.1441999.

Vincent, C., N. Rollock, S. Ball, and D. Gillborn. 2013. "Raising Middle-class Black Children: Parenting Priorities, Actions and Strategies." *Sociology* 47 (3): 427–442. doi:10.1177/0038038512454244.

Wun, C. 2016. "Against Captivity." *Educational Policy* 30: 171–196. doi:10.1177/0895904815615439.

DisCrit at the margins of teacher education: informing curriculum, visibilization, and disciplinary integration

Saili Kulkarni ⓘD, Emily Nusbaum ⓘD and Phillip Boda ⓘD

ABSTRACT
Teacher education is polarized. Traditionalists tend to center core practices, while justice-oriented scholars center ideologies embedded within our practices. Both, however, must consider how practices and ideologies can operate interdependently to disrupt inequity and cultivate agency among all students. Drawing on an intersectionally-aligned theory, DisCrit, we argue that practices and the ideologies they embody can be problematized vis-à-vis how racism and ableism operate to support hegemony bound in, and represented by, the normative center of schooling. In this paper, we unpack what DisCrit affords critical teacher education, how individuals with complex support needs are located within DisCrit's tenets, if at all, and the application of DisCrit in the disciplinary case of science education. By considering possibilities not yet explored within the literature, we further critical conversations about the relationship between DisCrit, silenced perspectives of populations unaddressed in teacher education for equity, and new disciplinary possibilities of what we mean by justice-oriented applications of theory and practice.

Challenging widespread deficit-oriented narratives based on race has remained a prominent area of research in teacher education for social justice, albeit the charge for radical shifts in socio-cultural ideology persistently rests on those populations frequently subjected to abuses of power and subordination. For example, Milner and Howard (2013) showcased the severe underdevelopment and lack of consistency in terms of racial theorizations among teacher education programs when conceptualizing and understanding the material realities students of color face in schools, and more broadly in society where racism leads to disproportionately liminal forms of self-determination. Their work, combined with Tolbert and Eichelberger's (2016) analysis including *deference to power* mantra in teacher education programs, provides a context for new teachers struggling to understand nuances of racism and ableism, in teacher education classrooms. They do this while also negotiating tensions around power across roles and contexts where multiply marginalized students may bear the brunt of oppression in silence.

Expanding the use of Critical Race Theory (CRT) taken up previously in teacher education contexts (cf. Solorzano and Yosso 2001; Sleeter 2017), Disability Studies was interwoven with race to further examine the interdependence between racism and ableism (Annamma, Connor, and Ferri 2013). Integrating disability studies and CRT, DisCrit is a theory focused on how schools and larger socio-cultural commitments sustain and mirror systems and structures that uphold the normativity of whiteness and able-bodies/minds (Leonardo and Broderick 2011). In other words, adopting a DisCritframework in education research and practice demands that scholars not only address racism as an isolated phenomenon but as part of the overall hegemony of understandings of acceptable personhood and studenthood. DisCrit, therefore, asserts that racism and ableism are never mutually exclusive and must be thought of interdependently if the promise of transformative schooling toward justice is to be actualized.

Among the most recent literature leveraging DisCrit to analyze school contexts and schooling cultures (Annamma et al. 2020), scholars have broached the tensions of racism and ableism more than had been done in the past. Examples of intersectional work highlights oppressive realities (Annamma and Handy 2020; Annamma et al. 2020), such as in disciplinary disparities, and their connection to racially muted conversations during manifestation determination reviews (Fisher, Fisher, and Railey 2020), the over-representation of students of color in special education (Connor et al. 2019), and the lack of critical praxis among teachers when thinking about students whose identities rest at the intersection of race and disability (Friedman, Hallaran, and Locke 2020). However, what is left wanting in much of this work is more complex investigations into how DisCrit can be used to explicitly support students with complex support needs,[1] and its applications to disciplinary fields. Below, we take up such nuanced positions to further expound the possibilities of DisCrit in education research and beyond.

Purpose

Annamma and Handy (2020) note that struggles to theorize educational justice have created 'dangerous realities for multiply-marginalized students even amid ostensible victories' (1). Victories such as recent increases in inclusive education for students with disabilities still often neglect any discussion of these students' identities and notions of self-determination. Such opportunities for inclusion are also often primarily reserved for white, middle-class children. The Convention on the Rights of Persons with Disabilities demands inclusive education be available for every student regardless of the complexity of their disability (UN 2006), yet far too often inclusive opportunities are denied to historically marginalized students. In fact, many students labeled as needing 'extensive' support, experience severely segregated settings (Cosier et al. 2020), rendering them largely/all but invisible.

Unsurprisingly, teacher education standards and credentialing mechanisms focus entirely on linguistic and cultural diversity (Naraian and Schlessinger 2017). These limited theorizations of difference often lead to pre-service teachers sustaining narrow views of race, sexuality, gender identity and disability, rather than exploring their intersections and interdependencies. Given the tendency of teacher education to avoid substantive conversations of racism and white supremacy (Milner 2010), there are a lack of complex discussions about overlapping markers of difference support mechanisms that sustain educational exclusion. Indeed, as Trent (1994) points out, one of the societal responses to significant disability is to institutionalize or segregate these dehumanizing positionalities from the mainstream, representing a larger exclusionary response to this marker of difference that has been mirrored in schools.

Scholars in disability studies in education (DSE), in response, have taken up a person-centered understanding of disability and identity but, unfortunately, this scholarship remains steeped in whiteness (Miles, Nishida, and Forber-Pratt 2017). While both special education and DSE have explicitly received criticism for their pathologization of Black people (Erevelles 2014), Disability Studies and Critical Race Theory (DisCrit) offers an alternative to these racist conceptualizations: An embrace and push toward decolonial, anti-oppressive, anti-ableist, intersectional approaches in teacher education. Below, we unpack what DisCrit's theorizations can contribute to critical teacher education. Specifically, we examine the invisibility of DisCrit in relation to students with complex support needs and the problematizations that emerge when trying to apply critical theories like DisCrit in one disciplinary field's cultural commitments (science education).

A Dis-Crit informed curriculum in teacher education

Engaging teacher education with disability is needed now more than ever, especially given the affordances and constraints of the global pandemic. One example of the operationalization of DisCrit by Annamma and Morrison (2018b) notes that a DisCrit-informed curriculum in schools must include a balance of historical and current ideas. These ideas should actively address the issues of redlining, judicial decisions, and how race, disability and deficit have resulted in exclusionary or punitive practices for multiply marginalized students. A breakdown of the existing structure of schooling and how teachers are educated and prepared is needed to embrace a DisCrit-informed curriculum and specifically center students of all disability identities, including those rendered invisible by their complex needs and supports. In what we outline below, there are specific impacts that a DisCrit-informed curriculum could have in teacher education, including how DisCrit itself may need to be re-envisioned to include all forms of disability across students, teachers, and teacher educators and intersectionality.

Incomplete curriculum and pedagogy can have detrimental effects on students. P-12 students enter a world in which they struggle to understand, or are directly oppressed by, power imbalances (Annamma and Morrison 2018a). For P-12 students, a DisCrit-informed curriculum in the classroom would mean building learning communities together, fighting and resistance to the oppressiveness of their existing school contexts. This means organizing and pushing back against existing curriculum, instruction and assessment practices that render disability, race, and all other forms of oppression invisible. In a DisCrit-informed curriculum, students would find connections to historical moments that emphasize the intersectional accomplishments of disabled people of color,[2] understand disability as an intersectional identity marker, and have access to lessons and units that specifically address the impacts of racism and ableism. For a DisCrit curriculum to become an integrated part of teacher education, pre-service students would need to be explicitly taught about intersectional identities and systems and engage disability in their classrooms beyond special education. Such a curriculum would, as Baglieri and Lalvani (2019) note, 'provide understanding that disability is varied' (71) and that there is a need to learn about disability and ableism in P-12 classrooms to benefit schools and society. Baglieri and Lalvani (2019) provide detailed opportunities to explore ableism and disability in the P-12 classroom. For example, the text asks students to deconstruct conceptions of normality, use film and multimedia to understand disability, and spotlights disabled activists of color. Given this knowledge, students could transform their learning environments: advocate for accessibility and begin operating from an intersectional stance when enacting anti-racist, anti-ableist change.

For teachers, a DisCrit-informed curriculum seeks to counter the persistent invisibility of the voices of disabled people of color beyond addressing cultural and linguistic diversity as othered in a special education context (Annamma and Morrison 2018b). This shift in curriculum would require challenging and dismantling existing curriculum while leveraging resources such as ethnic studies to re-center disability and race. Elder and Migliarini (2020) offer DisCrit as a way of rethinking inclusive education in post-colonial contexts as an example of this shift. They write, "Giving people the language and resources through which to advocate for educational justice can be transformative for people with disabilities and their families" (1859). Specifically, a DisCrit-informed curriculum offers that teachers must understand how schools are designed in hegemonic ways but can be reimagined to center multiply marginalized youth voice. Elder and Migliarini (2020) argue that this includes practices such as providing families with legal resources and engaging in person-centered planning. We argue that teachers must do this across teacher education disciplinary foci while also rethinking what is meant by the extensiveness and complexity of support needs. Rather than reserving disability, especially complex support needs, to a small subfield within special education, a DisCrit-informed curriculum requires that all teachers seek to listen to and engage with disabled people of color. This is done by teachers learning from community elders, especially those with complex support needs, at the same time, negotiating their own identity in their classrooms when trying to disrupt systems that have historically white, able-bodied positions.

Historically, teachers in schools have been positioned as managers of classroom behaviors and instructional practices. Philip et al. (2019) argue that the organizing around core practices 'peripheralizes equity and justice' (251). As Annamma and Handy (2020) note, the priority among educators often becomes management of behavior over learning and individual accomplishment as it connects to student compliance without considering the interdependent nature of teaching and learning. Students with complex support needs are particularly subject to hyper-structured environments in which teachers largely rely on practices grounded in positivism, such as applied behavior analysis and systematic instruction.[3] Therefore, a DisCrit-informed curriculum in teacher education would need to first involve teachers who upend existing harmful practices, such as systematic instruction and the primary focus of teacher education being to educate new teachers for (disciplinary) core practices (Philip et al. 2019). This shift would entail a move from behaviorist-aligned instruction that results in an expectation to 'teacher-proof' the classroom context to community-centered engagement of multiply marginalized youth across modes of access, discourse production, and assessment drawing directly on the assets of the students to evaluate success (Wilson 2017).

We specifically recommend incorporating the works of disabled people of color who have authored and produced important critiques of reductionist school-based practices designed for students with disabilities. For example, we recommend the books (among others) *Black Disabled Art History 101* by Moore (2017), and *Disability Visibility* by Wong (2020). These works feature prominent disabled scholars of color and speak directly to the practices that teacher educators and teachers can use to build asset-based classrooms. We additionally recommend teacher education programs model opportunities for teachers to engage emancipatory, anti-racist and ableist practices. Teachers need to see courses that restructure power dynamics between instructor and teacher candidate, provide opportunities for deep reflection, and engage critical readings across content. As Hooks (2014) explains in *Teaching to Transgress*, it is not enough to simply assign readings on liberatory and engaged pedagogy. Teachers must embody this way of being. Teacher educators must, therefore, engage disabled scholars and community activists of color, provide meaningful accessible instruction, and work with teacher candidates to create shifts in their beliefs about disability and race.

A DisCrit-informed curriculum is purposefully dynamic across space and time; it requires flexibility and shifting of power and agency among stakeholders to incorporate the immediate needs of students in the classroom. For teacher educators to truly embrace a DisCrit-informed curriculum, as noted above, would require a complete reshifting and breakdown of existing teacher education structures. A DisCrit curriculum, too, must examine practices that lead to the preparation of teachers. For example, DisCrit-informed curriculum must extend to examining gatekeeping mechanisms, such as admissions tests, financial costs, and hidden curriculum that have maintained a system of white, able-bodied, middle-class women as teachers, especially for students with disabilities at the intersections (Boveda and McCray 2020). Although the number of special education teachers of color are increasing in places like California (Cooc and Yang 2016), the field of special education itself continues to constrain more critical and intersectional understandings of disability as an identity upon which teachers of color could potentially draw on their own experiences and create connections with students (Sitter and Nusbaum 2018).

Generating DisCrit-informed curriculum and spaces are not without tension. Schooling structures and teacher education programs present significant challenges which must be reconciled by students, teachers, and teacher educators. Nusbaum and Steinborn (2019) highlight how even the standards used to teach content in schools are limited in their address of disability, continuing to render intersections of disability and race invisible. For example, statewide Common Core State Standards across disciplines overarchingly include generic statements about disability categories and access that are entangled with special education's limited definitions and lack any mention of any of the specific inequities that students of color with disabilities encounter in schools. Attempts at educational justice continue to pit disability and race against each other than in coordination. Oppressive structures of schooling highlight the need to rebuild systems in order to reimagine educational justice as intersectional. Teacher educators and university leaders need to reimagine teacher education through a DisCrit-informed curriculum to identify new, community-centered ways of nominating and identifying strong educators committed to social justice education that also push toward more complex meanings of disability and race. Finally, teacher educators must find new ways of undoing teacher preparation as a current form of racism and ableism to move toward a re-centering of disabled people of color across all disciplines and subdisciplines, as well as across all forms of disability identity (Kulkarni, in press, 2021). Below we expound further who is deserving of being 'seen', and how DisCrit could benefit from further development so those not currently part of research leveraging DisCrit are made more visible.

Vizibilzation of students labeled with complex support needs

Historically, knowledge production in traditional special education and associated educational practices for students with complex support needs has been grounded in limited (and limiting) positivist[4] ways of knowing (e.g. Browder and Spooner 2014). Even researchers in the field of inclusive education have largely relied on this paradigm to develop a wide body of research over the past 35 years that has focussed primarily on the technical implementation of practice, without an interrogation of reductionist and deficit-based thinking about disability that undergirds positivism or the ideologies of inclusive schooling (Nusbaum 2013). These bodies of research identify 'interventions' for students focused on person-fixing strategies and leveraging practices, such as systematic instruction and applied behavior analysis. In doing so, this work sustains deficit orientations toward student ability, achievement, and eventual social contribution (Ainscow et al. 2003). A positivist paradigm insists that both teaching and learning for students with complex support needs are primarily transactional, rely on a skills-based 'readiness' model, and are thus overwhelmingly oppressive in nature.

We assert that a DisCrit-informed theorization of schools and schooling can begin to shift these epistemological commitments toward more empowering, interdependent, and intersectional approaches. DisCrit can also begin to disrupt the positivist paradigm's distinct ownership of students with complex support needs. Specifically, (a) tenet two, troubling singular notions of identity; (b) tenet four, privileging voices of multiply marginalized populations; and (c) tenet seven, requiring activism and resistance, seem to present important starting points for positioning DisCrit as a possible avenue for reconceiving the experiences of students labeled with complex support needs, who experience multiple forms of marginalization that are often unrecognized, within educational contexts. This also offers the opportunity to reconceive educational opportunities and settings that remain highly segregated for these students, with little-to-no access to general curriculum, general school environments, and peers without disability labels (Cosier et al. 2020).

One might assume that scholars working among social justice traditions in education would offer disability (broadly) a home – as these bodies of work address both intersectional experiences and critical silences (Connor and Gabel 2010). Yet there is a glaring absence of the topic of disability – of students labeled with complex support needs and/or as 'low-incidence' disabilities – in social justice education (Lalvani et al. 2015; Pugach, Matewos, and Gomez-Najarro 2020). More importantly, Nusbaum and Steinborn (2019) note that the explicit absence of disability from most educational dialogues about diversity, marginalization, and equity in education is akin to the ontological erasure of disabled body minds from these spaces. As the beginning questions from Nusbaum and Steinborn (2019) ask us to contemplate 'Who's (still) not here yet? . . . What knowledge is of most worth? Who decides? Who benefits?' (24), this active (if not malicious) erasure of certain body minds from educational landscapes requires a process of vizibiling. Through this *vizibilization* disabled people become sites of political power and knowledge, in turn validating and asserting themselves and knowledge about their world (Hedva 2016).

The concept of ontological erasure is particularly useful to DisCrit as '. . . it denotes issues of agency and power, as well as the possibility of purposeful change' (Nusbaum and Steinborn 2019, 26). Thus, DisCrit allows us to consider the place of students with complex support needs within teacher education and curriculum, aligned with tenet seven. Through DisCrit tenets two and four, a purposeful 'vizibiling' of students and their intersectional identities that are almost unilaterally subsumed in the label of 'severe' disability is possible – 'troubling singular notions of identity' and 'privileging voices of (multiply) marginalized populations, traditionally not acknowledge within research' (Annamma, Connor, and Ferri 2013, 11). Although some education research that engages with disability in intersectional ways around forms of structural, political, and representational oppression (critical race theory, social justice in teacher education, and school choice, as some examples; cf. Gillborn 2015; Pugach, Matewos, and Gomez-Najarro 2020), unfortunately, this research has tended to focus on disability categories that are associated with disproportionately–specifically students with high-incidence labels like learning disability and emotional disturbance.

Critical inequities exist, without question, for students labeled with high-incidence disabilities at the intersections of race. Yet the erasure of low-incidence disability in intersectional work by reifying distinctions such as 'hard/soft' or 'socially-constructed /real-organic,' renders students with more complex needs invisible by drawing epistemological and ontological 'lines in the sand,' thereby dividing disability as an imposed label from disability as an identity (e.g. Artiles et al. 2011). Vizibiling then articulates the places of erasure that a DisCrit framework can surface. Specifically, how can DisCrit push back on this false binary for students with complex support needs in schools? As Erevelles (2014) notes '. . . even radical social theorists of difference distance themselves from any thoughtful discussion of disability because disability remains the acceptable line of separation between "us" and "them"' (83). As we critique this and the important work of inclusive education researchers, we also hold accountable all stakeholders in education such that we can begin to articulate, very explicitly, previously unseen patterns. We argue for an embodied, intersectional understanding that takes into account the complexity of the lived experiences of multiply marginalized students, especially those with complex support needs. Utilizing a DisCrit framework in this way presents the opportunity to push theoretical and methodological work forward in ways that honor Erevelles (2014) noticing above, by applying to 'not just the easily assimilated able-disabled but our brothers and sisters who have the most to lose in becoming visible – those who are completely socially marginalized, stigmatized, and hidden away in institutions . . . What they know, how they know, and why it matters is most threatening to the status quo' (Sandahl as cited in McRuer and Johnson 2014, 157).

Some representative publications offer possibilities for (co)constructing different ways of knowing about individuals with complex support needs (cf. Cowley 2016; Kliewer, Biklen, and Petersen 2015). Although work such as Kliewer, Biklen, and Petersen (2015) and Cowley (2016) do not specifically attend to race (or other identities), publications such as these offer critical considerations for expanding ways of knowing and being. In essence, these works bring into view epistemologies and ontologies concerning the lived experiences of students with complex support needs, while also actively offering alternatives to a positivist paradigm. They also reflect efforts towards *vizibiling* the lives of these individuals and attend explicitly to the questions asserted by Nusbaum and Steinborn (2019) above about whose lives matter, and why others may not be considered through such a purview. Other scholarships teach us to push boundaries even further. Miller (2020), for example, offers DisCrit as part of a theoretical and methodological framework to better understand the lived experiences of female students of color, labeled with intellectual disability, who live at the margins of multiply oppressed identities. This work brings forward the lived reality of multiply minoritized students and their access to dynamic literacy practices and spaces in schools. We argue that both approaches are significant and needed. These examples can also inform and propel future research that more explicitly incorporates a DisCrit framework. In this way, our contention does not fall prey to an either/or binary of epistemological and ontological commitments that, as we have argued, exclude. Adopting a both/and interdependentapproach would benefit both bodies of research as they transgress beyond their respective boundaries and push these boundaries in critical and creative ways.

In turn, akin to what Nusbaum and Steinborn (2019) has described as a 'vizibiling' project, the specific utilization of DisCrit tenets 2, 4, and 7 offer a potential a way to rehumanize and give voice to those students who have been deemed as less-than human, and whose educational (and societal) devaluation is justified, accepted, and promoted through continued absences, silence, and erasures in the educational research community. Perhaps even more importantly, applying a DisCrit informed framework to work that critiques the epistemological and ontological foundations of constructs like 'intellectual disability' or 'severe disability' could serve to do as Heshusius (1989) urges us, in exploring contours of alternatives: To push the edges of these contours even further to spaces on the horizon that render disability ' … desirable, and the structures which surround it, profoundly contested' (Kolářová 2014, 257). In articulating this standpoint, we seek to precisely combat what has been described as 'liberation for some at the expense of others' (Alim et al. 2017, 11). Finally, below, we unpack where the critical request embodied by DisCrit's tenets presents a uniquely difficult case to achieve this goal to think of possible futures in the application of DisCrit to disciplinary fields.

Conceptualizing DisCrit's application within disciplinary teacher education

Annamma, Connor, and Ferri (2013) suggest that, 'The aim of DisCrit is to push DS and CRT to academically and practically bridge commonalities utilizing the tensions between the theories as places for growth instead of resistance and separation' (6). They note explicitly that critical race analyses in special education journals have focussed primarily on disproportionality. Articles featuring disability as culture and identity, however, have not be published in general education journals, despite the fact that critical studies across race, class, and gender flourish in these venues. This pattern of publication and theorization in the discipline of science education is an exemplary case of how DisCrit could help build bridges between the binary of normal/abnormal that often operates to subordinate and segregate students (of color) labeled with disabilities. The 'general-special education division' can be disrupted by integrating DisCrit tenets (Annamma, Connor, and Ferri 2013), which makes often-rigid boundaries tenable to more porous understandings of the nuanced similarities between CRT and disability studies in order to engage with personhood, dignity, and the humanity of all students. In what follows, we explore the strengths and limitations of DisCrit to de-settle the formalized binary between special and science education.

DisCrit's first and arguably its central tenet brings to the forefront the notion that racism and ableism do not exist in a vacuum and that the normalcy by which they operate in schools and society more broadly goes unquestioned in part by the silencing of their interdependence. In science education, for example, there has been a long-standing lack of critical problematizations around race dating back 30 years (Atwater 1989). However, more recent scholarship showcases how race is troubled and racist systems sustained in science education (Mensah 2019; Morales-Doyle and Gutstein 2019; Walls 2016). Leveraging DisCrit's tenet two suggests that we engage with the multidimensionality of identity. Although studies around race intersecting with gender and class (Pinder and Blackwell 2014), or race and its nuance related to English-language learner designations (Sung 2018) have been prevalent in science education, there is a paucity of intersectional analyses related to race and disability; instead, disability inquiries in science education predominantly follow a resource accommodation approach wherein students labeled with a disability are merely engaged such that they are supported to learn science content in similar ways as students without such a label (e.g. Brigham, Scruggs, and Mastropieri 2011; Villanueva et al. 2012). There is also a tendency in science education to sustain deficit-based approaches toward disability and a deference to special education counterparts to lead and teach disciplinary content (Boda 2019b; Vannest et al. 2009), although such authority of who is the 'content teacher' has also shown to differ at times when inclusive co-teaching models are employed (King-Sears et al. 2014). The lack of critical theorizing in research on disability as it intersects with race within science education is also reflected in the type of research on disability in science education as shown above in the pragmatic 'strategies' approach illustrated above, further unpacked below.

Science education for students labeled with disabilities sustains a pragmatic focus on access and development of disciplinary acuity whose primary goal is not to disrupt the systems that position disability outside of other markers of difference but instead focus on 'the how' in terms of resource use and accommodation (cf. Mastropieri and Scruggs 1992; Taylor et al. 2020). This is not to say that positivism is unnecessary: Work exploring how science teachers take up their disciplinary teaching related to disability vary widely and are often framed by whether they can even conceptualize supporting this 'specific' population of students (Boda 2019a; Kahn and Lewis 2014). Disconcertedly, though, pragmatist approaches do not engage with the social construction of ability, which the third tenet of DisCrit explicitly demarks as impactful for understanding the intersection of racism and ableism. The disciplinary resources valued in science education, thus, do not interrogate power dynamics or systemic issues related to how race can be used as a proxy for perceptions of ability (Boda 2018; and see, e.g. Rule et al. (2011) for an example of a pragmatist-focused study). Disciplinary-specific commitments, such as those in science education related to 'inquiry' and 'scientific literacy' learning goals, therefore mediate how practices embody and embolden ideological commitments to whiteness and ability through hegemony, which DisCrit's sixth tenet makes evident that such a deconstruction of these affiliations should be part and parcel of any socially just research agenda.

Integrating DisCrit into disciplinary teacher education, however, is not merely a further conceptualizing of race but also involves interrogating the ability-profiling ingrained in the social construction of race, ability, and the normative center of schooling that sustains a specific type of student and personhood that is seen as 'teachable' (Collins 2013; Leonardo and Broderick 2011). We know hegemonic perceptions of ability get modeled by teachers and taken up by children as early as elementary school (Hatt 2012). For science teachers to understand race and its connection to disability, their engagement with how social positioning operates to produce inclusion/exclusion would need greater attention. DisCrit can provide one tool to think about these intersections with the commitment in its tenets to look beyond race and/or disability individually, as well as how these intersections converge in the capital afforded to whiteness and ableism. In addition to adopting a DisCrit lens, science teachers should also engage in critical conversations central to disrupting the accommodations-based disciplinary commitments of the field. Given that the tenets of DisCrit originated and were crafted without disciplinary focus, research suggests that such an integration of DisCrit without considering the tenets to be more explicit to disciplinary goals may not raise the consciousness of new science teachers (Boda 2019a, 2019b). We therefore contend that when science teachers are asked to negotiate disciplinary commitments that sustain practices that are actually antithetical to social justice orientations and commitments (i.e. Morales-Doyle et al. 2020), we must further unpack how a specific discipline orients its commitments related to teacher training. In other words, the discipline's approach, its research base, and its practices around disability must all be a part of this critical intervention.

Because science education lacks widespread critical theorizations around disability, despite a plethora of critical theorizations around race, class, and gender, DisCrit can provide a bridge between these two disparate approaches to identity and positionality. We see promising directions to challenge this *conceptual and disciplinary exclusion* of disability prominent in science teacher education (i.e. Boda 2019b) and in the larger field of the Learning Sciences as it grapples with disciplinary commitments and ideological alignments that sustain inequity and injustice in STEM education (de Royston and Sengupta-Irving 2019). However, these scholarly critical theorizations (consciously or not), while engaging intersectionally with critical standpoints of race, gender, class, and linguistic fluency, should also envision disability as a cultural component of social justice goals and as an identity/positionality that is subject to oppression and multiple marginalization. Indeed, as the larger educational research community moves beyond inclusion toward re-centering traditionally marginalized students, particularly around raciolinguistic, gendered, and contextual 'guests' in 'host' classrooms (Calabrese Barton and Tan 2020), what requires a more sensitive interrogation are children whose body/minds are not perceived as fitting within social justice and equitable education theories. Again, if we leverage DisCrit to recenter those who are multiply marginalized, then identity, capital, and the interests of schooling embodied therein can be more thoroughly interrogated.

We argue, then, with the hyper-focus on specific disciplinary fields like science education, STEM education, and computer science, DisCrit should be part of conversations about intersectionality to more critically engage identity frames necessary for justice-oriented disciplinary education research. In this way, we contend not only that disciplinary fields need DisCrit but also that such disciplinary considerations of critical theory applications would sharpen the power of DisCrit. However, given the current state of how disability is articulated and conceptualized in the field related to pragmatic solutions in lieu of inquiries around identity and agency, we emphasize a caution not to simply 'rubber-stamp' applications of critical theories generated with no disciplinary focus to disciplinary teaching and learning. If DisCrit is to have impact on disciplines like science education where disability continues to lack cultural and identity recognition, the integration of DisCrit within disciplinary teacher education will require more than merely applying social-justice oriented educational research or theory more broadly. Rather, to adopt critical, intersectional theories like DisCrit requires that we consider how and in what ways the tenets could be amenable to how disability is already theorized in disciplinary inquiries, taking the time to unpack if critical theorizations of disability and race are being discussed, and if not, thoroughly engaging with the work in such a disciplinary-like science education for students labeled with disabilities in ways that meet them where they are to push them forward. Below, we look toward possibilities to take up radical opportunities across teacher education, the lived experiences of students with complex support needs not yet conceptualized in DisCrit, and the disciplinary example of science education where the field has struggled to conceptualize disability beyond pragmatic accommodations and access to resources.

Moving toward radical possibilities without simplistic answers

Some questions must be considered when thinking about the margins in teacher education, as well as the argument we have sought to cultivate here. The intersectionally aligned arguments we have proposed do not come with simplistic and easily implemented transformations, especially given the complexities of the schooling system for disabled students of color at the margins. However, we argue that the tenets of DisCrit provide an initial framework for understanding how racism and ableism are interdependent systems that can inform the ways students labeled with disabilities are multiply marginalized and experience exclusion in education compounded with racism. Therefore, pushing and probing conceptual boundaries of such a promising theorization is part and parcel with the purpose of such a theory. As we conclude we urge "thinking and learning *with* and *through*" DisCrit as a way to become more sensitive and expansive in our applications of the original theorizations – we seek to open radical possibilities of how DisCrit informed research and practice can take form while asking questions that, right now, may have no well-developed answers by the field, or by DisCrit itself.

We first want to acknowledge the complexity of teacher education, as well as how disability and race are positioned vis-a-vis disciplinary content demands, and special education's history of segregating students of color and students with complex support needs. Therefore, we conclude by centering some questions around futures informed by the tenets of DisCrit that offer possibilities for expansive transformations within current pragmatist-driven education systems:

(1) What methods can we use to further social justice, activism, and resistance in order to reimagine a DisCrit-informed curriculum of teacher education, straddling margins and center, to re-envision the roles of students, teachers, and teacher education programs?

(2) How can the emphasis on multidimensional identities – on intersectional subjection to exclusion and violence – include those that are consistently positioned as less-important within and among justice-oriented theories (e.g. students with complex support needs), thereby reinforcing and sustaining ableist conceptions of normalcy?

(3) What radical possibilities could DisCrit theorizations promote among critical conversations happening in disciplinary-focused teacher education spaces?

In asking these questions, we probe further into arenas of ontological, epistemological, and ideological exploration within and among teacher education spaces. Doing this excavation work, thus, pushes us all toward the goal for further visibilization among those most likely to be subjected to exclusion and violence from the rhetoric and material realities always present and historically sustained through white ableist hegemony, and personhood more broadly.

Echoing these questions, we provide radical possibilities for futures not yet known, but that we can envision if the tensions we argue that exist when trying to integrate new, critical, intersectional theorizations like DisCrit in teacher education at the margins are considered:

(1) Requiring a DisCrit-informed curriculum of teacher education, which re-centers the knowledge, experience, and expertise of disabled people of color, is critical to the expansion of DisCrit *and* teacher education. Teachers must upend harmful and violent practices that inflict trauma on multiply marginalized youth and recognize the historical and current contexts of the lives of disabled people of color. We argue that DisCrit necessitates teacher education to center readings and products of BIPOC, disabled community scholars. Inevitably, a DisCrit-informed curriculum of teacher education means a complete restructuring of existing systems, and shifting power in this space to dismantle racism and ableism as they persist in schools, schooling, and teacher education;

(2) Using a DisCrit informed framework that also critiques the epistemological and ontological foundations of social constructs like 'intellectual disability' or 'severe disability' urges us to push the edges of these contours even further. *Vizibiling* is a way to articulate the places of erasure to which a DisCrit framework could afford nuance, although it would require attention from DisCrit and its current theorizations. Application and integration of DisCrit across disability cultures and identities thus requires working in tandem with philosophical approaches that have articulated alternative epistemological and ontological ways of knowing about students with complex support needs, and more specifically attend to those students who also embody multiple marginalization;

(3) Breaking through and beyond the *conceptual and disciplinary segregation* of disability from inquiries around race, class, and gender in disciplinary fields like science teacher education. This would shift the focus of this research beyond curricular modifications to align with legally required accommodations, toward also: considering the socio-cultural elements of ableism and its connection to racism; demand that the social positioning of disability in classrooms and society more broadly be engaged with; and a relinquishment of positivist commitments

among formative and summative assessments toward assessing student sense-making in science, and in their teachers' certification preparation programs.

In the end, our problematizations harken back to foundational questions in both Critical Race Theory and Disability Studies around love, liberation, and personhood: 'Who matters?'; 'Who is valued?'; 'Why do we fight?' By asking these questions, we are hopeful in quoting June Jordan's 1978 poem that 'we are the ones we've been waiting for' to begin to engage with the margins in teacher education for equity and social justice – not for some, but for all student body/minds.

Notes

1. This refers to students with low-incidence disabilities eligible for special education supports and services in categories such as (but not limited to): intellectual disability, multiple disabilities, deaf-blindness, and autism.
2. We use disabled people of color here to specifically highlight intersections of disability and race and curricular possibilities informed by DisCrit to assert disability as a reclaimed and political identity.
3. Systematic instruction and Applied Behavioral Analysis (ABA) have been used overwhelmingly in the field of special education in the United States context. These practices have been shown to be harmful and controlling of the bodies/minds, especially of multiply marginalized students (Roscigno 2019).
4. The process of *viziblization* refers to a concept posited by Nusbaum and Steinborn (2019) as it relates to their theory of *ontological erasure*: '... going beyond the *absence* of disability from curricular content or the *silence* regarding disability in educational justice conversations; rather, *ontological erasure* is the active erasing of certain body-minds from "being" in the educational landscape. This shift from considerations of *absence* or *silence*, which both imply passivity and neglect, to an analysis that arrives at the concept of *ontological erasure*, which is explicitly active, although not necessarily malicious' (26). Thus, we argue here that extending a DisCrit framework to students with complex support needs makes them *visible* within this specific, educational context.

Disclosure statement

No potential conflict of interest was reported by the author(s).

ORCID

Saili Kulkarni http://orcid.org/0000-0001-8133-7980
Emily Nusbaum http://orcid.org/0000-0001-8664-498X
Phillip Boda http://orcid.org/0000-0001-5797-8139

References

Ainscow, M., A. Howes, P. Farrell, and J. Frankham. 2003. "Making Sense of the Development of Inclusive Practices." *European Journal of Special Needs Education* 18: 227–242. doi:10.1080/0885625032000079005.
Alim, H. S., S. Baglieri, G. Ladson-Billings, D. Paris, D. H. Rose, and J. M. Valente. 2017. "Responding to "Cross-Pollinating Culturally Sustaining Pedagogy and Universal Design for

Learning: Toward an Inclusive Pedagogy that Accounts for Dis/ability".” *Harvard Educational Review* 87 (1): 4–25. doi:10.17763/1943-5045-87.1.4.

Annamma, S., and D. Morrison. 2018a. “Identifying Dysfunctional Education Ecologies: A DisCrit Analysis of Bias in the Classroom.” *Equity & Excellence in Education* 51: 114–131. doi:10.1080/10665684.2018.1496047.

Annamma, S., and D. Morrison. 2018b. “DisCrit Classroom Ecology: Using Praxis to Dismantle Dysfunctional Education Ecologies.” *Teaching and Teacher Education* 73: 70–80. doi:10.1016/j.tate.2018.03.008.

Annamma, S., T. Handy, A. L. Miller, and E. Jackson. 2020. “Animating Discipline Disparities through Debilitating Practices: Girls of Color and Inequitable Classroom Interactions.” *Teachers College Record* 122 (5). doi:10.3102/0013189x20953838.

Annamma, S. A., D. Connor, and B. Ferri. 2013. “Dis/ability Critical Race Studies (DisCrit): Theorizing at the Intersections of Race and Dis/ability.” *Race Ethnicity and Education* 16 (1): 1–31. doi:10.1080/13613324.2012.730511.

Annamma, S. A., and T. Handy. 2020. “Sharpening Justice through DisCrit: A Contrapuntal Analysis of Education.” *Educational Researcher*. Online first. doi:10.3102/0013189X20953838.

Artiles, Alfredo J. 2011.“Toward an interdisciplinary understanding of educational equity and difference: The case of the racialization of ability.”*Educational Researcher* 40(9): 431–445.

Atwater, M. M. 1989. “Including Multicultural Education in Science Education: Definitions, Competencies, and Activities.” *Journal of Science Teacher Education* 1 (1): 17–20. doi:10.1007/bf03032129.

Baglieri, S., and P. Lalvani. 2019. *Undoing Ableism: Teaching about Disability in K-12 Classrooms*. Routledge. doi:10.4324/9781351002868.

Boda, P. A. 2018. “Exclusion from Participation in Science: Confessions from an Ally on the Other Side of the Fence.” In *Toward Inclusion of All Learners through Science Teacher Education*, edited by M. Koomen, S. Kahn, C. Atchison, and T. Wild, 301–311. Sense/Brill Publishing. doi:10.1163/9789004368422_033.

Boda, P. A. 2019a. “Conceptualizing the Margins in Science Education: The Limits of Multicultural Analyses.” *Cultural Studies of Science Education* 14: 493–514. doi:10.1007/s11422-019-09926-x.

Boda, P. A. 2019b. “The Conceptual and Disciplinary Segregation of Disability: A Phenomenography of Science Education Graduate Student Learning.” *Research in Science Education*. (Online first). doi:10.1007/s11165-019-9828-x.

Boveda, M., and E. D. McCray. 2020. “Writing (For) Our Lives: Black Feminisms, Interconnected Guidance, and Qualitative Research in Special Education.” *International Journal of Qualitative Studies in Education*: 1–19. doi:10.1080/09518398.2020.1771465.

Brigham, F. J., T. E. Scruggs, and M. A. Mastropieri. 2011. “Science Education and Students with Learning Disabilities.” *Learning Disabilities Research & Practice* 26: 223–232. doi:10.1111/j.1540-5826.2011.00343.x.

Browder, D. M., and F. Spooner, eds. 2014. *More Language Arts, Math, and Science for Students with Severe Disabilities*. Paul H. Brookes Publishing Company. doi:10.1353/etc.2017.0018.

Calabrese Barton, A., and E. Tan. 2020. “Beyond Equity as Inclusion: A Framework of “Rightful Presence” for Guiding Justice-Oriented Studies in Teaching and Learning.” *Educational Researcher* 49 (6): 433–440. doi:10.3102/0013189x20927363.

Collins, K. M. 2013. *Ability Profiling and School Failure: One Child's Struggle to Be Seen as Competent*. Routledge. doi:10.4324/9780203802533.

Connor, D., W. Cavendish, T. Gonzalez, and P. Jean-Pierre. 2019. “Is a Bridge Even Possible over Troubled Waters? The Field of Special Education Negates the Overrepresentation of Minority Students: A DisCrit Analysis.” *Race Ethnicity and Education* 22: 723–745. doi:10.1080/13613324.2019.1599343.

Connor, D. J., and S. L. Gabel. 2010. “Welcoming the Unwelcome: Disability as Diversity.” In *Social Justice Pedagogy across the Curriculum*, edited by T. Chapman and N. Hobbel, 201–220. Mahwah, NJ: Erlbaum. doi:10.4324/9780203854488.

Cooc, N., and M. Yang. 2016. "Diversity and Equity in the Distribution of Teachers with Special Education Credentials: Trends from California." *AERA Open* 2 (4): 1–15. doi:10.1177/2332858416679374.

Cosier, M., A. Sandoval-Gomez, D. N. Cardinal, and S. Brophy. 2020. "Placement of Students with Extensive Support Needs in California School Districts: The State of Inclusion and Exclusion." *International Electronic Journal of Elementary Education* 12: 249–255. doi:10.26822/iejee.2020358218.

Cowley, D. M. 2016. "A Tale of Two Transitions." In *Enacting Change from Within: Disability Studies Meets Teaching and Teacher Education*, edited by C. E. Ashby and M. E. Cosier. New York, NY: Peter Lang. doi:10.3726/978-1-4539-1793-0/16.

de Royston, M., and T. Sengupta-Irving. 2019. "Another Step Forward: Engaging the Political in Learning." *Cognition and Instruction* 37: 277–284. doi:10.1080/07370008.2019.1624552.

Elder, B., and V. Migliarini. 2020. "Decolonizing Inclusive Education: A Collection of Practical Inclusive CDS-and DisCrit-Informed Teaching Practices Implemented in the Global South." *Disability and the Global South* 7: 1852–1872. https://disabilityglobalsouth.files.wordpress.com/2020/05/07_01_04.pdf.

Erevelles, N. 2014. "Crippin' Jim Crow: Disability, Dis-Location, and the School-to-Prison Pipeline." In *Disability Incarcerated*, edited by L. Ben-Moshe, C. Chapman, and A. C. Carey, 81–99. New York: Palgrave Macmillan. doi:10.1057/9781137388476_5.

Fisher, A. E., B. W. Fisher, and K. S. Railey. 2020. "Disciplinary Disparities by Race and Disability: Using DisCrit Theory to Examine the Manifestation Determination Review Process in Special Education in the United States." *Race Ethnicity and Education*: 1–15. doi:10.1080/13613324.2020.1753671.

Friedman, T. E., A. E. Hallaran, and M. A. Locke. 2020. "Rubberbanding in a Liminal Space: Teachers Contemplate Intersections of Dis/ability and Race in Inclusive Classrooms." *Race Ethnicity and Education*: 1–21. doi:10.1080/13613324.2020.1753677.

Gillborn, D. 2015. "Intersectionality, Critical Race Theory, and the Primacy of Racism: Race, Class, Gender, and Disability in Education." *Qualitative Inquiry* 21: 277–287. doi:10.1177/1077800414557827.

Hatt, B. 2012. "Smartness as a Cultural Practice in Schools." *American Educational Research Journal* 49: 438–460. doi:10.3102/0002831211415661.

Hedva, J. 2016. *Sick Woman Theory*. Mask. http://www.maskmagazine.com/not-again/struggle/sick-woman-theory

Heshusius, L. 1989. "The Newtonian Mechanistic Paradigm, Special Education, and Contours of Alternatives: An Overview." *Journal of Learning Disabilities* 22: 403–415. doi:10.1177/002221948902200702.

Hooks, B. 2014. *Teaching to Transgress*. Routledge. doi:10.4324/9780203700280.

Jordan, J. 1980. "Poem for South African Women." *Passion New Poems 1977–1980*.

Kahn, S., and A. R. Lewis. 2014. "Survey on Teaching Science to K-12 Students with Disabilities: Teacher Preparedness and Attitudes." *Journal of Science Teacher Education* 25: 885–910. doi:10.1007/s10972-014-9406-z.

King-Sears, M. E., A. E. Brawand, M. C. Jenkins, and S. Preston-Smith. 2014. "Co-Teaching Perspectives from Secondary Science Co-Teachers and Their Students with Disabilities." *Journal of Science Teacher Education* 25: 651–680. doi:10.1007/s10972-014-9391-2.

Kliewer, C., D. Biklen, and A. J. Petersen. 2015. "At the End of Intellectual Disability." *Harvard Educational Review* 85 (1): 1–29. doi:10.17763/haer.85.1.j260u3gv2402v576.

Kolářová, K. 2014. "The Inarticulate Post-Socialist Crip: On the Cruel Optimism of Neoliberal Transformations in the Czech Republic." *Journal of Literary and Cultural Disability Studies* 8 (3): 257–274. doi:10.3828/jlcds.2014.22.

Kulkarni, S. (*in press*, 2021). "Shifting special education teacher beliefs about dis/ability and race: Counter stories of goodness and smartness." *Journal of Curriculum Inquiry*. doi:10.1080/03626784.2021.1938973.

Lalvani, P., A. A. Broderick, M. Fine, T. Jacobowitz, and N. Michelli. 2015. "Teacher Education, in Exclusion, and the Implicit Ideology of Separate but Equal: An Invitation to a Dialogue." *Education, Citizenship and Social Justice* 10: 168–183. doi:10.1177/1746197915583935.

Leonardo, Z., and A. Broderick. 2011. "Smartness as Property: A Critical Exploration of Intersections between Whiteness and Disability Studies." *Teachers College Record* 113: 2206–2232.

Mastropieri, M. A., and T. E. Scruggs. 1992. "Science for Students with Disabilities." *Review of Educational Research* 62: 377–411. doi:10.3102/00346543062004377.

McRuer, R., and M. Johnson. 2014. "Proliferating Cripistemologies: A Virtual Roundtable." *Journal of Literary & Cultural Disability Studies* 8 (2): 149–170. doi:10.3828/jlcds.2014.13.

Mensah, F. M. 2019. "Finding Voice and Passion: Critical Race Theory Methodology in Science Teacher Education." *American Educational Research Journal* 56: 1412–1456. doi:10.3102/0002831218818093.

Miles, A. L., A. Nishida, and A. J. Forber-Pratt. 2017. "An Open Letter to White Disability Studies and Ableist Institutions of Higher Education." *Disability Studies Quarterly* 37 (3). doi:10.18061/dsq.v37i3.5997.

Miller, A. L. 2020. "Disabled Girls of Color Excavate Exclusionary Literacy Practices and Generate Promising Sociospatial-Textual Solutions." *International Journal of Qualitative Studies in Education*: 1–24. doi:10.1080/09518398.2020.1828649.

Milner, H. R., IV. 2010. "What Does Teacher Education Have to Do with Teaching? Implications for Diversity Studies." *Journal of Teacher Education* 61: 118–131. doi:10.1177/0022487109347670.

Milner, H. R., IV, and T. C. Howard. 2013. "Counter-Narrative as Method: Race, Policy and Research for Teacher Education." *Race Ethnicity and Education* 16: 536–561. doi:10.1080/13613324.2013.817772.

Moore, L. 2017. *Black Disabled Art History 101*. San Francisco, CA: Xochitl Justice Press.

Morales-Doyle, D., and E. R. Gutstein. 2019. "Racial Capitalism and STEM Education in Chicago Public Schools." *Race Ethnicity and Education* 22: 525–544. doi:10.1080/13613324.2019.1592840.

Morales-Doyle, D., M. Varelas, D. Segura, and M. Bernal-Munera. 2020. "Access, Dissent, Ethics, and Politics: Pre-Service Teachers Negotiating Conceptions of the Work of Teaching Science for Equity." *Cognition and Instruction*: 1–30. doi:10.1080/07370008.2020.1828421.

Naraian, S., and S. Schlessinger. 2017. "When Theory Meets the "Reality of Reality": Reviewing the Sufficiency of the Social Model of Disability as a Foundation for Teacher Preparation for Inclusive Education." *Teacher Education Quarterly* 44: 81–100. doi:10.1016/j.tate.2017.12.012.

Nusbaum, E. A. 2013. "Vulnerable to Exclusion: The Place for Segregated Education within Conceptions of Inclusion." *International Journal of Inclusive Education* 17: 1295–1311. doi:10.1080/13603116.2013.826292.

Nusbaum, E. A., and M. L. Steinborn. 2019. "A "Visibilizing" Project: "Seeing" the Ontological Erasure of Disability in Teacher Education and Social Studies Curricula." *Journal of Curriculum Theorizing* 34 (1): 24–35.

Philip, T. M., M. Souto-Manning, L. Anderson, I. J. Horn, D. Carter Andrews, J. Stillman, and M. Varghese. 2019. "Making Justice Peripheral by Constructing Practice as "Core": How the Increasing Prominence of Core Practices Challenges Teacher Education." *Journal of Teacher Education* 70: 251–264. doi:10.1177/0022487118798324.

Pinder, P. J., and E. L. Blackwell. 2014. "The "Black Girl Turn" in Research on Gender, Race, and Science Education: Toward Exploring and Understanding the Early Experiences of Black Females in Science, a Literature Review." *Journal of African American Studies* 18 (1): 63–71. doi:10.1007/s12111-013-9255-4.

Pugach, M. C., A. M. Matewos, and J. Gomez-Najarro. 2020. "Disability and the Meaning of Social Justice in Teacher Education Research: A Precarious Guest at the Table?" *Journal of Teacher Education*. doi:10.1177/0022487120929623.

Roscigno, R. 2019. "Neuroqueerness as Fugitive Practice: Reading against the Grain of Applied Behavioral Analysis Scholarship." *Educational Studies* 55: 405–419. doi:10.1080/00131946.2019.1629929.

Rule, A. C., G. P. Stefanich, R. M. Boody, and B. Peiffer. 2011. "Impact of Adaptive Materials on Teachers and Their Students with Visual Impairments in Secondary Science and Mathematics Classes." *International Journal of Science Education* 33: 865–887. doi:10.1080/09500693.2010.506619.

Sitter, K. C., and E. A. Nusbaum. 2018. "Critical Disability Studies and Community Engagement." In *The Wiley International Handbook of Service-Learning for Social Justice*, 191–202. doi:10.1002/9781119144397.ch8.

Sleeter, C. E. 2017. "Critical Race Theory and the Whiteness of Teacher Education." *Urban Education* 52 (2): 155–169. doi:10.1177/0042085916668957.

Solorzano, D. G., and T. J. Yosso. 2001. "From Racial Stereotyping and Deficit Discourse toward a Critical Race Theory in Teacher Education." *Multicultural Education* 9 (1): 2. doi:10.1080/09518390110063365.

Sung, K. K. 2018. "Raciolinguistic Ideology of Antiblackness: Bilingual Education, Tracking, and the Multiracial Imaginary in Urban Schools." *International Journal of Qualitative Studies in Education* 31: 667–683. doi:10.1080/09518398.2018.1479047.

Taylor, J. C., J. Hwang, K. L. Rizzo, and D. A. Hill. 2020. "Supporting Science-Related Instruction for Students with Intellectual and Developmental Disabilities: A Review and Analysis of Research Studies." *Science Educator* 27: 102–113. https://eric.ed.gov/?redir=https%3a%2f%2fwww.nsela.org%2fscience-educator-journal-

Tolbert, S., and S. Eichelberger. 2016. "Surviving Teacher Education: A Community Cultural Capital Framework of Persistence." *Race Ethnicity and Education* 19: 1025–1042. doi:10.1080/13613324.2014.969222.

Trent, J. W., Jr. 1994. *Inventing the Feeble Mind: A History of Mental Retardation in the United States.* doi:10.1080/13613324.2014.969222.

UN (United Nations). 2006. *Convention of Rights of Persons with Disabilities and Optional Protocol.* New York: United Nations.

Vannest, K. J., B. A. Mason, L. Brown, N. Dyer, S. Maney, and T. Adiguzel. 2009. "Instructional Settings in Science for Students with Disabilities: Implications for Teacher Education." *Journal of Science Teacher Education* 20: 353–363. doi:10.1007/s10972-009-9135-x.

Villanueva, M. G., J. Taylor, W. Therrien, and B. Hand. 2012. "Science Education for Students with Special Needs." *Studies in Science Education* 48: 187–215. doi:10.1080/14703297.2012.737117.

Walls, L. 2016. "Awakening a Dialogue: A Critical Race Theory Analysis of US Nature of Science Research from 1967 to 2013." *Journal of Research in Science Teaching* 53: 1546–1570. doi:10.1002/tea.21266.

Wilson, J. D. 2017. "Reimagining Disability and Inclusive Education through Universal Design for Learning." *Disability Studies Quarterly* 37 (2). doi:10.18061/dsq.v37i2.5417.

Wong, A., ed.. 2020. *Disability Visibility: First-Person Stories from the Twenty-First Century.* New York: Vintage.

Extending DisCrit: a case of universal design for learning and equity in a rural teacher residency

Beth S. Fornauf and Bryan Mascio

ABSTRACT
The Rural Teacher Residency (RTR) program prepares teachers to work in 'high need' rural schools in the northeastern United States, and specifically works to establish a counter-narrative to the commonly-held deficit lens applied to these schools and communities. Framed by theory and research on DisCrit and Universal Design for Learning (UDL), we share our experiences as rural teacher educators using UDL to help preserve teachers disrupt assumptions about rurality, socioeconomics, race, ability, gender identity, and privilege. We explain how our gradual incorporation of the tenets of DisCrit improved our ability to support pre-service teachers' examination of structural inequities in school practices, including but not limited to norms of race, ability, and rurality. We conclude by offering our ongoing planning in RTR as a model for how teacher educators interested in working with DisCrit can expand its use as a transformative and liberatory framework that includes, but also extends beyond race and ability.

Calls for explicit and critical engagement with racism embedded in the curriculum and structure of educational systems have become more urgent in recent years. In the United States, events of the past year – including multiple murders of unarmed Black citizens by police, the rise of militant White supremacists, and disproportionate coronavirus-related deaths among minoritized groups (e.g., Black, Latinx, disabled) – have spurred growing conversations about systemic racism, White supremacy, and inequity in multiple spheres. In response to these conversations, many educators have opted to re-evaluate and redesign their curricula and practices in an effort to name and dismantle systems that perpetuate discrimination (Minor et al. 2020). The urgency of these actions has redoubled interest among educators and the public alike in endorsing the efforts of many scholars who have long advocated for explicit acknowledgement and abolition of the ways racism, ableism, heterosexism, and other oppressive forces intersect in education (e.g., Annamma, Connor, and Ferri 2013; Leonardo and Broderick 2011; Love 2019), and specifically within teacher education (e.g., Annamma, 2015; Young 2016).

This paper is premised on the necessity of DisCrit as both a disruptive and central organizing framework for teacher education in the United States. As teacher educators who work with preservice teachers in a rural region of the northeastern United States, we actively work to disrupt stereotypes of 'imagined Whiteness' of rural places that perpetuate 'a view that race is not a concern' in these places (Pini and Bhopal 2017, 20). In addition, because of our background in special education, we are acutely aware of the often subtle yet disturbingly acceptable ways in which ableism manifests in taken-for-granted norms of schooling.

As rural teacher educators invested in DisCrit, we initially framed this paper as an argument for critically considering rurality through a DisCrit lens. While we remain committed to attending to issues of place, and interrogating stereotypes about rural places, schools, and knowledge (e.g., Azano and Stewart 2016; Heldke 2006), our goal here extends beyond this original aim. Inspired by the variability and complexity of rural schools and communities across the globe, we offer a conceptual argument that illuminates how DisCrit can better enable us all to disrupt norms of schooling – including but not limited to norms of race, ability, and rurality. In doing so, we draw upon our experience applying Universal Design for Learning (UDL) in a rural teacher residency (preparation) program.

Framed by theory and research on DisCrit and UDL, we share our experiences as practitioners who use UDL to help preservice teachers interrogate assumptions about rurality, socioeconomics, race, ability, gender identity, and privilege. We describe how we have used UDL in our own courses to try to disrupt and shift paradigms of normativity that support inequitable practices and systems (e.g., ability grouping, exclusionary discipline). We then explain how educators can draw on tenets of DisCrit to complement and enhance UDL's use as a pedagogical framework that foregrounds variability of students' identities, backgrounds, and geographies. We conclude by offering our ongoing planning as a model for how teacher educators interested in working with DisCrit can expand its use as a transformative and liberatory framework that includes, but also extends beyond race and ability.

Theoretical framework

In framing this work, we draw on tenets of DisCrit, and research in UDL. In addition, the contexts in which we work – in rural schools and communities in the northeastern United States – play a significant role in how we engage with concepts of race and ability in teacher education. Thus, we begin by describing the landscape of rurality and rural education in the United States.

Rurality and rural education in the United States

Rural is an ambiguous and often contentious term in many countries, and the United States is no exception. Defined by their distance to urban centers, and categorized accordingly (i.e., rural fringe, rural remote), rural areas of the United States have seen a slight population decrease in recent years (Aud et al. 2013). Still, recent estimates show that more than one-quarter of the country's students are educated in rural schools; of these students, roughly 25% are students of color, and approximately 14% have been identified with disabilities (Showalter et al. 2017). Although all regions of the country (e.g., northeast, west, south) include rural areas, racial and linguistic demographics vary by region,

In the wake of recent presidential elections (2016 and 2020), the country's rural vs. urban dichotomy has been thrust into the public sphere; yet rural education policy continues to be inconsistent, disjointed, and viewed through a deficit lens (Schafft 2016). While 'urban education' has often been employed as a deficit-based and racialized euphemism to describe schools that are largely non-White (e.g., Watson 2011), discourses of rural schools largely position them as White and culturally static (Anthony-Stevens and Langford 2020), while rural people are stereotyped as uneducated or possessors of 'stupid' knowledge (Heldke 2006). Further, tropes of rural communities and schools as either pastoral and idyllic (Azano and Stewart 2016) or backwards and in decline (Reid et al. 2010) highlight an oversimplified dichotomy which we, as rural teacher educators, consciously reject.

DisCrit

From our perspective, DisCrit lays the theoretical groundwork for paradigmatic shifts in how teachers view the role of race and ability in schools. We view these shifts as crucial in the contexts described above, in which rural and urban have been racially codified (as White and Black respectively) and used to dichotomize an already polarized population along a geopolitical divide. Just as attention to race has been problematized as absent in rural education and curriculum (e.g., Pini and Bhopal 2017; Straubhaar 2017), we believe that the interrelationship of race and ability put forth by DisCrit tenets must be foregrounded in rural teacher education, and among place-based – and largely White – identities.

DisCrit's first tenet problematizes deeply entrenched cultural standards of normativity, including Whiteness and ability, that 'lead to viewing differences among certain individuals as deficits' (Annamma, Connor, and Ferri 2013, 12). This, along with DisCrit's other tenets, offers a stance from which to interrogate assumptions of neutrality, many of which are embedded in schools and curricula, that have historically privileged White, middle class, non-disabled bodies. Rejecting such assumptions is particularly crucial in teacher education, given that a majority of teachers in the United States identify as White. Of further concern are limited opportunities for preservice teachers to engage with concepts of race and ability – beyond course requirements highlighting euphemistic concepts of 'diversity' and 'exceptionality.' In contrast, DisCrit's tenets highlight intersectional identities and foreground the perspectives of historically marginalized individuals as valuable sources of knowledge. We draw on DisCrit not simply to argue that it ought to attend to rurality, but to imagine an extension of its tenets to account for and aspire to a centering of variability in all of its forms.

Universal design for learning

UDL is an approach to teaching and learning that was developed by researchers from the Center for Applied Special Technology (CAST; Meyer, Rose, and Gordon 2014). It has emerged as a framework for inclusive instructional design and pedagogy, with an emphasis on reframing disability. Several of its core concepts are consistent with social models of disability that counter notions of individual deficiencies by emphasizing the disabling effects of the environment (Meyer, Rose, and Gordon 2014).

Complementary to DisCrit's theoretical framing, UDL offers a practical approach to redesigning curriculum that rejects conceptions of an 'average' student and emphasizes variability among learners (Rose and Meyer 2002). Our own work, in a rural-focused teacher residency, aims to center UDL as a framework for both our students' practice, as well as our own. We have increasingly drawn on UDL as a platform for questioning norms of schooling. Consistent with DisCrit's problematization of the ways in which Whiteness and ability exert power and define boundaries of 'normalcy,' we have centered core UDL concepts in our work supporting pre-service teachers to interrogate and reject practices that marginalize and oppress students on the basis of identity and place (i.e., race, gender, ability, rurality, urbanicity).

In recent years, the UDL framework has evolved to adopt a more nuanced stance on ability that foregrounds variability in student learning patterns, backgrounds, and identities as a starting point for (re)designing curriculum, courses, and schools (Gravel et al. 2015). Additionally, a number of researchers (e.g., Fritzgerald 2020; Waitoller and King Thorius 2016) have explored how UDL can take on an actively anti-racist and/or anti-ableist stance. As we will discuss, we support these efforts and argue that DisCrit tenets offer a theoretical grounding for UDL pedagogy that has the potential to act as a transformative force in teacher education.

UDL and DisCrit in action: rural teacher residency

The Rural Teacher Residency (RTR)[1] is a 15-month teacher preparation program based in the northeastern United States. It is associated with a major university and specifically designed to prepare teachers for 'high-need' rural[2] schools, including those in geographically distant areas several hours away from the university campus (Reagan et al. 2018). It explicitly centers the need to counter commonly held deficit notions of rural communities, and recognize the strengths of the families and communities as importantly valuable to educating all children. RTR begins with a summer institute comprising three graduate courses, and a 30-hour internship with a community-based organization. Students in the program, known as 'residents,' then co-teach for the whole school year with a mentor teacher while continuing full-time graduate coursework, and end the second summer with their remaining courses. Upon successful completion of the program, residents earn a Master's of Education as well as teaching certification in either elementary education, or secondary math or science.

Over the course of the program, we have worked with approximately 40 residents across four cohorts. The residents are somewhat distinct from nationwide teacher demographics in the United States. In the U.S., approximately three-quarters of the teaching force identifies as female, while nearly 80% identifies as White (Hussar et al. 2020). In RTR, we had a higher proportion of males (37%), and almost all residents identified as White. Additionally, the program recruited residents with a range of professional experiences; this included former teacher's assistants, military veterans, and small business owners, ranging in age from 22 to 55 years old. While a number of the residents grew up in the region where RTR operates, many were from other areas of the country.

Likewise, the northeastern region is somewhat distinct in terms of rural demographics in the United States. Although nationally there is racial and linguistic diversity among rural students as discussed above, this is unevenly distributed. Student and teacher populations in RTR are predominantly White and English-speaking. There is also significant socioeconomic variability in this area; many towns that once thrived in wood-based industries have experience a decline in recent years, resulting in a shift to tourism-driven seasonal economies and residents (Vernikoff et al. 2019). In general, rural areas in the region have nearly double the poverty rates of suburban areas (Mattingly, Carson, and Schaefer 2013). Additionally, while there are small cities in this area, none qualify as large urban centers.

In addition to supporting the residents in their placements and teaching program courses, several members of the RTR leadership team participate in related research projects focused on notions of place, rurality, and curriculum. Among these projects is a self-study that took place from 2018 to 2021, in which faculty (ourselves included) and doctoral students analyzed our experiences operationalizing UDL in our practice, and which introduced us to DisCrit. In the following section, we share our lessons learned, and how our gradual incorporation of the tenets of DisCrit, in conjunction with UDL, improved our ability to support pre-service teachers' examination of structural inequities in school practices, including but not limited to norms of race, ability, and rurality.

'Collaborating with families' course: UDL and DisCrit tenet 1

One course which underwent significant revision in the RTR program was entitled 'Collaborating with Families of Individuals with Exceptionalities.' I (Beth) taught this course during the summer term in 2018 and 2019. A White, monolingual, cisgender woman, originally from the greater Philadelphia area of the United States, I resided primarily in the city's suburbs while growing up. My interest in disability arose from seeing firsthand how disabled family members' experiences with barriers in the built environment, communication, and the educational system limited and shaped their social participation.

I began my teaching career in a rural school district in the far northeastern United States. While much of my teaching experiences have been in areas that meet the federal definitions of rural, I have mostly lived in middle-class, suburban communities since moving to this part of the country. Shortly after beginning my first teaching position as a special education teacher, I realized that I knew little about my students or their families. As a novice teacher, I also had the jarring experience of realizing that while my teacher education program had prepared me well in terms of pedagogical knowledge, I lacked a clear sense of the rural community's values, interests, and priorities that was necessary to foster meaningful connections (Corbett 2010). Having never lived in a rural place, I had not previously considered the unique benefits and challenges of teaching in a rural school, or how I might familiarize myself with the particular community in which I taught.

It was this gap in my own development as a teacher that compelled me to join the RTR team several years later, while pursuing my doctoral degree in teacher education. I was offered the opportunity to teach Collaborating with Families, which was required of residents in RTR, and also a certification requirement for those who wished to pursue a teaching credential in special education. A number of assignments met standards required by the Council for Exceptional Children (CEC).[3] The course was offered during the final month of the RTR program (the 15th month of coursework).

When I first taught the course in 2018, I made a concerted effort to embed UDL and accessibility into the course content and pedagogy, often offering students multiple modalities of resources (rather than relying on text), and encouraging students to express their learning in a variety of formats (e.g., presentations, videos). In other words, I wanted to model UDL while also teaching about it. I also attempted to connect the content of the course with the specific rural contexts in which residents lived and taught. For example, one assignment asked students to research local resources for families, and to map them to highlight the assets and needs of the community.

After the course ended, I realized that while I had emphasized UDL and accessibility, and introduced students to multiple models of disability (e.g., medical, social) in order to highlight deficit-based practices, I neither questioned nor critiqued the establishment of such practices in schools. Additionally, while we had discussed how systems of ability-based privilege define some students as normal and others as disabled, I offered no concrete means of supporting students to push against this in their practice. Furthermore, while I had read about issues of inappropriate identification of students of color as disabled (e.g., Harry and Klingner 2014), Whiteness as property (Leonardo and Broderick 2011), and the intersections of race and disability as theory (Annamma, Connor, and Ferri 2013), I had not centered DisCrit in my practice. Although I emphasized the power of ableism in schools and curriculum, I did not attend enough to race, or ways in which racism and ableism functioned simultaneously (Annamma, Connor, and Ferri 2013). I realized that *not* addressing race in the context of special education provided residents with an incomplete, and ultimately irresponsible analysis, and elected to redesign the course to address these gaps.

My goal for improving the course was to engage more intentionally with the intersection of disability and race in schools, and in rural schools in particular. I realized that in order to truly disrupt the normative center of my practice I needed to re-evaluate content, and work with students to challenge our own understandings of ability and normalcy. During my time as a special education teacher, I had developed a beginning understanding of the medicalized and often deficit-laden discourse around disability that permeated special education processes and solidified an invisible barrier between students who were positioned as disabled and those who were not. Additionally, as a former rural teacher myself, I was aware of similarly negative discourses ascribed to rurality.

The similarities in how disability and rurality play out in schools became more pronounced in my work in RTR. The othering of both disability and rurality in schools speaks to an assumed neutrality of education – and teacher education – that is neither required nor expected to attend to either concepts outside of specialized courses or programs. Such othering allows both to be positioned as one-dimensional, and fails to acknowledge the ways that disability and rurality vary significantly across contexts. As DisCrit's first tenet suggests, this false neutrality allows 'general' education to function as a standard of normalcy that assumes nondisabled, White, middle-class, suburban or 'placeless' ways of being. I wanted to highlight the othering of disability and rurality in my teaching, and examine the causes and consequences while also attending to the relationship between racism and ableism.

Although UDL does not (as of yet) explicitly address issues of equity, one of its principles – engagement – does highlight the importance of optimizing relevance in content offered to students (CAST 2018). When I taught the Collaborating with Families course for a second time in 2019, I sought out sources of knowledge that addressed the significance of geography, and rurality as they related to issues of race and ability. I chose *Ability Profiling and School Failure* (Collins 2013) to provide a narrative-like account of how students are profiled in schools, and constructed via racism, ableism, and exclusionary practices. I also felt the need to have a 'handbook' text, which students could refer back to in their future practice. Rather than rely on the 'big glossies' (Brantlinger 2006) that follow a disability-of-the-week structure that highlights medicalized categories, I used a text that approached family collaboration through an asset-based orientation, *Cultural Reciprocity and Special Education* (Kalyanpur and Harry 2012).

My aim in selecting these texts was to provide teacher residents with the opportunity to examine the ways in which race and ability function interdependently (Annamma, Connor, and Ferri 2013), particularly in the realm of special education. It also gave us a platform for interrogating assumptions about the Whiteness and perceived racial homogeneity of the rural context in which many residents taught. We began by analyzing special education processes of referring and diagnosing disabilities, and discussing how such processes pathologize student differences in perceived ability, race, and socioeconomic status. Students facilitated weekly discussions of the Collins (2013) text, and were encouraged to share their responses to the text, as well as any connections to their own experiences.

Looking back on the course, I felt that while I addressed some theoretical elements of DisCrit, I fell short of explicitly centering its tenets in the curriculum. Although I provided residents opportunities to discuss and critique the disproportionate representation of students of color in special education, the engagement was limited and from a distance; none of us considered the direct implications of racism and ableism on our practice. In other words, we stopped short of considering the ways we, a group of educators who largely identified as White and non-disabled, might be complicit in perpetuating and supporting systemic inequities.

A deeper engagement with UDL had compelled me to increase the relevance of resources in the course, and I had some success in supporting residents to problematize the marginalization of disability and rurality in schools. When it came to intentionally engaging residents with the intersection of race, ability, and rurality however, I only partially met my goals. I had drawn on UDL to reframe ability, and begun to explore the role of racism in shaping disability in schools in general; yet more explicit opportunities to unpack the role of race in the specific – and predominantly White – rural places where residents lived and taught was underexplored.

Summer institute: UDL and DisCrit tenets one through four

In the hopes of building upon Beth's progress and setting up the next cohort of residents for even greater growth, we turned our sights to the summer institute which begins new residents' experience. In the summer institute, the three courses students take are: Introductory Seminar; Human Development and Education; and, Sociocultural Perspectives and Education. I (Bryan) teach the latter two summer institute courses, in collaboration with another colleague. I am a cisgender, monolingual, White man who grew up near the rural region that RTR serves – a region that has wide diversity in socioeconomic status (of which I later came to understand that I had been towards the lower end of), but a dearth of racial diversity.

My preparation as a special education teacher – at the same University where RTR is now housed – led to a 12-year classroom career in various educational settings, typically working with adolescents who had been removed from their original school setting because of their behaviors. During these years, I clearly came to see that my students (and their families) were deeply disadvantaged by the systems and institutions that upheld traditional normative assumptions and thus deemed those people who fell outside of those norms, as deficient. It was not until I left the classroom to pursue my doctoral studies elsewhere that I encountered more diversity – among my classmates, professors, and academic thought – and realized that the normative forces that I had been fighting on behalf of my students were a part of a much bigger problem of equity that is tied to systemic racism. It is from this perspective that, working as a postdoctoral associate in RTR, teaching courses, and supervising residents, I made changes to the summer institute courses using UDL and DisCrit to bring issues of equity to the forefront.

Like other members of RTR's self-study project on UDL, I also continued to increase my explicit incorporation of UDL into my own practices. I rewrote the syllabi to center the required competencies for the courses, and then allowed for flexibility and choice much as has been described in the Collaborating with Families course. The use of UDL in my practice was regularly explicitly explained to the residents, so that they could examine and critique my use of UDL and the resulting impact on their learning, and use that as a lever to develop designs of UDL in their own emerging practice.

My participation in the self-study research had also introduced me to seminal writings of DisCrit, which both resonated with the misgivings I held regarding many common school practices, and informed curricular changes I introduced for the summer institute courses. In addition to DisCrit's first tenet (discussed above) and aligned with its second and third tenets, I wanted the residents to explore the ways that intersectional identity can, through socially constructed systemic discrimination, greatly disadvantage those who do not match an imagined 'normal.' In particular, I wanted to help residents move beyond the inclination to dismiss people's real experiences of discrimination by comparing themselves on the basis of a single dimension of identity.

In collaboration with the other members of the teaching team, I designed a series of activities to take place in the first several weeks, focused on laying a foundation for social justice and equity to be at the core of the rest of the curriculum. This started with residents exploring their own multifaceted identity and juxtaposing that with an examination of the deficit lens commonly applied to rural communities (e.g., Heldke 2006). The efforts continued with a week of activities on the concepts of equity, privilege, bias, social justice, intersectionality, and critical examination of classroom disciplinary practices. While this recentering of intersectional equity was planned months beforehand, it felt prescient when the start of our summer institute coincided with the national and international protests in response to the killing of George Floyd and systemic racism in policing and society.

We also began a weekly assignment which many residents later described as being central to the evolution of their thinking about race and equity in their rural setting. Inspired by the fourth DisCrit tenet, the need to privilege otherwise-marginalized voices, the Social Justice Entertainment assignment asked residents to partake in and discuss selected popular media (tv shows, movies, podcasts, comic books, etc.) that centers characters who are typically marginalized due to race, disability, gender, gender identity, sexual orientation, religion, class, or other characteristics. One resident remarked at how this assignment prompted introspection on their[3] past experiences which in turn informs their future intentions:

> All the books I have read over the past 2 years have been written by White men, the shows I tend to watch are usually about White people. Considering this I find it important to recognize that White, straight and male is not the default or 'normal' that other identities exist and should be heard and given the same consideration ... Having grown up in a rural town myself I feel like it was hard to speak up about issues of race and identity because straight and White were perceived as the norm or default ... My hope is that by providing students these new perspectives it might equip them with the tools to address a comment or racist idea that they encounter.

After the intensive week on social justice and equity, the conceptual groundings of UDL were taught, using the same language and imagery that had been a part of the discussions of equity the previous week. This was followed up with a guest speaker discussing practical applications of UDL, including how to conduct a 'barrier analysis' – a deliberate examination of curricular materials to identify potential barriers for learners using UDL's principles and guidelines (Beck et al. 2014; Fornauf et al. 2020). The combination of UDL's conceptual centering of variability, along with its practical approach to planning for that variability, resonated with many of the residents. One resident later reflected, ' ... if variability is the norm, then we make these modifications and room for multiple means of expression/representation in the planning process before we even know what group of people we'll be serving. It becomes proactivity rather than reactivity.'

While we have yet to fully understand the longer-term impact of these changes, our attempts of incorporating the first four tenets of DisCrit seem to be very promising. The residents' work has shown a strong use of UDL, an appreciation for their rural communities, and a widely inclusive pedagogical stance that incorporates many ways of supporting otherwise-marginalized students. In reflections on social justice and equity at the conclusion of the summer institute, residents were very open about their starting points being an acknowledgment of their own identity (largely White, Christian, middle class, able-bodied) as the 'norm,' and about taking for granted the traditional school and societal practices designed for that norm. They all described a recognition that de-centering a 'normal' identity is key to improving school and society. One resident connected this explicitly to the current events during the summer institute:

> Learning about social justice and equity in class concurrently with current events helped me realize racism is deeper than individual beliefs; it's a systemic problem in this country. It also helped me understand that as a teacher it's important to have awareness of and promote diversity in the classroom regardless of how diverse the student body is ... Once I began to think about social justice and equity (and UDL, human development theories, etc.) it was hard not to think about it. It's in the forefront of my mind.

Extending DisCrit to strengthen UDL

While we believe that UDL has been a potent tool in the RTR program for promoting and supporting more equitable and inclusive teaching, we are not claiming that it is a panacea for educational equity. In recent years, UDL has been rightly criticized for falling short in its attention to issues of privilege and bias that create structural inequities in school systems. Waitoller and King Thorius (2016) offered a 'loving critique' of UDL urging it 'to actively address how power and privilege shape and block learning opportunities at the intersection of raced/abled identities' (p. 376). In a moderated forum in *Harvard Educational Review (HER)*, Alim et al. (2017) responded by recognizing that many ubiquitous concepts in education are actually undergirded by ideologies of White supremacy and eugenics, and admitting that UDL and other equity-aspiring approaches must more explicitly call out and counter those premises. In late summer of 2020, CAST focused its annual symposium on addressing this very issue, launched a new initiative which seeks to extend the UDL guidelines to counter systems of oppression in schools, and published *Antiracism and Universal Design for Learning* (Fritzgerald 2020).

As rural teacher educators who are currently planning ongoing improvements of our courses, and in the hopes of continuing the conversation of loving critique, we offer ways that DisCrit can further strengthen UDL in these efforts. Waitoller and King Thorius (2016) critiqued UDL on three accounts: (1) UDL does not explicitly examine whether the curriculum being offered in school is itself promoting justice and equity, (2) UDL does not explicitly address the inequitable and discriminatory context of schools, and (3) UDL does not explicitly challenge the concept of a desirable normativity. We will start by addressing the first two critiques together – not because we believe them to be synonymous, but because in our context we imagine addressing them in tandem – then go on to discuss the third critique, and conclude with our path forward in using DisCrit to address these challenges.

Access to what? And what about the context?

While UDL's stated goal is to help students become expert learners, it has been agnostic as to what they are learning. Waitoller and King Thorius (2016) suggest that instead, UDL should strive, 'to nurture expert learners who interrogate multiple forms of oppression and who apprentice to be key participants in a pluralistic democracy' (p. 375). We believe that our incorporation of the first four tenets of DisCrit in RTR's most recent summer institute was a valuable step in preparing residents to critically examine curricular content. However, what we see throughout subsequent coursework and conversations is that those who entered the program already questioning the commonly prejudiced depictions of minoritized and oppressed populations in textbooks and classroom lessons, have used their experience in the summer institute to bolster their insistence that more equitable and inclusive curriculum take its place. However, residents for whom the summer institute marked their first exposure to such critical examination reported difficulty reconciling this new valuing of equity and inclusion with the lessons they were taught as children and the ways that their own (White, rural) identities are interwoven with those lessons.

Before turning our focus to how we intend to address this shortcoming and its manifestation in RTR, we want to bring it into conversation with the second of the aforementioned critiques of UDL. Despite its emphasis on engagement and relevance, UDL fails to consider the prejudices and structural inequities that exist in schools. UDL advocates call for engagement to take into account students' culture, but Waitoller and King Thorius point out that this call 'is informed by a static and oppression-free conceptualization of culture. Schools are fraught with ableist, racist, and classist practices' (p. 376). Context matters, and if UDL is telling teachers to have students collaborate and interact as part of their learning experience, it must do so with knowledge of the oppressive relationships that exist in schools and communities and the ways that the school structures exacerbate those inequities. Alim responded to this critique, agreeing that, "... in some ways that's the problem with the terms 'include' and 'inclusion' in the first place, that they assume that the goal is to be included into a system that's always already oppressive, as opposed to transforming it ... ' (Alim et al. 2017, pp. 18–19). Fritzgerald (2020) opens her book on UDL and Anti-racism by providing evidence of racism in statistics of disproportionate suspension rates, overidentification for special education services, and denial of access to desirable programs.

When we look within our context of RTR, this lack of explicitly examining school practices initially appears to manifest in similar ways as the lack of explicitly examining curriculum. Some of the residents who had previously questioned the structural oppression in school practices are actively pushing against the continuation of those practices, while others openly struggle to examine the ways that their upkeep of traditional practices may be replicating that discrimination. A significant difference between how residents are examining school curriculum versus school structure and practices, however, may be the way that race, ability, and class intersect differently for the residents and in the schools that RTR serves.

As described earlier, both the school population in the region that RTR operates and the residents themselves are overwhelmingly White. When it comes to critically examining the oppressive nature of curriculum such as history lessons – a topic largely charged with problematic representations of race – any subsequent changes may be seen by some of the residents as being at odds with both their own identity and what they understand to be the identity of their students and families. We hear evidence of this conflict in their contributions in class and individual conversations. In contrast, examination of inequitable school practices and structures (e.g., exclusionary discipline practices, ability grouping) within a predominantly White school still reveals discrimination, although largely along lines of ability and class. Since many residents report being attracted to RTR because of a commitment to helping students who are disadvantaged along lines of ability and class, we wonder if their attendance to these inequities presents far less conflict with their own identities. The potential exceptions to this are the residents who have been highly successful in past schooling and have an identity of value that is conflated with that success.

What is normal?

While UDL charges teachers with teaching to the margins, it does not directly challenge the fundamental concept of there being a curve with margins. Waitoller and King Thorius insist, ' ... such use of language reinforces the faulty assumption on which special education is predicated – the normal curve – even when UDL attempts to dismantle ability hierarchies' (p. 376). In the *HER* forum, Ladson-Billings reflected on the foundational work in education that was done by scientists who held highly problematic views about human worth, stating, ' ... even the whole field, for example, of gifted and talented education – rests on a eugenics premise' (Alim et al. 2017, 6).

We must admit that when we first encountered this particular critique of UDL, we questioned it, feeling that UDL does already directly challenge the concept of normativity, and replaces it by centering the concept of variability. Three of the core ideas of UDL that RTR draws on are: variability is the norm, variability is predictable to some extent, and it is the context which is disabling rather than a child who is disabled. Conceptually, we felt that these interdependent messages were a repudiation of the White supremacist and eugenic foundations that underlie so many problematic assumptions of normalcy. However, our recent incorporation of DisCrit has provoked introspection that reveals the weakness that we and UDL share in this matter.

Our realization may be exemplified by a teaching resident's concern about their first-grade classroom, explaining that only four of the 15 students were 'typical' learners, and the rest were struggling with the curriculum for a variety of reasons. Having been told that this ratio was commonplace in many schools in the area, the resident wanted to know what to do about the rest of the students. We have come to realize that this question in no way conflicts with the concepts of UDL as we have taught them; it expects the commonality of variability among students in the classroom, it acknowledges that the expectation of that variability should inform instruction, and it accepts the responsibility for the teacher to create a context that fits the variability. All of these are drastic paradigm shifts from commonly held assumptions of schools, and they can be valuable in making a teacher's practices more equitable and inclusive. But the fact that residents are not questioning what is meant by 'typical,' even when the majority of their students rarely fit the description, makes it clear that we have not yet enabled our residents to truly challenge the concept of normativity as desirable.

Implications

We now revisit the tenets of DisCrit through our plans to address the identified ways that RTR's use of UDL has fallen short in our mission to prepare teachers for equity and inclusion. We hope that sharing this process can also serve other teacher educators who may wish to combine DisCrit and UDL to do the same.

DisCrit and improving RTR

While some of the RTR residents may have different challenges when interrogating inequitable curricular content versus inequitable school practices, we intend to address these challenges together in our forthcoming courses. First, we revisit the first tenet of DisCrit, in particular the interdependency of racism and ableism and how those can be seen in schools and society jointly othering populations in an effort to disempower them. Second, we explicitly incorporate lessons aligned with the fifth and sixth tenets, examining the legal and historical evidence of this othering that has been purposefully used to advantage some while disadvantaging others, and has been reified in countless structures throughout school and society.

We want residents to recognize that the 'grammar of schooling' (Tyack and Cuban 1995) – established school norms that are commonly taken for granted – are not natural phenomena that should be unquestioned. Every part of the curriculum and school structure were created by individuals who had multiple unexamined biases and were part of groups that stood to gain from establishing those norms. Acceptance or rejection of these norms serve purposes of upholding or undermining the power structures that they were created within. Our hope is that these activities directly connecting current curriculum and practices with the history of their discriminatory purpose will help our residents continue to grow in their thinking.

Many of those activities revealing the foundational problems with commonly accepted curriculum and school norms may also help residents critically examine the underlying concept of desirable normativity. However, we believe that in order to support residents' interrogation of the fundamentally discriminatory ideas of typicality and normalcy, we must return to DisCrit's third tenet and further examine what is meant by race and ability being socially constructed. The third tenet states, 'DisCrit emphasizes the social constructions of race and ability and yet recognizes the material and psychological impacts of being labeled as raced or dis/abled, which sets one outside of the western cultural norms' (Annamma, Connor, and Ferri 2013, 11). We utilized multiple resources that make the point of race and ability being socially constructed and we included that language in our lessons, but discussions with the residents give us the impression that we have fallen short of this tenet's intention. Many of our resources and lessons have been focused on the 'material and psychological impacts' of racism, ableism, and other oppressive forces. Perhaps because of that focus, residents seem to have interpreted that the justification for someone to mistreat others based on race and/or ability is what is socially constructed. We wonder whether they believe that racism and ableism are socially constructed, rather than the foundational ideas of race and ability being socially constructed themselves. The latter is a more abstract idea, but is necessary to meet the intended goal of dismantling ability hierarchies. When a resident speaks about their first graders not being 'typical,' they may be dedicated to treating all students well, but are not questioning the assumption that the end goal is still to turn them into typically abled students as defined by ableist societal standards.

We are currently exploring resources and activities that will revisit the third tenet and help residents interrogate the social construction of the very ideas of race, ability, gender, rurality, and other forms of identity. One possible avenue is to have residents jointly investigate how each of these identities has been defined differently over time and across cultures, and another is to discuss how changes in context can redefine whether differences become disabling. We know that there are many texts written for teachers (e.g. Baglieri and Lalvani 2019; Valle and Connor 2019) as well as firsthand accounts written for the general public (e.g., Mooney 2007; Valente 2011) that can be used for these purposes. We look forward to continuing on this journey with the residents, and hope that as other teacher educators join us in using UDL and DisCrit together, we can learn from each other.

Notes

1. All names, with the exceptions of the authors, are pseudonyms.
2. Because the examples in this paper are drawn from an educator preparation program funded in part by a United States Department of Education Teacher Quality Partnership Grant, we refer to federal definitions of rural and high-need as outlined by the terms of the grant (retrieved from https://www2.ed.gov/programs/tqpartnership/faqeligibility.html).

3. Please note that the singular 'they/their' is used throughout this document. Despite not being formally recognized in academic writing, we choose to use this nomenclature out of respect for gender diversity and because of its alignment with societal speaking norms outside of the academy.

Disclosure statement

No potential conflict of interest was reported by the author(s).

References

Alim, H. S., S. Baglieri, G. Ladson-Billings, D. Paris, D. H. Rose, and J. M. Valente. 2017. "Responding to 'Cross-pollinating Culturally Sustaining Pedagogy and Universal Design for Learning: Toward an Inclusive Pedagogy that Accounts for Dis/ability.'" *Harvard Educational Review* 87 (1): 4–25. doi:10.17763/1943-5045-87.1.4.

Annamma, S. A. 2015. "Whiteness as Property: Innocence and Ability in Teacher Education." *The Urban Review* 47 (2): 293–316. doi:10.1007/s11256-014-0293-6.

Annamma, S. A., D. Connor, and B. Ferri. 2013. "Dis/ability Critical Race Studies (Discrit): Theorizing at the Intersections of Race and Dis/ability." *Race Ethnicity and Education* 16 (1): 1–31. doi:10.1080/13613324.2012.730511.

Anthony-Stevens, V., and S. Langford. 2020. "What Do You Need a Course like that For?" Conceptualizing Diverse Ruralities in Rural Teacher Education." *Journal of Teacher Education* 71 (3): 332–344. doi:10.1177/0022487119861582.

Aud, S., S. Wilkinson-Flicker, P. Kristapovich, A. Rathbun, X. Wang, and J. Zhang. 2013. "The Condition of Education 2013 (NCES 2013-037). U.S." Washington, DC: Department of Education, National Center for Education Statistics. https://nces.ed.gov/pubs2013/2013037.pdf

Azano, A. P., and T. Stewart. 2016. "Confronting Challenges at the Intersection of Rurality, Place, and Teacher Preparation: Improving Efforts in Teacher Education to Staff Rural Schools." *Global Education Review* 3: 1.

Baglieri, S., and P. Lalvani. 2019. *Undoing Ableism: Teaching about Disability in K-12 Classrooms.* New York: Routledge.

Beck, T., P. Diaz Del Castillo, F. Fovet, H. Mole, and B. Noga. 2014. "Applying Universal Design to Disability Service Provision: Outcome Analysis of a Universal Design (UD) Audit." *Journal of Postsecondary Education and Disability* 27 (2): 209–222.

Brantlinger, E. 2006. "The Big Glossies: How Textbooks Structure (Special) Education." In *Who Benefits from Special Education? Remediating (Fixing) Other People's Children*, edited by E. Brantlinger, 45–76. Mahwah, NJ: Lawrence Erlbaum Associates.

CAST. 2018. "Universal Design for Learning Guidelines Version 2.2." http://udlguidelines.cast.org

Collins, K. M. 2013. *Ability Profiling and School Failure: One Child's Struggle to Be Seen as Competent.* 2nd ed. New York: Routledge.

Corbett, M. 2010. "Backing the Right Horse: Teacher Education, Sociocultural Analysis and Literacy in Rural Education." *Teaching and Teacher Education* 26 (1): 82–86. doi:10.1016/j.tate.2009.08.001.

Fornauf, B. S., T. Higginbotham, B. Mascio, K. McCurdy, and E. M. Reagan. 2020. "Analyzing Barriers, Innovating Pedagogy: Applying Universal Design for Learning in a Teacher Residency." *The Teacher Educator* 1-18. doi:10.1080/08878730.2020.1828520.

Fritzgerald, A. 2020. *Antiracism and Universal Design for Learning: Building Expressways to Success.* Wakefield, MA: CAST Professional Publishing.

Gravel, J. W., L. A. Edwards, C. J. Buttimer, and D. H. Rose. 2015. "Universal Design for Learning in Postsecondary Education: Reflections on Principles and Their Application." In *Universal Design in Higher Education: From Principles to Practice*, edited by S. E. Burgstahler, 81–100. 2nded. Cambridge, MA: Harvard Education Press.

Harry, B., and J. Klingner. 2014. *Why are so Many Minority Students in Special Education?* New York: Teachers College Press.

Heldke, L. 2006. "Farming Made Her Stupid." *Hypatia* 21 (3): 151–165. doi:10.1111/j.1527-2001.2006.tb01118.x.

Hussar, B., J. Zhang, S. Hein, K. Wang, A. Roberts, J. Cui, M. Smith, F. Bullock Mann, A. Barmer, and R. Dilig. 2020. "The Condition of Education 2020 (NCES 2020-144)." *National Center for Education Statistics.* https://nces.ed.gov/pubsearch/pubsinfo.asp?pubid=2020144

Kalyanpur, M., and B. Harry. 2012. *Cultural Reciprocity in Special Education: Building Family-professional Relationships.* Baltimore, MD: Paul H. Brooks.

Leonardo, Z., and A. Broderick. 2011. "Smartness as Property: A Critical Exploration of Intersections between Whiteness and Disability Studies." *Teachers College Record* 113 (10): 2206–2232.

Love, B. L. 2019. *We Want to Do More than Survive: Abolitionist Teaching and the Pursuit of Educational Freedom.* Boston: Beacon Press.

Mattingly, M. L., J. A. Carson, and A. Schaefer. 2013. "2012 National Child Poverty Rate Stagnates at 22.6 Percent. New Hampshire Child Poverty Jumps 30 Percent since 2011." *Carsey School of Public Policy, University of New Hampshire.*

Meyer, A., D. H. Rose, and D. T. Gordon. 2014. *Universal Design for Learning: Theory and Practice.* Wakefield, MA: CAST Professional Publishing.

Minor, C., C. Miller, Dingle, C. Minor, L. Fortin, and J. Mundorf. 2020. "UDL Rising: Naming, Disrupting, and Dismantling Barriers to Equity [Conference Keynote]." CAST Symposium, August 5.https://www.youtube.com/watch?v=TdSnI7orfJQ&t=2s

Mooney, J. 2007. *The Short Bus: A Journey beyond Normal.* New York: Henry Holt and Company.

Pini, B., and K. Bhopal. 2017. "Racialising Rural Education." *Race, Ethnicity and Education* 20 (2): 192–196. doi:10.1080/13613324.2015.1115620.

Reagan, E. M., A. Coppens, L. Couse, E. Hambacher, D. Lord, K. McCurdy, and D. Silva Pimentel. 2018. "Toward a Framework for the Design and Implementation of the Teacher Residency for Rural Education." In *Innovation and Implementation: School-University- Community Collaboration in Education*, edited by M. Reardon and J. Leanord, 81–106. Charlotte, NC: Information Age Publishing.

Reid, J. A., B. Green, M. Cooper, W. Hastings, G. Lock, and S. White. 2010. "Regenerating Rural Social Space? Teacher Education for rural—Regional Sustainability." *Australian Journal of Education* 54 (3): 262–276. doi:10.1177/000494411005400304.

Rose, D. H., and A. Meyer. 2002. *Teaching Every Student in the Digital Age.* Alexandria, VA: ASCD.

Schafft, K. A. 2016. "Rural Education as Rural Development: Understanding the Rural School—community Well-being Linkage in a 21st-century Policy Context." *Peabody Journal of Education* 91 (2): 137–154. doi:10.1080/0161956X.2016.1151734.

Showalter, D., R. Klein, J. Johnson, and S. L. Hartman. 2017. "Why Rural Matters 2015-2016: Understanding the Changing Landscape. A Report of the Rural School and Community Trust." *Rural School and Community Trust.*

Straubhaar, R. 2017. "Trying to Build a Classless Utopia in the Land of Racial Democracy: The Lack of Racial Discussion within the Educational Materials of the Brazilian Landless Rural Workers' Movement." *Race Ethnicity and Education* 20 (2): 264–276. doi:10.1080/13613324.2015.1110341.

Tyack, D. B., and L. Cuban. 1995. *Tinkering toward Utopia: A Century of Public School Reform.* Cambridge, MA: Harvard University Press.

Valente, J. M. 2011. *d/Deaf and d/Dumb: A Portrait of A Deaf Kid as A Young Superhero.* New York: Peter Lang.

Valle, J. W., and D. J. Connor. 2019. *Rethinking Disability: A Disability Studies Approach to Inclusive Practices.* 2nd ed. New York: Routledge.

Vernikoff, K., T. Schram, E. M. Reagan, C. Horn, A. L. Goodwin, and C. J. Couse. 2019. "Beyond Urban or Rural: Field Based Experiences for Teacher Residencies in Diverse Contexts." In

Handbook of Research on Field-based Teacher Education, edited by T. E. Hodges and A. C. Baum, 256–279. Hershey, PA: IGI Global. doi:10.4018/978-1-5225-6249-8.ch011.

Waitoller, F. R., and K. A. King Thorius. 2016. "Cross-pollinating Culturally Sustaining Pedagogy and Universal Design for Learning: Toward an Inclusive Pedagogy that Accounts for Dis/ability." *Harvard Educational Review* 86 (3): 366–389. doi:10.17763/1943-5045-86.3.366.

Watson, D. 2011. "What Do You Mean When You Say "Urban"? Speaking Honestly about Race and Students." *Rethinking Schools* 26 (1): 48–50.

Young, K. S. 2016. "How Student Teachers (Don't) Talk about Race: An Intersectional Analysis." *Race Ethnicity and Education* 19 (1): 67–95. doi:10.1080/13613324.2013.83182.

Traerás tus Documentos (you will bring your documents): navigating the intersections of disability and citizenship status in special education

Lilly B. Padía and Rachel Elizabeth Traxler

ABSTRACT
DisCrit has illuminated the interconnectivity of racism and ableism, though the experiences of undocumented youth and families enrolled in special education are largely unknown. In this paper, we explore the experiences of students at the intersection of disability and migratory status, examining the interplay of fear, schooling, and language use as students pursue college. We use DisCrit to help us understand historical patterns surrounding citizenship and how race, ableism, and documentation status continue to intersect and shape the acknowledgment of which bodies – with which papers – are rendered deserving. Examining interviews with students, researcher memos and fieldnotes, and researcher reflections, we consider the cases of Fernanda, an undocumented high schooler, and Daniel, a 9th grader from a mixed-citizenship status family. We highlight how students at the intersection of migratory status and disability are met with care by teachers and schools, yet remain unsupported in several domains. We also highlight how students experience the movement from entitlement to eligibility in schools, and discuss complications surrounding documentation of disability for disclosure and language. In light of our findings, we suggest implications for research and practice.

If you have a disability, you can register with disability services to get accommodations and extra help in college. You make an appointment with them and you provide your documentation.

Si tienes una discapacidad, puedas registrarte con la oficina de servicios de discapacidad para obtener acomodaciones y ayuda extra en la universidad. Harás una cita con ellos y traerás tu documentación.

In an instant, the rustling in the room stopped. It was as if the air had been sucked out of the auditorium. Our presentation continued for a few minutes before concluding. Some families took fliers with our website information, but no one asked us any questions.

We were presenting at an informational workshop session for undocumented high school students with disabilities. We were there to present on how to access disability services in college, regardless of citizenship status. Rachel, with a background in disability services in higher education, was the primary presenter, while Lilly, with a background in bilingual special education in K-12 schools, translated the information into Spanish. The audience was comprised of teenagers and their adult caregivers. Several women sitting with teenagers nodded upon hearing words like 'IEP' and 'servicios de educación especial'/'special education services.' It seemed clear that some of the students in the room received special education services and that their caregivers were familiar with the special education system.

After we left the event, we stood in the sunshine and unpacked what had just occurred. Our use of the word documentation/documentación, such a mainstay in the field of special education and disability services in higher education, had triggered the very fears and dangers we were seeking to assuage through the information we shared. As special educators and researchers working at the intersections of disability and language development, we were accustomed to being the only disability representatives in rooms focused on language, race, and citizenship. That day, we realized how very much we still need to learn from undocumented students with disabilities and their families. Something seemingly so small as one word that is used so frequently in special education discourse, transformed into an arm of a carceral nation-state when put in conversation with migration status.

We take up DisCrit, specifically tenets five and seven, which state the ways race and disability have been utilized to deny rights and identifies activism and resistance as crucial (Annamma 2018). We further complicate and extend DisCrit, however, by examining how citizenship status, disability, race, and language are co-constructed when students are both dis/abled and un/documented[1] in the United States school system. We put DisCrit in conversation with Undocumented Critical Theory (UndocuCrit) to explore the intersections of disability and documentation status in the United States school system (Aguilar 2019). UndocuCrit draws on TribalCrit (Brayboy 2005) and the legacy of Critical Race Theory to make sense of the experiences of undocumented people living in the United States today. Aguilar exposes the reality that U.S. immigration policies have their roots in capitalism, White supremacy, ideas of material acquisition, and assimilation and directly impact undocumented people (2019).

The tenets of UndocuCrit include:

> 1. Fear is endemic among immigrant communities; 2. Different experiences of liminality translate into different experiences of reality; 3. Parental sacrificios become a form of capital; 4. Acompañamiento is the embodiment of mentorship, academic redemption, and community engagement (Aguilar 2019, 3–6).

When we think about fear in relation to the school system, as well as parental sacrificios, it leads us to understand and view the school as an extension of the carceral state. We are also reminded of the barriers for families in the special education system, given the lack of access to clear information about their rights and legally mandated supports (Wilgus, Valle, and Ware 2013). These factors implicate a school system that does not provide access and justice to all; the burden often falls on parents/guardians to advocate for what they and their children are legally entitled to.

Struggles over access magnify when parents/guardians experience fear related to documentation status in schools, by virtue of schools being state institutions. Althusser describes the school as an ideological state apparatus (1971), where we cannot separate schooling from the state. Within contemporary calls to defund the police (e.g. Akbar

2020; Williams and Paterson 2020) and the removal of police and resource officers from schools is an opportunity to acknowledge that schooling is itself an ideological state apparatus meant for control and reification of social strata. In response to anti-immigrant political rhetoric and policies, schools and cities around the country have declared themselves sanctuaries for immigrants, rejecting U.S. Immigrations and Customs Enforcement (ICE) to keep students and families safe. By presuming that removing police or blocking ICE from schools will deliver justice, the embedded assumption is that schools are safe spaces where violence does not occur.

We address the following research question: In what ways do disability status and migratory status intersect for two high school students who receive language and disability services? The purpose of this paper is twofold: (1) we offer an examination of schools as arms of the carceral state, used as a lens to unpack the experiences of undocumented students with disabilities and (2) share our analysis of interviews with high school students who receive both special education and English language services. In asking this question, we assert that that students with disabilities who are undocumented are not markedly different from other students. For instance, students of all identities share aspirations, dis/abilities, strengths, and needs, though the arms of the state through the school that act upon students at this particular intersection create different and unique experiences within schools and beyond.

Citizenship, disability, and documentation

Citizenship refers to the reciprocal relationship between individuals and the state (Heywood 1994) and refers to the rights, duties, and obligations afforded by this status. While there are several definitions of citizenship, we are concerned with the tangible responsibilities and affordances for citizens and the nature of power, policies, and pedagogies enacted within schools (see Ramanathan 2013). Citizenship can bring belonging and a sense of unitedness, though aspects of citizenship – including the extension of schooling – are marginalizing for undocumented students with disabilities and present a dichotomy of inclusion/exclusion.

Historically and presently, race and disability have been conflated to create and uphold White supremacist norms and hierarchies of power, including links drawn between disability and Blackness to justify enslavement of Black people in the United States (Davis 1995; Erevelles 2011) and refusal of certain immigrant groups' entrance to the country (Dolmage 2018). The relationships between disability, race, and immigration have a long and sordid history that inform how schools approach undocumented students with disabilities today.

Legislation protects disabled and undocumented youth from outright discrimination in schools, such the Americans With Disabilities Act of 1990 (1990) and policies extending from *Plyler v. Doe* (1982), discussed below. Mechanisms fueled by systemic racism, such as disproportionality, inequitable disciplinary practices, and the de-prioritization of academics, compound with the limitations of *Plyler v. Doe* to further limit student participation (Gonzales, Heredia, and Negrón-Gonzales 2015). Access to economic and social mobility for undocumented students is further compounded by the inaccessibility of work, lack of financial assistance for postsecondary education, and limits on voting rights. These barriers exist both within and without public schooling and resources remain inaccessible for students who are often doubly stripped of their rights and duties afforded by citizenship.

Schools, citizenship, and disclosure

The Supreme Court decision *Plyler v. Doe* (1982) placed responsibility on schools to avoid questions about immigration status and social security numbers. However, what has transpired in many schools is that students' experiences and identities continue to be hushed and silenced in the name of neutrality. Schools have taken on the responsibility outlined in Plyler by adopting a culture of silence, reminiscent of 'don't ask, don't tell' (Mangual Figueroa 2011). Different experiences of citizenship status translate to different experiences of liminality for students (Aguilar 2019). Understanding policies like Plyler v. Doe helps shed light on the theoretical hopes of United States schooling and the differential experiences of liminality that students experience because of policies targeted towards language, dis/ability, and citizenship.

Schools reproduce civic identities through their practices and pedagogies, though little is known about how schools work with undocumented students within K-12 (see Gonzales, Heredia, and Negrón-Gonzales 2015) and even less is known about students at the intersection of disability and migratory status. Like undocumented students who are othered in schools, being disabled in schools requires navigation through disclosure and othering, though students are often 'outed' as disabled through participation in special education services. Undocumented students with disabilities receive multiple services from schools, including special education or English language (EL) services. A few scholars have attended to the intersection of language education and special education (see Harry and Klingner 2006; Baca and Cervantes 1998; Artiles and Ortiz 2002, Hoover and Collier 2004) and a small body of critical work is emerging that addresses students living at these intersections (e.g. Cioè-Peña 2017; Phuong 2017), but the intersection remains underexplored in many ways.

Theoretical framework

DisCrit is helpful for examining the ways that race and ableism are interconnected, but to date, few researchers have considered the experiences of undocumented students with disabilities. In this paper, we extend DisCrit to take up migratory status using empirical data, to examine how schools and structures deny citizenship affordances to undocumented youth with disabilities. We place DisCrit in conversation with UndocuCrit (Aguilar 2019), the history of eugenics in immigration policy (Dolmage 2018), and constructs of deservingness and innocence in migration discourse (Patel 2015).

To place our work within a larger context, we envision the integration of theory using the visual of a braid. The hands braiding the strands represent the State and its arms– including schools. The strands braided together represent the different systems and dynamics present in the schooling experiences of undocumented students with disabilities (i.e. special education, English language services, policies and/or supports for undocumented students and families). These braided strands are woven together to create the distinct experiences of undocumented dis/abled students. We use a bricolage of theories as a lens to understand this braid, including DisCrit, UndocuCrit, deservingness, and heterotopias of deviation (Foucault 1986), to show how the state and the schooling systems experienced by these students and families create a particular liminal reality. We consider these braided experiences within a larger context that extends through categorizations of 'the state.' We also acknowledge the fringe emerging within the braid – elements of these strands that have frayed and come loose with time – representing disruptions to these systems. Among these frays are individual teachers who support students and families with their advocacy and actions to counter state control to the degree that is possible within the current system.

Aguilar's focus on acompañamiento (2019) as embodiment of mentorship, academic redemption, and community engagement as particularly salient for disabled undocumented students and their communities. The idea that IEPs, special education services, and English language services should serve to promote student success via individualism and independence upholds White supremacist ideals. The myth of meritocracy suggests that White, upper-middle class young people who achieve do so of their own accord, rather than recognizing the webs of networks, resources, and wealth that bolster their success. Acompañamiento aligns with community care accentuated within the disability justice movement (Piepzna-Samarasinha 2019). We recognize that care webs support both disabled students and students navigating the endemic fear of un/documentation status.

Jay Dolmage cites Foucault's heterotopias of deviance to understand intersections of immigration, race, and disability in the U.S. (2018). He writes:

> .... a heterotopia of deviation divides and isolates difference, suggesting that this situation (of purifying by extraction) is ideal for the 'normals' in mainstream society, yet also creating a dystopian space for the minoritized .... (2018, 10)

We suggest that schools are heterotopias of deviation, specifically in their construction and regulation of disability and citizenship. Schools serve to uphold ableist notions of normalcy (Davis 1997) and ideals of success aligned with a medical model of disability (Shakespeare 1995), wherein anyone who deviates from said norm is punished, regulated, subjected to 'cure,' and/or marginalized; 'racism and ableism circulate interdependently, often in neutralized and invisible ways, to uphold notions of normalcy' (Annamma, Connor, and Ferri 2013, 11–12). Regulation of bodies and identities that 'deviate' from the norm are disciplined and removed. Disabled students of color are hyper-surveilled, hyper-labelled, and hyper-punished. (Annamma 2018). The policing, controlling, silencing, and managing of disabled undocumented students directly links to tenet five of DisCrit, wherein race and disability have been employed individually and collectively to deny the rights of some citizens (Annamma, Connor, and Ferri 2013; Connor, Ferri, and Annamma, 2016).

Recognizing schools as ideological state apparatuses (Althusser 1971) helps highlight their role as heterotopias of deviation. Fear is understood as something cultivated and imposed by the state. The fear that undocumented families experience when interacting with the school system is important to recognize in the context of parental advocacy for what their children are entitled to under IDEA. Aguilar (2019) acknowledges the perseverance that emerges alongside fear. The interplay between fear related to documentation status and the infantilizing or devaluing of disabled students can help us understand the unique experiences that undocumented students with disabilities face in our schools. We want to be mindful of romanticizing traumatic and oppressive realities when we discuss the transformational potential of fear, while also recognizing that undocumented communities in the United States consistently engage in resilience and persistence.

Patel highlights the discourse of deservingness surrounding immigration when she writes that the debates, policies, and rhetoric about immigration frames migrants as lacking in worth (2015). The question of worth under a White settler capitalist society is inextricably bound to conversations of productivity. Special education programming often evaluates students in terms of their productive capacity. Historically, for instance, students with disabilities were categorized as 'educable' or 'trainable' (Wehmeyer 2013) and to this day transition programming is centered in large part around the vocation, career, and/or education that a student will obtain after secondary school to earn money and contribute to a capitalist economy and society.

Patel identifies language fluency as a proxy for race, wherein programming centered around English language development is rooted in the premise that acquiring and adhering to the dominant codes of power will enable students, even undocumented students, to access social mobility and well-being. She identifies '[w]hite settler anxieties that seek to discipline subalterns' practices and delimit the very possibilities of those practices' (p. 17). The parallels between English language programming and special education programming that funnels students into 'less restrictive' settings are premised on the same White settler anxieties that privilege particular ways of being (neurotypical, White, middle class, monolingual English speaking) and criminalize, infantilize, and/or devalue others (disabled, BIPOC, multilingual/speakers of languages other than English).

We see these theoretical approaches intersecting and braiding together to extend DisCrit to conceptualize the experiences of undocumented students with disabilities. Our use of theory in this paper is intended to further uplift and explore the experiences of students living at these intersections as they experience state violence through schooling. DisCrit's recognition of Whiteness and ability as property highlights the ways that schools obscure and marginalize disabled students. Examining the relationships between citizenship, deservingness, racialization, and disability centers the experiences of undocumented disabled students and their families to offer new possibilities for schooling and learning.

Methods

This study is a part of a larger mixed-methods examination of the experiences of high school and college students dually identified as multilingual with disabilities, using both qualitative interviewing and quantitative measures data from the National Longitudinal Transition Study 2012 (NLTS2012). We collected data for this larger study in high schools located in New York City and interviewed students who received both English Language (EL) and special education services. For this study, we are focused on two cases within the larger qualitative study. IRB approval was obtained from the Department of Education and from New York University. The research team for this study was made up of 6 people, with a range of experiences in special education k-12, special education teacher training, multilingual education, disability services in higher education, and occupational therapy. The research team for this project was committed to engaging in reciprocal relationships with participants and employed a researcher-as-activist paradigm. We developed professional development sessions for local teachers to address the needs identified by students in this study and partnered with local institutions (both high school and college) to provide information about students with disabilities attending college to families. No data was collected from participants at these events.

The present study

One primary research question guided this study: in what ways do disability status and migratory status intersect for two high school students who receive language and disability services? We relied on qualitative methods to explore the experiences of two undocumented students identified with disabilities during the transition from high school to adulthood. We drew from three primary data sources: (1) interviews with two high school students, chosen purposively from a larger sample due to knowledge or self-disclosure about students' or family's documentation status, (2) researcher field notes and analytic memos, (3) a collection of researcher reflections. Using these data sources, we describe some of the ways disability status and migratory status intersect for students engaged in transition.

Interviews

We interviewed high school students face-to-face at two time points, utilizing semi-structured interviewing at their high schools. Each semi-structured interview lasted about 45 minutes. In the first interview, we asked students questions about their goals and plans for life after high school. In the second interview, we asked students about their involvement in IEP meetings, their participation in schools, and the supports they received. Interviews were recorded with participants' consent and were translated when necessary and transcribed.

Researcher field notes and memos

We wrote field notes about the interviews and campus visits, where we detailed our impressions of context, features of the environment, and our experience within and around the interviews. In addition to describing our observations, these notes also included researchers' past experiences as they related to the interviews and surrounding context. We also wrote analytic memos where we discussed coding choices and emergent patterns, themes, and concepts (Saldaña 2016) and reflected on the interviews, theory, and coding, discussed discontinuities that arose during the coding process, and connected our thoughts across interviews. We share researcher reflections that emerged from our field notes and include ourselves as participants to recognize the role that our identities, interpretations, and experiences play in relationship to the study. Participant narratives shared during interviews are distinct from the researcher reflections; we analyzed both our researcher reflections, researcher fieldnotes and memos, and participant interviews to uncover insights about disability and citizenship status in education.

Participants

We take this opportunity to provide a brief description of both our participants and to position ourselves as researchers and participants.

Fernanda

Fernanda was a 12th grader at a New York City high school, the oldest of three siblings, a speaker of Spanish and English, and saw herself being a teacher or a nurse's assistant. She identified her disability as hearing loss and shared that she migrated with her family from Mexico. We came to learn about her documentation status through conversations with her mother and school staff. When given the option to share three identity components from a list of ten in a written icebreaker activity, Fernanda shared with Lilly, the interviewer, that she was female, 19 years old, and learned Spanish as her first language.

Daniel

Despite feeling unprepared and uncertain about his next steps after high school, Daniel shared that he is the only one in his family pursuing college – he was the one with papers. He was a 9th grader at a high school in New York City and was the middle child. He shared with his IEP team that he aspired to be an animator but wasn't currently involved in technology or art classes. Daniel shared with Lilly during the icebreaker activity that he was male, 16 years old, and identified his ethnicity as Salvadorian and Guatemalan.

Rachel

I am a White woman from the South with an emerging and non-linear identity as disabled. I grew up outside county lines, bordering conservative farm country and the suburbs, about 15 miles from a major liberal city. My upbringing was saturated within explicit and visible anti-Blackness (confederate flags sprinkled my neighborhood), the treatment of undocumented folks as other ('Why can't they speak English? This is America'), intense gentrification (railroad tracks separated the classes), the privileging of certain discourses and accents (White Texan, but take out the drawl), and the segregation of the disabled (Partners 'n PE, a partnership between general education and the Resource room, got me out of gym class). As I have engaged with critical discourses, I am reminded about the dangers of beliefs, policies, and educational philosophies guised as neutral or apolitical, and how I have been – and am – an active contributor in positioning 'the other.' I believe that unchecked neutrality, especially for students with minoritized identities in schools, actively works against goals of equity and belonging.

Lilly

For most intents and purposes, I experience the world as a White woman. My mother's family from Belarus is Russian-Jewish and immigrated to the Bronx and then Los Angeles. My father's family is mixed White and Mexican. Our Mexican family is specifically Chicanx, having been in Southern California since it was México; 'We never crossed the border; the border crossed us,' was a common phrase I heard growing up. My notions of citizenship were complicated by this constant adage, as well as constant reminders that we were on Ohlone land (in Oakland, California) my whole life. My experiences led me to the understanding that it is not our identities that determine one's access, but rather the ideological, institutional, interpersonal, and internalized messages, policies, practices, and beliefs that impose specific meanings on people's identities.

Analysis

We used NVIVO software to conduct analysis with participant interviews, researcher reflections, fieldnotes, and analytic memos. Migration status emerged during analysis of the larger data set, particularly with the interviews with Daniel and Fernanda and their parents. We coded the three sources of data, identified themes across sources, and tested our themes across data used for this study (Ryan and Bernard 2000). We developed a codebook utilizing both deductive (pulling from our theoretical framework) and inductive methods (Saldaña 2016). We referred back to and continued to shape our theoretical framework throughout analysis. Codes and categories were created iteratively and recursively, placed within context and extracted from the data sources. Examples of codes included IEP meetings, student beliefs about disability, concerns about college, and their engagement in schools. We visited about codes as a team and when disagreement arose, discussed extensively and came to agreement. Following creation of codes, we sorted codes into categories and examined these categories for thematic trends. We developed themes across data sources by tracing continuities and discontinuities in the data and identifying patterns and themes related to students' experiences as undocumented and disabled.

Findings

In the following section, we report on our findings, discussing student and family experiences with liminality and citizenship in schools, the notion of symbolism tied to college-going, and the connection between entitlement, eligibility, and fear.

Liminal experiences with citizenship in schools

The following outlines an interaction Lilly had at one of the schools in the study. Lilly's fieldnotes outline the experience.

> "So, we have one parent in particular, the mother of a student who might be in your study," a staff member said to me in hushed tones.

> "We are running the Free Application for Federal Student Aid (FAFSA) workshop and, because of her status and her daughter's status, they cannot fill out the FAFSA. So, we are going to have her come and talk to you when we start talking about the FAFSA."

> [staff member to the mother of student]

> "Puedes confiar en ella. She is someone you can trust. We would never put you in touch with someone that you couldn't trust. We work closely with her and she will not share your information with anyone. You can trust her to help you get information about this process."

Fernanda's mom arrived at the event expecting to learn how to complete FAFSA for her daughter. Instead, the school presented her with the opportunity to talk to Lilly, a researcher there to do recruitment for a study on the transition of emergent bilingual students with IEPs. Lilly's field notes from that day detail her perception of how the interactions unfolded:

> The school counselors pulled me to the side to let me know that they thought undocumented parents and students were unable to fill out a FAFSA using the outline they were providing that day. Because of their status, some parents might come to talk to me instead of participating in the FAFSA workshop. When Fernanda's mother came to the office, another school staff member introduced us and told her that I was going to talk to her about college for bilingual students with IEPs. I had stacks of fliers that offered insights via our research team's website, but beyond that, I was there to recruit participants for our study, not to provide expertise on the college-going process.

Tenet two of UndocuCrit proposes that 'Different experiences of liminality translate into different experiences of reality' (Aguilar 2019, 4). The liminality that both Fernanda and her mother experienced regarding their (un)documented status impacted the school's approach to them. We read this liminality and differential experience(s) in conversation with DisCrit tenet five, which posits, 'DisCrit considers legal and historical aspects of dis/ability and race and how both have been used separately and together to deny the rights of some citizens' (Annamma, Connor, and Ferri 2013, 11). This denial of rights–such as information about FAFSA–is thinly veiled under the guise of ignorance or lack of knowledge; the school, typically positioned as the beacon of expertise, abdicated responsibility for a family that did not have nation-state-conferred citizenship. Here, the school staff member assumed that undocumented students would be ineligible to complete the FAFSA to gain financial aid in college and did not provide additional resources, information, or options for students. In tandem, they opted out of responsibility and instead, positioned Lilly as an expert and mediator of the 'complications' extended from undocumentation. This scenario highlights questions of deservingness in schools: who is positioned as deserving of the time, research, and resources necessary to support a student's dreams and transition to life after high school, and who gets denied these rights?

In her interview, Fernanda talked extensively about wanting to be a teacher and had experience tutoring young children and working as a teacher's assistant. Her commitment to education and public service might be read as a testament to her faith in the education system, despite school staff feeling unequipped to support her college-going process due to her documentation status. Despite performing a deep care for Fernanda and her mother, the school simultaneously engaged in a paternalistic dismissal of them when they asserted they did not have any resources or guidance to offer them in the FAFSA and financial aid process. Fernanda maintained hope and commitment to her goals of educating young people.

Acompañamiento: symbolic college-going

> Such as me . . . I don't like, like going to college. But like years ago when I was little, I told my mom that I don't want to go to college because it seems like it's pretty impossible for me to do. But mom was like it's your opinion but I'm telling you that you have to go because your older brother hasn't gone to college. He doesn't have the papers when he was born he doesn't have any. . . . So that's why they couldn't apply to college . . . I'm the only one because I have the papers of course. And my little brother of course. –Daniel, age 16

Acompañamiento is defined by Aguilar 'not only as a "way to *acompañar* . . . students in their journeys through school" and life, but also to *acompañar* and be *acompañados* by our communities as we create knowledge (Sepúlveda 2011, 568)' (Aguilar, 2019, 6). Daniel came from a mixed citizenship-status family, which he chose to disclose in the context of explaining why he had to go to college. He explained that life had been hard for his older brother, and that finding work has been difficult. Daniel was formerly in one of the most restrictive programs for autistic students in the district and moved to what is considered one of the least restrictive for high school.

College-going might feel like a natural progression because Daniel experienced a move from a class setting of 'less capable' students to the 'most successful' in special education in his district. Daniel lived at the intersections of problematic doling out of worthiness and deservingness from the system; he was a 'high functioning' student with autism who has 'successfully' moved across restrictive environments, and he has the legal status of 'belonging' in the United States. Upward social mobility and assimilation into White, middle class economic and behavioral norms is often considered a marker of successful acculturation (Bui 2015; Padia and Traxler 2021), but this simplification of success obscures the emotion and nuance undocumented students with disabilities face in their educational journeys.

Tenet three of UndocuCrit posits that '*Parental sacrificios become a form of capital . . .* parental sacrificios have been shown to motivate undocumented individuals to excel academically and engage civically' (2018, 5). Daniel's statement of college as mandatory because of his conversations with his mother and his awareness of his differential status in relation to his family members signaled an understanding of familial responsibility, both on his part but also in terms of the status that he has due to his mother's sacrificios.

Aguilar (2019) writes about the coworkers who told him that he was meant for academia rather than hard labor because of his 'gentle hands.' The conflation between manual labor and lack of citizenship might be evident in Daniel's assertion that he was the one who must go to college, because he was the one with papers. The responsibility of college-going that Daniel shares was not just an individual goal, but a familial one, symbolic of the opportunities he had access to by virtue of citizenship. While not explicitly stated, this mandate of college-going may also point to parental sacrificios. The dynamic of what his mother has sacrificed for her children's opportunities may be a driving force in his life choices. Daniel shared that he told his mom that college was pretty impossible for him when he was in middle school, a time when he was in a more restrictive special education environment. His movement to a less restrictive environment and his college-going trajectory speak back to expectations that schools often hold for students in more restrictive environments (i.e. that they will enter the workforce and not continue to higher education after secondary school). The recognition that he is the one with papers so he has to go to college, citing that his brother was not able to, reflects his understanding that attending college is not purely about his personal success, but a collective college-going for his mixed citizenship-status family (Mangual Figueroa 2011). He claimed that path for himself–and, by proxy, his family–despite his internalized assertion that college would be 'pretty impossible' for him–a notion likely instilled through his experiences with the special education system.

Fernanda shared that she tutored the child of a neighbor in her apartment building. This role of tutoring combined with her experience working as a teaching aide at her church, as well as her desire to become a teacher long-term, demonstrate her leveraging her education for communal learning and benefit. She is embodying acompañamiento in her learning experiences. This speaks directly back to the ways that her citizenship is literally and figuratively denied due to her disability status, racial identity, national origins, and status as an English learner in the school system. Fernanda's resistance to what DisCrit tenet five identifies as the denial of the rights of some citizens is not just for her individual rights and citizenship status; she is ensuring her community accompanies her as she grows and seeks resources and opportunities.

Documentación: entitlement, eligibility, and fear

K-12 students are protected under IDEA and deemed *entitled* to special education services and supports, provided that they have approved documentation of disability. Once students age out of the K-12 system, however, they become *eligible* for services and supports rather than entitled. Disability service personnel provide accommodations (e.g. extra time on exams, reduced distraction testing environment) and additional services (e.g. peer tutoring, academic counseling) for disabled students who seek out the support and qualify. To be eligible for support in college, schools request documentation from students, which can include medical paperwork, school evaluations, or other professional documents. Students disclose their disability and negotiate with support staff to determine applicable supports. In special education, these services are initiated by school staff.

Students may opt out of disability services in college to renounce a label, because they are uncomfortable sharing disability information, or fear of being misunderstood by faculty (Wagner et al. 2005; Getzel and Thoma 2008; Hill 1994). As we experienced firsthand during our presentation, this language used to access services can be inaccessible for undocumented students. Relying on language rooted in the medical model of disability that simultaneously implies tracking and proof is not an equitable practice. We had not proactively considered the interplay of migratory status with the language and 'norms' of postsecondary disability services – specifically, the word 'documentation' and its myriad meanings – and mediated trust between presenter and attendees. Here, our language choice accompanied the endemic fear surrounding citizenship (Aguilar 2019).

Students without documentation experience challenges and pressures in the pursuit of college including fewer financial resources and assistance options, and as Lilly encountered, completing the FAFSA. This difference between entitlement and eligibility requires an extensive shift in the advocacy of students and families and involves a recentering of responsibility. This shift in responsibility is drastic and mirrors the tropes of innocence and criminality tied to immigrant children and adults respectively (Patel 2015). In childhood, youth are disconnected from the 'blame' of not having documentation, both related to medical records and migratory documentation. As children move into adulthood, this innocence shifts to responsibility. For instance, undocumented adults are deemed criminals. Academics and activists addressing the discourse around DREAMers, recipients of the Deferred Action for Childhood Arrivals (DACA), have identified the tensions of innocence versus culpability that traffic through these seemingly benevolent policies that absolve young people whilst continuing to demonize their parents and families (López 2020). The shift from innocence to responsibility continues in the sphere of postsecondary education, as support moves from school-initiated special education, where teachers and stakeholders individualize for students, to disability services in higher education, where students are responsible for proving and disclosing disability.

Conclusion

We believe that reading DisCrit in conversation with UndocuCrit illuminates aspects of the experiences of undocumented students identified with disabilities in the U.S. school system. We traced Aguilar's (2018) tenets of UndocuCrit through two cases – Daniel and Fernanda – of high school students with IEPs who experienced direct interaction with citizenship in their schooling experiences, transition plans, and long-term goals. Additionally, frameworks like deservingness and heterotopias of deviation helped to further illuminate DisCrit tenet five's message of how systems of power work to confer or deny rights on some citizens.

Implications for research

In addition to taking up DisCrit as an analytic tool and theoretical framework, researchers should work to understand the experiences of students at the intersection of migratory status and disability, and to understand the ways in which our systems, schools, and stakeholders are complicit in denying students access to rights and affordances of citizenship. Identifying how teachers and other school stakeholders within K-12 systems approach students' experiences with migratory statuses, particularly disclosure and confidentiality, is important for informing future policies and practices in schools.

While researchers have investigated students' hesitations to disclose disability in college (e.g. Wagner et al. 2005; Getzel and Thoma 2008; Hill 1994), little is known surrounding how and why undocumented students disclose disability. Future research should examine how students at this intersection navigate disclosure, share their experiences, and what supports and services are helpful during the transition from high school to college. Further, we acknowledge that while DisCrit is helpful for examining inequity and historical issues in schools and some researchers have examined this phenomenon (e.g. Annamma, Connor, and Ferri 2013), application should not be limited to the investigation and critique of schools. We call for research that critically examines the systems and structures outside of the context of schooling.

Implications for practice

Fernanda's experiences reveal a direct need for schools to consider the needs of undocumented students in transition planning. As an undocumented student, Fernanda will need support navigating systems that will permit her to teach without requiring citizenship documentation. Fernanda's mother, as the guardian of an undocumented student with an IEP, needed transition support specific to the intersections of (un)documentation and disability. Educators and researchers must examine the ways systems are at odds with various student identities and be intentional about communicating this to families and students. For example, disability disclosure is essential for accessing special education services, but documentation status disclosure is not required. Educators' and schools' awareness of differential access and providing resources can support all students – including undocumented students with disabilities – in working towards their goals and dreams, from logistical items like financial aid applications to larger projects like securing work as a future educator.

A call to critical reflection

We acknowledge the real and human tendency to absolve responsibility for our role within these systems. We continue to grapple with the reality that we did harm at this event by using a word embedded in a culture of policing and fear. Working within oppressive systems means we are all culpable and responsible for perpetuating harm to students, regardless of our intentions. Acknowledging this reality is not enough, but this acknowledgement holds transformative power for students and for all who participate in upholding and extending the violent arms of the state. We leave stakeholders, including educators, disability service staff, and researchers with essential critical questions to facilitate acknowledgement of the roles we actively play within these systems.

We call on educational stakeholders to consider the following critical questions: How are teachers/schools complicit in furthering the culture of silence (Mangual Figueroa 2017) and shame around disability and documentation status? How can schools foster environments of trust and belonging for all students, including for undocumented youth with disabilities? Disability service offices and K-12 educators can resist and transform the culture of silence, fear, and state violence by explicitly examining their language use and explicitly laying bare the differential meanings of words like 'documentation' in the interlocking systems of disability services and nation-state citizenship. DisCrit tenet seven is a call to action for educators to engage in activism and resistance.

We call on disability service providers and admissions professionals to participate in this activism and resistance by engaging with these critical questions: In what ways do current practices actively omit students who are hesitant to share aspects of their identity to get necessary support? How can individual providers work to help students feel safe, seen, and heard within practice? How can providers help omit barriers to participation by challenging social norms within programs?

Finally, educational researchers can consider: What elements of your identity do you include in your research? What have you bracketed in the name of 'objectivity?' How do you make space for participants to remind you of what you don't know? How do you honor participants' silence and refusal? And lastly, acknowledging the work of Tuck and Yang (2014), what forms of knowledge, identity/ies, and participant narrative does the academy not deserve?

Note

1. In the same way we employ dis/abled to recognize the false binary between abled and disabled, we use un/documented at times to highlight how documentation is specific to a given nation-state. For example, a student who is considered 'undocumented' in the United States who has citizenship in their home country has documentation, just not the 'right' kind in the eyes of the state. Additionally, a student in a mixed-citizenship status family might experience this spectrum of documentation, even if they themselves are 'documented' by the state.

Acknowledgment

Our heartfelt thanks to Professor Audrey Trainor and the PSSIEP research team at New York University for their support, encouragement, and collaboration. We wish to thank the reviewers who provided helpful suggestions to improve and clarify the manuscript. Finally, many thanks to David Connor, Subini Annama, and Beth Ferri for their guidance throughout this process. The authors would like to acknowledge that this paper was equally coauthored together.

Disclosure statement

No potential conflict of interest was reported by the author(s).

Funding

The research reported here was supported by the Institute of Education Sciences, U.S. Department of Education, through Grant R305A170259 to New York University. The opinions expressed are those of the authors and do not represent views of the Institute or the U.S. Department of Education.

References

Aguilar, C. 2019. "Undocumented Critical Theory." *Cultural Studies ↔ Critical Methodologies* 19 (3): 152–160. doi:10.1177/1532708618817911.

Akbar, A. A. 2020. "An Abolitionist Horizon for (Police) Reform." *California Law Review* 108 (6): 1781–1846. Ohio State Legal Studies Research Paper No. 560.

Althusser, L. 1971. "Ideology and Ideological State Apparatuses." In *Lenin and Philosophy and Other Essays*, edited by L. Althusser, 104–140. New York and London: Monthly Review Press.

Americans With Disabilities Act of 1990. 1990. "Pub. L. No. 101-336, 104 Stat. 328."

Annamma, S. A. 2018. *The Pedagogy of Pathologization: Dis/abled Girls of Color in the School-prison Nexus.* London: Routledge.

Annamma, S. A., D. Connor, and B. Ferri. 2013. "Dis/ability Critical Race Studies (Discrit): Theorizing at the Intersections of Race and Dis/ability." *Race Ethnicity and Education* 16 (1): 1–31. doi:10.1080/13613324.2012.730511.

Artiles, A. J., and A. A. Ortiz, eds. 2002. *English Language Learners with Special Needs: Identification, Assessment, and Instruction.* Washington, D.C.: Center for Applied Linguistics.

Baca, L. M., and H. T. Cervantes. 1998. *The Bilingual Special Education Interface.* Upper Sale River, NJ: Merill Pub.

Brayboy, B. J. M. 2005. "Toward a Tribal Critical Race Theory in Education." *Urban Review* 37 (5): 425–46. doi:10.1007/s11256-005-0018-y.

Bui, H. N. 2015. "Behavioral Outcomes." In *Transitions: The Development of Children of Immigrants*, edited by C. Suárez-Orozco, M. M. Abo-Zena, and A. K. Marks, 239–258. New York, London: New York University Press. doi:10.1080/15348431.2017.1337577.

Cioè-Peña, M. Winter 2017. "Disability, Bilingualism and What It Means to Be Normal." *Journal of Bilingual Education Research & Instruction* 19 (1): 138–160.

Connor, D. J., B. A. Ferri, and S. A. Annamma. 2016. *DisCrit: Disability Studies and Critical Race Theory in Education.* New York: Teachers College Press.

Davis, L. J. 1995. *Enforcing Normalcy.* New York: Verso. doi:10.13023/DISCLOSURE.06.04.

Davis, L. J. 1997. Constructing normalcy. In The disability studies reader, edited by L. J. Davis, 9–28. New York: Routledge.

Dolmage, J. 2018. *Disabled Upon Arrival:Eugenics, Immigration, and the Construction of Race and Disability.*

Erevelles, N. 2011. *Disability and Difference in Global Contexts.* New York: Palgrave MacMillan.

Foucault, M. 1986. "Of Other Spaces." *Diacritics* 16 (1): 22–27. doi:10.2307/464648.

Getzel, E. E., and C. A. Thoma. 2008. "Experiences of College Students with Disabilities and the Importance of Self-determination in Higher Education Settings." *Career Development for Exceptional Individuals* 31 (2): 77–84. doi:10.1177/0885728808317658.

Gonzales, R., L. L. Heredia, and G. Negrón-Gonzales. 2015. "Untangling Plyler's Legacy: Undocumented Students, Schools, and Citizenship." *Harvard Educational Review* 85 (3): 318–341. doi:10.17763/0017-8055.85.3.318.

Harry, B., and J. K. Klingner. 2006. *Why are so Many Minority Students in Special Education?: Understanding Race & Disability in Schools.* New York; London: Teachers College Press.

Heywood, A. 1994. *Political Ideas and Concepts: An Introduction.* New York: St. Martin's Press.

Hill, J. L. 1994. "Speaking Out: Perceptions of Students with Disabilities at Canadian Universities regarding Institutional Policies." *Journal of Postsecondary Education and Disability,* 11 (1): 1–14.

Hoover, J. J., and C. Collier. 2004. "Methods and Materials for Bilingual Special Education." In *The Bilingual Special Education Interface,* edited by L. M. Baa and H. Cervantes, 276–297, Columbus, OH: Merrill.

López, R. M. 2020. "Discursive De/humanizing: A Multimodal Critical Discourse Analysis of Television News Representations of Undocumented Youth." *Education Policy Analysis Archives* 28 (47). doi:10.14507/epaa.28.4972.

Mangual Figueroa, A. 2011. "Citizenship and Education in the Homework Completion Routine." *Anthropology & Education Quarterly* 4 (3): 263–280. doi:10.1111/j.1548-1492.2011.01131.x.

Mangual Figueroa, A. 2017. "Speech or Silence: Undocumented Students' Decisions to Disclose Citizenship Status in Schools." *American Educational Research Journal* 54 (3): 485–523. doi:10.3102/0002831217693937.

Padia, L., and R. Traxler. 2021. "'We Don't Kiss in School': Policing Warmth, Disciplining Physicality, & Examining Consent of Latinx Students in U.S. Special Education Classrooms." In *Centering Dis/ability in Latin America,* edited by C. Figueroa and D. Saca-Hernandez, 195–216, London: Palgrave Macmillan.

Patel, L. 2015. "Deservingness: Challenging Coloniality in Education and Migration Scholarship." *Association of Mexican American Educators Journal* 9: 11–21.

Phuong, J. 2017. "Disability and Language Ideologies in Education Policy. Working Papers." *Educational Linguistics* 32 (1): 47–66.

Piepzna-Samarasinha, L. L. 2019. *Care Work: Dreaming Disability Justice.* Vancouver, BC, Canada: Arsenal Pulp Press.

Ramanathan, V. 2013. "Language Policies and (Dis)citizenship: Rights, Access, Pedagogies." In *Language Policies and (Dis)citizenship: Rights, Access, Pedagogies,* edited by V. Ramanathan, 1–18, Briston, UK: Multilingual Matters.

Ryan, G. W. & H. R. Bernard. 2000. "Data management and analysis methods." In *Handbook of qualitative research,* edited by N. K. Denzin, and S. L. Yvonna. Thousand Oaks, CA: Sage Publications.

Saldana, J. 2016. *The coding manual for qualitative researchers.* SAGE.

Sepúlveda, E. 2011. "Toward a Pedagogy of Acompañamiento: Mexican Migrant Youth Writing from the Underside of Modernity." *Harvard Educational Review* 81: 550–573.

Shakespeare, T. 1995. "The Social Model of Disability." In *The Disability Studies Reader.* 2nded., edited by L. J. Davis, 197–204. New York: Routledge.

Tuck, E. and K. W. Yang. 2014. "R-Words: Refusing Research." In *Humanizing Research: Decolonizing Qualitative Inquiry with Youth and Communities,* 223–48. London: SAGE Publications, Inc.

Wagner, M., L. Newman, R. Camento, and P. Levine. 2005. *After High School: A First Look at the Postschool Experiences of Youth with Disabilities.* Menlo Park, CA: SRI International.

Wehmeyer, M. L. 2013. *The Story of Intellectual Disability: An Evolution of Meaning, Understanding, and Public Perception.* Baltimore: Brookes Publishing.

Wilgus, G., J. Valle, and L. Ware. 2013. "Algorithms of Access: Immigrant Mothers Negotiating Educational Resources and Services for Their Children." *Review of Disability Studies: An International Journal* 9 (2–3).

Williams, A., and C. Paterson. 2020. "Social Development and Police Reform. Some Reflections on the Concept and Purpose of Policing and the Implications for Reform in the UK and USA." *Policing: A Journal of Policy and Practice.* doi:10.1093/police/paaa087.

Bringing DisCrit theory to practice in the development of an action for equity collaborative network: passion projects

Tammy Ellis-Robinson 🆔

ABSTRACT

Disability Critical Race Theory (Dis/Crit) was useful as a tool and a lens for the development of a collaborative network of educators, community providers, and community stakeholders including educators, community members, parents, and individuals. Initially I engaged these stakeholders in action research sessions to inform planning for developing contextualized cultural competence among pre-service special education teachers. Examining equity and inequity in educational and community experiences for people representing minoritized identities including disability, race, ethnicity, language, immigrant status, gender, sexual orientation and socioeconomic status broadened our focus and passion for change. Expanding the process of building collective narrative inquiry, our network built projects to disrupt inequities at the intersections of disability and race in schools and community spaces. I discuss the utility of finding common ground in the theoretical framing lens Dis/Crit provides for planning action and collaboration among stakeholders. Finally, I share projects developed through our process to illustrate the influence of specific tenets of DisCrit theory in practical collaborative action.

Educators, researchers, and theorists can adopt an activist stance, and work with community members to disrupt systems of inequity. Theory is a useful tool for understanding initiating, implementing and institutionalizing equity in education and recognizing the ways that complex identities experience multiple oppressions (Annamma, Connor, and Ferri 2013; Collins 1990). To ground my work as a researcher, educator, and activist, I integrate theory, practice, and community engagement to promote action for equity. With a commitment to transformation, Disability/Critical Race Theory (Dis/Crit) (Annamma, Connor, and Ferri 2013) highlights the interrelated exacerbation of oppressions as they affect black and brown bodies with disabilities. As an action-aware theory, Dis/Crit is a useful tool to create common ground and provide accessible guidance on the path to foster equity focused policy and practice. In this article, I will share the journey from invitation to inquiry and inquiry to the ignition of passion projects for change. To activate theory, I sought collaborators from among community members who would engage in transformative learning (Freire 2000) and share context for theoretical applications of equity-focused theories in education. Together we built a network committed to enacting meaningful change to mitigate oppressions in real spaces.

Positionality

As a Black and multi-ethnic, cisgender, female teacher educator, I approach my work through a racialized lens steeped in the intersections of my identity. Race, religion, and cultural combinations, and caregiving relationships with family members with disabilities have heightened my attention to the navigation of multiple identities. As a teacher educator and former special education teacher, I have noticed a disconnection of identities in the field. In the planning of services, and interactions in schools, classrooms, and community the focus on disability is often a solitary factor foregrounding one aspect of identity in the interpretation of experiences (Leonardo and Broderick 2011). For example, I have heard practitioners declare that students with disabilities served by Individualized Education Programs (IEPs), are protected and have *all* of their rights preserved. This belief oversimplifies the complexity of what it means to navigate systems that have historically fostered inequity. A singular focus veils the pervasive intersections of oppression when individuals represent multiple marginalized identities minoritized based on race, disability and other categories of identity (Annamma, Connor, and Ferri 2013; Migliarini and Stinson 2020).

Compartmentalizing categories of marginalization belies the statistical realities of disproportionate representation of students of color in particular special education categories and disallows a recognition of inherent systemic inequities evident at the intersection of racism and ableism (Triplett and Ford 2019; Leonardo and Broderick 2011). Despite the promise of the Individuals with Disabilities in Education Act (IDEA), the persistence of disproportionality is evidence of the continuing effects of systemic inequity for people with disabilities. Disproportionality in special education includes the existence of disproportionate numbers of Black, Latino and Indigenous people in more stigmatizing categories of disability and disproportionally harsher disciplinary measures for the same groups. Inequities are deeply rooted in a social framework that otherizes, and marginalizes Black, Latino, and Indigenous people (Kramarczuk Voulgarides, Fergus, and King Thorius 2017). The absence of ability in many conversations about inequity renders invisible those who live at the juncture of race and ability (Annamma, Ferri, and Connor 2018). Labeling and oversimplification of complex identities limits the rights of multiply minoritized youth in special education. (Murugami 2009). Self-determination is a universal right (U.N. ICCPR 1966) that should include the right to self-identify, yet regulations and practices have delimited its exercise, feeding societal prejudices (Murugami 2009). Socio-cultural attitudes often prescribe fixed and limiting identities. To protect universal rights and promote a culture of inclusivity, individuals must be free to determine how they will identify themselves and the relevance of those definitions to their own experience. Educational practice must encourage young people to self-categorize from among scores of identities for a meaningful conceptualization of self (Murugami 2009). Reframing self-categorization theory (Turner 1985) as an ethic means individuals define themselves and all aspects of their identity according to their experience.

Experiences often provide a point of entry for critical inquiry of theory and practice. Researcher and educator identity and positionality combine with experience to create a lens for a critique of practice and impetus for action. To effect change, activists must address disenfranchisement through action rather than problematizing outcomes. In my role as a researcher activist, the integration of Dis/Crit theory with action research, and community connections has been instrumental, providing segue from scholarship to practical action and community building.

Theoretical frames

For my initial foray into the development of a community approach to institutionalization of equity practice, I convened stakeholders in special education. Stakeholders included educators working with pre-service teachers in our teacher preparation program, graduate students, teachers and administrators, parents and individuals with disabilities, and community members representing a range of socio-cultural groups.

The framing of our collaborative work began with sharing several equity-focused theories. Equity literacy (Gorski 2014) is an approach for developing equitable schools through a deepening of individual and institutional understanding of equity and inequity in organizations, to identify and eliminate inequities while actively building opportunities. In addition, we focused on cultural competence (Cross et al. 1989) characterized by lifelong development of cultural understanding and deepening proficiency to work with others. Culturally responsive teaching (Gay 2000), includes specific classroom practices that honor and address a variety of cultures in the classroom. Culturally sustaining pedagogy (Paris 2012) promotes cultural pluralism and values perspectives of non-dominant cultures. In a series of gatherings, we discussed these theories and applied them to our contexts. With attention to each theory, stakeholders engaged in productive conversations, but their passions ignited when we turned to tenets of Dis/Crit. Tenets address systemic oppression, multidimensional identities, material impacts of ableism and racism, legal and historical impact of oppressions, the privileging of marginalized voices, White supremacy and ableist perspectives, and activism (Annamma, Connor, and Ferri 2013). Dis/Crit provided a meaningful integration encompassing ideas from each of the theories we had discussed previously. Recognizing all of the various stakeholders present as actors, who could work within and through their stakeholder roles to initiate change, I called on our new network to act.

Dis/Crit theory, as contextualized in schooling experiences, energized the group (Annamma & Morrison 2018). Though all tenets of Dis/Crit Theory were shared, unpacked, and considered in the context of lived experiences across settings, a few of the tenets (two, three, and seven, specifically) were most central to our discussions. Tenet two emphasizes the valuing of multidimensional identities. Tenet three recognizes the material and psychological impacts (oppressions) of being labeled as raced and disabled, and tenet seven calls for redressing and action to mitigate the impact. These three tenets emphasize the importance of holistic and self-determined identity appreciation and the pervasive negative impact of misrepresentations and oversimplification.

The inquiry began with the following research questions.

(1) What is the role of special education teachers in the development of critical multicultural citizenship for their students (defining culture broadly to include multiple components of identity)?

(2) What information, skills, and understandings are necessary for preservice teachers to be prepared to provide effective educational experiences to students whose identities include intersections of disability and other marginalized social groups, as well as those whose experiences represent dominant culture and social strata?

(3) How are schools addressing the needs of students and families as they relate to diversity and concerns for marginalizing factors of identity?

The process unveiled an additional central question that led to collaborative cohesion.

(4) How can education stakeholders across settings collaborate toward educational equity working with and across fields and areas of expertise?

The last question evolved organically to include extension projects created with stakeholders. In the next section, I will share the development process of a collaborative network.

Method

The development of our collaborative network started with participant stakeholders and myself engaging in an iterative process (Yull et al. 2014) of self and group study through emancipatory action research (Feldman, Paugh, and Mills 2004). Our organic process is evident retrospectively through the artifacts and notes from several related collaborative gatherings listed in Figure 1. At each gathering, we engaged in critical inquiry, which inspired shifts in practice, beginning with self-reflection and uncovering the

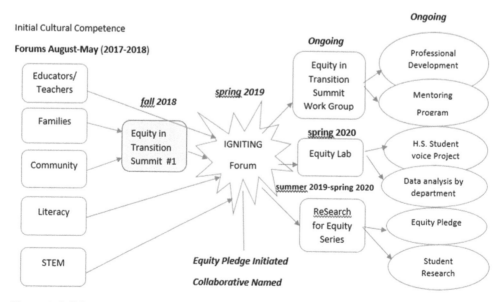

Figure 1. Collaborative network development process timeline. Figure 1 illustrates the sequence and timeline of gatherings that led up to the formal naming of a collaborative network and subsequent planned action-focused project.

reproduction of power evidenced in inequities in systems and processes (Miller 2019). Our collaborative network engaged in research, action, and forged connections across professional domains and social groups. Through this process, we generalized theory to applications in schools, adult service agencies, the community, and families (Annamma, Ferri, and Connor 2018). Throughout, we engaged collectively in a dialogic spiral reflecting on (Kinloch and San Pedro 2014) identity exploration activities, our practices, and developing action projects (McNiff 2013).

Participants/stakeholders

Across the many gatherings and projects that led to the development of the collaborative network, participants/stakeholders included individuals with disabilities, teachers, and administrators from public and charter schools in rural, sub-urban and urban districts that host our practicum placements, community agencies for individuals with disabilities, business owners, university professors and students, and parents representing a range of socio-cultural groups. Initially, I invited stakeholders to gatherings using flyers and invitations throughout the university, K-12 schools, and organizations that serve diverse individuals with and without disabilities in the communities near the university. Motivated by interest in the development of our preservice teachers and/or deepening their own cultural competence a shifting group of stakeholders engaged in each of the first five sessions with the smallest having 10 and the largest 25 collaborators. In total 38 stakeholders engaged across all five initial forums. The number of stakeholders in subsequent events and gatherings increased with project momentum. We shared the collaborative process through our individual networks, bringing in new collaborators throughout the process. By the time, we named the collaborative; approximately 50 collaborators had joined the effort.

Collaborative context

At the outset of the first five forums, I invited stakeholders to gather to address cultural competence and equity in our institutions. Initially I sought to survey the nature of the preparation and support needed for pre-service special education teachers in their practicum, student teaching and, internship experiences inviting participants to build knowledge while assisting this effort. Our development process began with a focus on identity. First, I asked participants to consider the intersections of their own identities as they affected their work, lives, and decision to engage in our project, centering stakeholder voices and fostering community knowledge building (Freire 2000; Wenger 1998). Next, we focused on cross-categorical experiences of students and adults across minoritized groups. We interrogated practices such as cultural responsiveness and inclusivity and their connection to resultant equitable outcomes such as inclusion in social activities, college attendance, and career participation. Stakeholders explored educator, student, community, and family narratives of injustices across the lifespan (Souto-Manning and Winn 2017). Through collaborative conversations and information sharing, we examined social justice, cultural competence, and equity in the development of educators (Gorski 2014; Siuty 2017; Staratt 1994). Topics ranged from shared concerns, promising practices and needs related to specific curricular domains including literacy, STEM (Science, Technology, Engineering,

Mathematics), and transition to post-secondary opportunities for people with disabilities. I began each forum with explanations of theory, sharing articles and discussing concepts with the group. We followed these discussions with interactive pairings and group conversations to apply elements of theories to various settings and experiences taking notes and reporting out to one another. Stakeholders shared examples from their schools, organizations, and their personal lives. We recorded comments and ideas through shared writing and note taking. Inspired by shared stories of lived experiences, stakeholders and I drew on our personal passions and professional influence to promote transformation through action. Together, our goal shifted from focusing on teacher preparation alone to identifying and refining processes for the initiation, implementation, and institutionalization of practices to promote equity and disrupt institutionalized oppression at all levels of service, across contexts, and across the lifespan (Fullan 1985; Kelly and Varghese 2018). The newly formed, still informal collaborative network continued to gather and correspond to plan ongoing projects, adding in new collaborators through events focused on transition, research, and K-12 settings.

At each gathering, I shared a summary of ideas, activities and outcomes from previous gatherings to encourage continuity. This way, new members came into the conversation and helped us collectively evaluate our unfolding plans for action. Addressing each of the key topics and theories I shared, stakeholders identified success stories and needs related to equity, highlighting professional and personal applied experiences from sharing of policy and practice by the school officials, and personal experiences among practitioners, families, and individuals. Figure one shows the timeline of gatherings and projects which ultimately resulted in the formalization of our collaborative network after the igniting forum.

Data

Data consisted of residual artifacts from each gathering. These included collaborative written responses to questions about practice and problem identification in schools and communities, individual written reflective responses after each forum, and my field notes and reflections from forums and subsequent gatherings. My reflection and analysis of the data reveals the process for development of a community collaborative network.

Analysis

In creating this collaborative network, I engaged in reflective discourse and an integrated analysis that was both deductive and aligned with targeted theory (Mayring 2014) and inductive. My observations and reflections of stakeholders and applied experiences focused on how to use participants' perspectives to bring nuance to the critical theories (Bradley, Curry, and Devers 2007). I applied codes derived from Dis/Crit tenets to the ideas shared in the collaborative writings, individual reflections, field notes, and subsequent planned action projects.

Trustworthiness

Trustworthiness includes elements of credibility, transferability, confirmability and dependability (Lincoln and Guba 1985). By focusing on action research, I achieved credibility through developing the project in collaboration with participants and contextualizing the research in their lived experiences. I applied ideas and findings across a number of projects and then shared them among the collaborative community showing transferability of findings. Drawing on multiple sources of information across time and involving a close comparison of theory to practice and participant experiences, I established rigor in the findings (Creswell 2013; Dick 1999). I triangulated the analysis of the collaborative process by embedding member checking through consensus in collaborative network building and project design (Creswell 2013).

Findings

In the following sections, I first present the findings of this project through connections to key tenets of Dis/Crit theory. I then discuss additional findings related to some of the material manifestations of the collaborative network, addressing research questions.

Connections to tenet two

Tenet Two states, 'DisCrit values multidimensional identities and troubles singular notions of identity such as race or dis/ability or class or gender or sexuality and so on' (Annamma, Connor, and Ferri 2013, 11). In our many gatherings, we identified and acknowledged those who were unseen and absent in the authorship of narratives of identity and motivation. Tenet two guided our action and supported the need for self-determination of identity. Self-examination and self-analysis of the interplay of multi-dimensional identities and holistic views of individuals (Cross et al. 1989; Miller 2019) evoked empathy and shared responsibility among stakeholders.

When I asked stakeholders how often they thought about marginalized and intersecting identities, and how their own identities affected their thinking and experiences, one White community member shared, ' . . . being a mother is what I think of most; I've never thought about these [intersections].' Others, particularly those who were Black or members of non-dominant groups including categories of dis/ability, indicated the pervasiveness of their group membership and its marginalizing effect on many aspects of their lives. Still others struggled and sat with a blank page in front of them. Most often, these individuals identified as white cisgender males who were unaccustomed to thinking about themselves as gendered, raced, etc. Considering their professional or work identities, educators and community providers shared their relationships with students, clients, and families. Some highlighted bonding over shared activities, while others addressed feeling a need to learn more about languages, cultures, ethnicities, families, and experiences that differed from their own. One stakeholder, a Black special education teacher said, ' . . . relationships matter, but it's more than that.' She reminded the group that the personal interactions count, but systemic change must include and move beyond those interpersonal interactions.

Stakeholders seemed ready to move beyond naming and identifying problems (and people) to taking actions. Collaborative knowledge building and information sharing soon gave way to scrutinizing material and psychological impacts of oppression in our respective spaces. Explorations of identity shifted to pursuit and acknowledgement of practices designed to disrupt these negative impacts.

Connections to tenet three

Tenet three states, 'DisCrit emphasizes the social constructions of race and ability and yet recognizes the material and psychological impacts of being labeled as raced or disabled, which sets one outside of the western cultural norms' (Annamma, Connor, and Ferri 2013, 11). We used a critical lens to help us consider the material and psychological impacts such as life satisfaction, academic and behavioral outcomes, as well as environmental conditions in various settings. As one White high school special education teacher stated, 'I can see that I don't understand the experience of my students, but I must do something about the experiences they have when they are with me.' The group's discussion of tenet three focused on data, including grades and employment outcomes. By critically examining these data, the group was able to consider ways to improve the experiences of multiply minoritized students, and to adjust policy to meet their needs, rather than simply justifying the status quo and deficit perspectives.

One middle school special educator described her self-contained classroom. She noted that she taught 'moderately disabled' students who had immigrated to the United States from Africa, Latin America, and Southeast Asia. She described half of her students as nonverbal and shared that families of her students spoke a variety of different languages. Although the district had supplied an English as a New Language (ENL) teacher to support her students, the ENL teacher had no experience with nonverbal students and did not know how to engage them. We could see from her example the impact that compartmentalizing identity led to substandard resource provision.

Connections to tenet seven

Tenet seven states, 'DisCrit requires activism and supports all forms of resistance' (Annamma, Connor, and Ferri 2013, 11). Tenet seven inspired our collaborative to act. One elementary special educator stated, 'This one makes theory live.' Our network recognized and lauded the opportunity to engage in activism that included a critical examination of practice, which then led to strategizing about how to best leverage pockets of personal power to invoke, promote, and institutionalize equitable practices. Stakeholders discussed how they could use their positionality to disrupt systems of oppression in their work within schools, communities, and agencies. One school district administrator shared that cultural competency was a priority in her district and had resulted in changes to hiring practices and the language of job descriptions. Advertisements for new teachers named a requirement to model 'culturally appreciative' and 'sensitive' behavior and to show an understanding of various cultures, backgrounds, orientations, and religions. Despite formalizing this new policy, the administrator identified cultural competence among educators as space for further action. Despite naming a new policy, the increase in cultural competence could not become institutionalized change without explicit efforts to develop this appreciativeness and complexity of thinking about intersections of identity among existing employees. Our collaborative space provided an opportunity for stakeholders to imagine and consider the effects their choices within existing power structures in this case a critical examination revealing the need to do more. Over the course of meetings, our collaborative network found shared missions and motivation, and moved from discussion and awareness, to plans for action. Next, I describe a few of these collaboratively initiated projects.

Material manifestations of Dis/Crit: passion projects

The infusion of DisCrit theory helped us to engage in interactive brainstorming about the actions our network might take. The initial research questions combined with stakeholder-initiated priorities resulted in several collaborative projects further codifying the work of our collaborative network. In the next section, I share details and theoretical underpinnings of a few of our passion projects, including work with pre-service teachers, the Action for Equity Pledge and an Equity Lab project.

Work with pre-service teachers

During the process of building a collaborative, the group addressed the initial research questions focused on teacher preparation. In light of the focus on identity in the collaborative work of this project, I adjusted the curricula of courses I teach. Validated by the authentic input of the network, I now ask pre-service teachers to examine their identities, perceptions, and positionalities related to ability, race, language and culture. I ask them to think about the way students experience schooling and the importance of building of meaningful teacher student relationships (Annamma, Ferri, and Connor 2018). Combining the study of cognitive psychology and culturally responsive practices (Hammond and Jackson 2015) with case studies of inequities (Gorski and Pothini 2018), I ask pre-service teachers to explore the connections and disconnections between these frameworks and their application to classroom practice. After the forums our field experience supervisor, a stakeholder in our collaborative network process, and I brought some of our discussions and tools to promote cultural competence and culturally responsive teaching to university supervisors of applied experiences for our preservice special education teachers. Through an interactive training, we highlighted how acknowledging the intersections of identity and the impacts of oppression on students, they could use their own influence to enact change and inspire change making.

Action for equity pledge

At the Igniting Forum (see Figure 1), a Black member of a local board of education suggested that we, as a newly forming collaborative, author a pledge to share our equity mission and invite others to commit. She said, 'You need a pledge. It will get this message out.' A few months later at the first 'ReSearch for Equity' gathering, stakeholders revised the Action for Equity Pledge that I had drafted. A graduate student suggested a blast in social media to bring the theoretical perspectives we were engaging to active prescriptions throughout the community: 'We need a [clear set] of concrete actions … and we need a hashtag.' Drawing from an Equity of Care pledge in the health field (American Hospital Association 2015) and our collaborative discussions, the Action for Equity Pledge (see Figure 2) defines three concrete actions that agencies, schools, and individuals can take. Inherent in the language and purpose of the pledge is activism to transform experiences. Through the pledge, collaborators share a commitment to disrupt the – isms that interfere with self-determined and equitable outcomes.

> *The Action for Equity Pledge*
>
> **I pledge to promote equitable outcomes and the elimination of disparities in experiences and opportunities in both education and community settings.**
>
> **I pledge to take action for at least one of the following goals:**
>
> > Intentional collection and ethical use of data on race, ethnicity, language preference, socio-economic status and other sociodemographic data to improve quality and safety in schools, communities, and their partnerships.
> >
> > Promoting in-depth culturally responsive and sustaining professional development to promote equitable and culturally responsive and sustaining instruction, dialogue and care.
> >
> > Advancing diversity and inclusivity in educational professionals and leadership to reflect the communities served.
> >
> > Improve and strengthen community partnerships by
> >
> > > Consider each individual race, ethnicity, ability, gender, language group, sexual orientation's perspectives and experiences in planning and programming.
> > >
> > > Create and/or maintain spaces for people of diverse backgrounds to gather and share their experiences and concerns.

Figure 2. The action for equity pledge. Constructed to unite and expand collaborative attention to action steps to promote equity across the lifespan.

In concert with the pledge, momentum for the action called for in tenet seven of DisCrit to support 'activism' and 'resistance' (Annamma, Connor, and Ferri 2013) unfolded quickly. The collaborative network connected through an evolving social media repository for information sharing and a constant presence to enact change. Collaborators continue to circulate the pledge and share it across networks, events, and gatherings. The district administrator who shared the change in hiring practices at an earlier gathering committed to the pledge and came to the collaborative network with the desire to expand capacity for equitable practice to her district faculty through the Equity Lab.

Equity lab

The administrator, an assistant superintendent who attended the initial forums and I collaborated to develop the Equity Lab Project in her suburban school district. She initiated the collaboration out of a concern for how her own positionality affected her conversations with district educators regarding the ideals of the Action for Equity Pledge within the district. She wanted to promote buy-in to an equity charge in her district and inspire her staff to take up this work. Together we designed an interactive process with k-12 academic administrators to plan for and commit to standards of equity in their work. Three pillars were key to the Equity Lab: access, opportunity, and outcomes. We met with the group to discover, analyze, and plan. The specific objectives aligned with the key tenets of Dis/Crit and centered on identity, oppressions, and plans for mitigating action.

Identity and experience. Introducing the lab, in alignment with Dis/Crit tenet two, academic administrators completed an intersecting identities activity to consider their own identities. The activity encouraged them to think about intersections of identity in their work with students and centered on value added outcomes that would occur through honoring multidimensional identities. Turning toward material and psychological impacts (tenet three) educators dug deeper to examine how their identity might affect their relationships and educational practices. One administrator acknowledged that the intersections of his LGBTQ, educator, and White male identities affected how he interacted with students and even what he chose (or did not choose) for music for school concerts. He had not previously considered these intersections in himself or in his students. The group discussed a previously held belief that they should keep their identities separate from their work, replacing this with a new understanding that acknowledging identities of self and others improves experience and practice.

Culturally responsive practice and equity literacy. In the Equity Lab, we discussed changing demographics as well as adjustments to educational practice according to political and social mores in their school district. They examined who among their students were benefitting from the practices in their classrooms, and who seemed left out. Several mentioned the absence of Black and Latino students in honors classes. One educator spoke about the experiences of students with disabilities in relation to innovative programs and the general perception of excellence for students in the district, which did not include students with disabilities: 'They don't count the same or get seen the same,' she said. 'Do people even care about their success?' In this suburban district, although some students who were raced and disabled were able to access some opportunities within the system, administrators reported that disaggregated data revealed they were disproportionately disciplined, kept from AP courses, and more likely to experience failure or lower levels of achievement than their peers. A look at policy, practice, and outcome data revealed the pervasiveness of these inequities.

Equity standards. To examine the equity standards for the district within the dialectical view of the Equity Lab participants, I asked the group to consider a few questions: 'What is the goal of school?' and, 'Why are you an educator?' They answered: 'to make a difference;' 'because I love kids;' and, 'to share knowledge.' Career passion (Berg 2015) as conceptualized in these responses uncovers educators' motivation for choosing their career and their intent to act according to ethical standards.

I then asked, 'Where does equity fit in with your worldview and perspective on your career/role?' Educators responded that equity was an 'essential' component of their work. Conversations exploring bias and institutionalized barriers followed, coming back to access, opportunity, and outcomes for multiply minoritized students. Together we brainstormed methods to right the inequities we documented. One idea explored peer pairings between students with disabilities and students traditionally in honors and AP classes, broadening inclusive opportunities to interact around course themes. The educators, representing the special education department, lamented the lower levels of achievement among the students in their caseloads, particularly those who represented intersecting marginalized categories. As a group, the special educators exhibited a disheartened weariness around the ideas of bringing greater inclusion opportunities to their students. One special educator responded, 'I've heard it before.' Not to be dissuaded, the general educators committed to looking more closely at their practices and impact on specific students. Uncovering practices of exclusion and otherizing must precede their dismantling.

I asked, 'What content area matters most?' This contentious question invited a powerful argument from the literacy coordinators about the importance of reading to all other disciplines, though social studies and music teachers made compelling arguments about their disciplines as well. The difference in perspective among educators helped me to connect to considering what their students might feel matters most.

Together, we explored thinking beyond the mandates, to focus on the values they embody. Considering demographics, educators brainstormed and together shared lists of the subgroups of students within their school as they analyzed each of the three pillars, access, opportunity, and outcomes for each group. They identified specific groups that experienced inequity. Consensus emerged that Black and Latino, students with disabilities, and students from lower socio-economic status all lacked access, opportunity, and positive outcomes as compared to non-marginalized peers. In a suburban, mostly-White school district with a high graduation rate detailed and disaggregated analysis of the data was required to reveal inequities.

The administrators discussed particular students and explored how to promote self-determination of future outcomes and opportunities compared to current outcomes. They underscored how changing outcomes required asking and then listening to their students. The academic administrators planned for strategic approaches to provide financial support for Advance Placement test fees for all students, considering non-traditional peer and inclusion roles for students with disabilities, and work with classroom teachers to promote transformation of practice to acknowledge intersections of identity. The Equity Lab project exemplified our collaborative network's understanding and explicit call to action. The process in the district continues as other concerns and differing levels of commitment affect buy-in. Our collaborative network group provided an infusion of energy, support, and perspective that both inspired and pushed the initiating administrator activist to use her influence to affect change in policy and practice. Despite the successful development of an interprofessional and cross-sectional collaborative network, there remain some limitations, tensions, or confounds in the process to address.

Collaborative confounds

The happenstance of the organic collaborative network development process belies an organizational system or hierarchy. Collaborators participate and engage at different levels and in different ways. Some moved on from work together, however, the strength of the process is its responsiveness and fluidity. The tensions inherent in a collaborative meeting of the minds are indicative of the critical nature of the topics and issues we discussed. Perspectives entrenched in historical views and practices occasionally interfere with stakeholders' commitment to honoring identity, eradicating oppression, and taking an active approach to equity. The complexity and pace of perspective taking within our collaborative network has included some buy in and some push back. The practice of 'admiring the problem' (talking about a problem but not doing anything to solve it) was a concern among our group, who were 'sick' of this phenomenon. For some the pace and the need to discuss in order to collaborate was sometimes a frustration.

As many of the educators explicitly shared and analyzed policy and practices in their settings, lack of time, and resistance to change brought out a difference in commitment between members of our collaborative network and some of their colleagues. Persistence, clarity of mission and concrete methods have been the best response to these concerns. Through examples in practice, members of the network discovered that despite differences in focus, professional terminology and traditions of inequity, we have peered in the same waters in search of clear answers to support the ultimate goal of improved and equitable outcomes for people with disabilities across socio-cultural groups.

Conclusion

Ignited by DisCrit theory, the Action for Equity Collaborative began as an inquiry space and evolved to become a network of passion projects among committed professionals. In organizing the project, we centered our work on the acknowledgement of identity and the capital we all possess to advantage our various positionalities to effect change. Through an examination of inequitable access and outcomes that have plagued individuals at the intersections of identity, a call for action through interprofessional and community collaborations led to deepening processes and engaging in several collaborative projects. Collaborators focused attention on the gifts indicative of cultural funds of knowledge (Rodriguez 2013) and perceptive understanding, that people who are multiply marginalized have that White practitioners do not (Annamma, Ferri, and Connor 2018). These minoritized voices must be a part of any similar effort. Community stakeholders' comments, ideas, and problem identification provided the context for innovation in their respective settings of influence. Shifting concentration on those left behind and ill served in the educational system inspired resistance to the pervasive influence of systems that strip away opportunities and possibilities. Paradigmatic shifts promoting inclusive and reflective thinking require adjusting both habits of thinking and points of view (Mezirow 2002). Educators can enact and create educational spaces that provide access to and support for all students through liberation practices (Freire 2000). To redress the damage caused by systems of oppression in education settings, educators must embrace their positionality as activists and commit to equity-focused pedagogy centered on stances that respect history, address race and language, and recognize the elusiveness of justice while relentlessly seeking it (Annamma and Winn 2019).

The dialogic spiral of interactive conversations to interpret and apply theory to living spaces collaboratively, while implementing actions that serve to mitigate oppressions and promote equitable outcomes, provides a road map for sharing perspective and planning.

The actionable DisCrit theory served as practical guidance to transform stakeholders and institutionalize equitable practices. The strength in a collaborative process is the range of perspectives, resources, and solutions applied across contexts. Theoretical approaches and commitments provide the fire and fuel for educators to build new frames of reference, rejecting deficit ideologies and complacent indoctrination to existing systems, with a critical evaluation of the resulting outcomes. Concentrating on intersections of identity, Dis/Crit has been instrumental in our development of a collaborative action network, fostering equity focused practitioners, and community members who seek to operate in solidarity across difference. The theory that underlies projects serves to align and unify stakeholders in pursuit of equitable outcomes as they initiate, implement and institutionalize practices to disrupt oppression (Annamma, Connor, and Ferri 2013) thereby liberating all individuals.

Acknowledgments

Recognition and appreciation to the Collaborative for Action for Equity.

Disclosure statement

No potential conflict of interest was reported by the author(s).

ORCID

Tammy Ellis-Robinson http://orcid.org/0000-0003-1857-008X

References

American Hospital Association. 2015. *#123 for Equity Pledge to Act to Eliminate Health Care Disparities.* https://ifdhe.aha.org/system/files/media/file/2020/02/EOC_Pledge_Packet_Aug2017_FINAL.pdf

Annamma, S., B. Ferri, and D. Connor. 2018. "Disability Critical Race Theory: Exploring the Intersectional Lineage, Emergence and Potential Futures of DisCrit in Education." *Review of Research in Education* 42 (1): 46–71. doi:10.3102/0091732X18759041.

Annamma, S., and D. Morrison. 2018. "Dis/Crit Classroom Ecology: Using Praxis to Dismantle Dysfunctional Education Ecologies." *Teaching and Teacher Education* 73: 70–80. doi:10.1016/j.tate.2018.03.008.

Annamma, S. A., C. Connor, and B. Ferri. 2013. "Dis/ability Critical Race Studies (Dis/crit): Theorizing at the Intersections of Race and Dis/ability." *Race, Ethnicity and Education* 16 (1): 1–31. doi:10.1080/13613324.2012.750511.

Annamma, S. A., and M. Winn. 2019. "Transforming Our Mission: Animating Teacher Education through Intersectional Justice." *Theory into Practice* 58 (4): 318–327. doi:10.1080/00405841.2019.1626618.

Berg, J. L. 2015. "The Role of Personal Purpose and Personal Goals in Symbiotic Visions." *Frontiers in Psychology* 6 (443): 1–8. doi:10.3389/fpsyg.2015.00443.

Bradley, E. H., L. A. Curry, and K. J. Devers. 2007. "Qualitative Data Analysis for Health Services Research: Developing Taxonomy, Themes, and Theory." *Health Services Research* 42 (4): 1758–1772. doi:10.1111/j.1475-6773.2006.00684.x.

Collins, P. H. 1990. *Black Feminist Thought: Knowledge, Consciousness, and the Politics of Empowerment.* Boston: Unwin Hyman.

Creswell, J. W. 2013. *Qualitative Inquiry and Research Design.* 3rd ed. Sage.

Cross, T., B. Bazron, K. Dennis, and M. Isaacs. 1989. *Towards a Culturally Competent System of Care*. Vol. I. Washington, DC: Georgetown University Child Development Center, CASSP Technical Assistance Center.

Dick, B. 1999. "Sources of Rigour in Action Research: Addressing the Issues of Trustworthiness and Credibility." A paper presented at the Association for Qualitative Research Conference "Issues of rigour in qualitative research", Melbourne, Victoria, 6–10.

Feldman, A., P. Paugh, and G. Mills. 2004. "Self-Study through Action Research." In *International Handbook of Self-Study of Teaching and Teacher Education Practices*, edited by J. Loughran, M. Hamilton, V. LaBoskey, and T. Russell, 943–977. Springer. doi:10.1007/978-1-4020-6545-3_24.

Freire, P. 2000. *Pedagogy of the Oppressed*. Continuum.

Fullan, M. 1985. "Change Processes and Strategies at the Local Level." *Elementary School Journal* 85 (3): 391–421. doi:10.1086/461411.

Gay, G. 2000. *Culturally Responsive Teaching: Theory, Research, and Practice*. Teachers College Press.

Gorski, P., and S. G. Pothini. 2018. *Case Studies on Diversity and Social Justice Education*. Routledge.

Gorski, P. S. 2014. *Reaching and Teaching Students in Poverty: Strategies for Erasing the Opportunity Gap*. Teachers College Press.

Hammond, Z., and Y. Jackson. 2015. *Culturally Responsive Teaching and the Brain: Promoting Authentic Engagement and Rigor among Culturally and Linguistically Diverse Students*. Corwin, a SAGE Company.

Kelly, D. C., and R. Varghese. 2018. "Four Contexts of Institutional Oppression: Examining the Experiences of Blacks in Education, Criminal Justice and Child Welfare." *Journal of Human Behavior in the Social Environment* 28 (7): 874–888. doi:10.1080/10911359.2018.1466751.

Kinloch, V., and T. San Pedro. 2014. "The Space between Listening and Storying: Foundations for Projects in Humanization." In *Humanizing Research: Decolonizing Qualitative Inquiry with Youth and Communities*, edited by D. Paris and M. T. Winn, 21–42. SAGE. doi:10.4135/9781544329611.n2.

Kramarczuk Voulgarides, C., E. Fergus, and K. A. King Thorius. 2017. "Pursuing Equity: Disproportionality in Special Education and the Reframing of Technical Issues to Address Systemic Inequities." *Review of Research in Education* 41 (1): 61–87. doi:10.3102/0091732X16686947.

Leonardo, Z., and A. Broderick. 2011. "Smartness as Property: A Critical Exploration of Intersections between White Ness and Disability Studies." *Teachers College Record* 113 (10): 2206–2232. https://www.tcrecord.org/Content.asp?ContentId=16431

Lincoln, Y. S., and E. G. Guba. 1985. *Naturalistic Inquiry*. Sage Publications.

Mayring, P. 2014. "Qualitative Content Analysis: Theoretical Foundation, Basic Procedures, and Software Solutions." *Klagenfurt PID*. https://nbn-resolving.org/urn:nbn:de:0168-ssoar-395173

McNiff, J. 2013. *Action Research: Principles and Practice*. Routledge.

Mezirow, J. 2002. "Transformative Learning: Theory to Practice." [ITAL:] *New Directions for Adult and Continuing Education* 1997 (74): 5–12. doi:10.1002/ace.7401.

Migliarini, V., and C. Stinson. 2020. "Inclusive Education in the (New) Era of Anti-Immigration Policy: Enacting Equity for Disabled English Language Learners." *International Journal of Qualitative Studies in Education* 34 (1): 72–88. doi:10.1080/09518398.2020.1735563.

Miller, A. L. 2019. "(Re) Conceptualizing Family-School Partnerships with and for Culturally and Linguistically Diverse Families." *Race Ethnicity and Education* 22 (6): 746–766. doi:10.1080/13613324.2019.1599339.

Murugami, M. W. 2009. "Disability and Identity." *Disability Studies Quarterly* 29 (4). doi:10.18061/dsq.v29i4.979.

Paris, D. 2012. "Culturally Sustaining Pedagogy: A Needed Change in Stance, Terminology, and Practice." *Educational Researcher* 41 (3): 93–97. doi:10.3102/0013189X12441244.

Rodriguez, G. 2013. "Power and Agency in Education: Exploring the Pedagogical Dimensions of Funds of Knowledge." *Review of Research in Education* 37 (1): 87–120. doi:10.3102/0091732X12462686.

Siuty, M. E. 2017. "(Re) Constituting Teacher Identity for Inclusion in Urban Schools: A Process of Reification and Resistance." Doctoral diss., ProQuest LLC. https://www.semanticscholar.org/paper/(Re)Constituting-Teacher-Identity-for-Inclusion-in-Siuty/cbb0a33756809195c83fe5c06a6295c50e29704f

Souto-Manning, M., and M. T. Winn. 2017. "Foundational Understandings as "Show Ways" for Interrupting Injustice and Fostering Justice in and through Education Research." *Review of Research in Education* 41 (1): ix–xix. doi:10.3102/0091732X17703981.

Staratt, R. 1994. *Building an Ethical School.* Palmer Press.

Triplett, N. P., and J. E. Ford. 2019. "E (Race)ing Inequities: The State of Racial Equity in North Carolina Public Schools." 42–49. https://www.ednc.org/wp-content/uploads/2019/08/EducationNC_Eraceing-Inequities.pdf

Turner, J. C. 1985. "Social Categorization and the Self-Concept: A Social Cognitive Theory of Group Behavior." In *Advances in Group Processes: Theory and Research*, edited by E. J. Lawler, Vol. 2, 72–121. JAI Press.

UN General Assembly, *International Covenant on Civil and Political Rights.* 1966 December 16. "United Nations, Treaty Series." Vol. 999, 171. https://www.refworld.org/docid/3ae6b3aa0.html

Wenger, E. 1998. *Communities of Practice: Learning, Meaning, and Identity.* Cambridge University Press.

Yull, D., L. V. Blitz, T. Thompson, and C. Murray. 2014. "Can We Talk? Using Community-Based Participatory Action Research to Build Family and School Partnerships with Families of Color." *School Community Journal* 24 (2): 9–32. https://psycnet.apa.org/record/2014-56242-001

Global conversations: recovery and detection of Global South multiply-marginalized bodies

Shehreen Iqtadar (iD), David I. Hernández-Saca (iD), Bradley S. Ellison (iD)
and Danielle M. Cowley

ABSTRACT
This paper problematizes, in the spirit of loving critique, the paucity of global intersectional dis/ability politics in the fields of Disability Studies and Critical Race Theory. In this paper, we attempt to account for a more global and humane, liberatory theoretical positioning of Disability Critical Race Theory (DisCrit) by analyzing the human rights discourses employed by the United Nations Convention on the Rights of People with Disabilities (UNCRPD). DisCrit scholars emphasize 'the social construction of race and ability ... which sets one outside of the western cultural norms'. We push DisCrit further to (a) account for the impact of these western cultural norms and ideals in global and local contexts, and (b) problematize how the binary between the Global South-Global North gives impetus for and further reifies the global racist and ableist hegemony of western cultural norms, domination, and violence identified within human rights discourses.

The United Nations Convention on the Rights of Persons with Disabilities (UNCRPD), along with its preamble and optional protocol, is an international treaty which addresses the universal human rights of people with disabilities globally. As the first comprehensive United Nations (UN) treaty of the 21st century, it was adopted by the UN General Assembly in 2006 and was opened for state signatories in March, 2007. The major contribution of the convention was to highlight and eradicate the discrimination experienced by people with disabilities. Following a number of UN declarations (e.g., Declaration of the Rights of Disabled Persons in 1975), the convention adopted a social model of disability in reaffirming that all people with disabilities must enjoy human rights and fundamental freedom.

Our use of the term 'bodies' or 'disabled body' in this paper is *not* to dehumanize the human body and mind in any capacity nor to extend the able/disabled conception of human difference. Rather, we understand that language in the written word is important in order to call out the dehumanizing ideologies around it. We use the term to focus how human bodies are a) the primary focus of scientific correction to align with a 'normed' body, b) holistic to identify the interrelationship between the mind and body mediated by discursive, emotive and material human reality, c) considered an intersection for 'social relations of production and consumption in transnational capitalism' (Erevelles 2011, p. 7), and d) labeled to practice the hegemony of social and economic productivity of 'abled' bodies. Goodley and Runswick-Cole (2013) further theorize the productivity, demands, and practicalities of non-normative bodies as an imaginative possibility of difference. For this reason, and to question the existence of 'able/disabled bodies' we have added quotation marks when using the term.

In recent years, scholars have argued that the Convention – akin to the UN declaration of Human Rights – represents Eurocentric, individualistic approaches to being and living in a society, which contrasts with the morals and values of the Global South[1] (Meekosha and Soldatic 2011; Mutua 2002). For example, the meanings associated with the UNCRPD's understanding of dis/ability[2] (through the social model) follow the historical development of the disability rights movement and critical consciousness as well as dis/ability activism in the Global North, especially the United States (Heyer 2015). In contrast, dis/abled people in the Global South are poorly represented in the convention by universalizing this 'dis/ability knowledge' imported from the Global North, which represents only a fraction of the one billion people living with dis/abilities globally (Meekosha and Soldatic 2011). Further, the convention's language has stark similarities and is consistent with language embedded in U.S. civil rights and educational laws such as the American with Disabilities Act (ADA) of 1990 and the Education for All Handicapped Children Act of 1975 (Public Law 94–142), now known as the Individuals with Disabilities Education Act (IDEA) (Ribet 2011; Walker 2014). A cursory read of the two documents reveal many similarities between the CRPD and IDEA, in that they both represent and highlight the rights of individuals with dis/abilities to education on an equal basis and access to resources without much emphasis on the production and/or emergence of dis/ability in local and global contexts.

At this point, we acknowledge some fundamental differences between IDEA and CRPD. The convention: 1) is more expansive in recognizing the multiple ways that students across a range of contexts are disadvantaged, excluded, and denied an education; 2) presents a much stronger discourse around inclusion; and, 3) advances a social model of disability in contrast to IDEA and ADA. However, in this paper, we concur with scholars that the text of the convention historically aligns and is consistent with the language of IDEA and ADA (Ribet 2011; Walker 2014). Further, the CRPD does not account for the intersectionally-rich, depth of experiences of disabled people in the Global South and it uses language embedded in U.S. laws to further implement the defined understandings of dis/ability from the Global North.

In this paper, we model our expansion and application of Disability Critical Race Studies (DisCrit) after Paris and Alim's (2014) notion of *a loving critique*. Paris and Alim (2014) define *a loving critique* as 'a position of deep respect from which we [engage in] problematiz[ing] and exten[tion]' of theory (p. 85). Our loving critique will account for a global and humane, liberatory theoretical positioning of the seven tenets of DisCrit theory by critically exploring and analyzing the role of the UNCRPD in the education of people and students with dis/abilities in the Global South. We begin by reviewing some of the conceptual underpinnings of the convention, specifically Article 24, which describes education for students with dis/abilities. This section also includes a summary of some existing critiques of the convention.

In the next section, we will place the work of DisCrit in conversation with the convention text to explore how race, dis/ability, and immigration and/or refugee status impact the lives of those living at these intersections in global contexts. DisCrit, a recent theory, method and praxis to understand the lived and educational experiences of people and students of color with dis/abilities, will be used here to account for a critical analysis of the UNCRPD and its role in the life of subaltern people/individual with dis/abilities in the Global South. We acknowledge that this paper is a beginning conversation to engage DisCrit with a global intersectional dis/ability politics.[3]

In this context, the UNCRPD's example helps us underscore and extend DisCrit to a global intersectional dis/ability politic by: a) locating dis/ability in today's geopolitical context; b) problematizing the existing binary between the Global North-South divide in relation to dis/ability politics; and, (c) including the voices of subaltern people with dis/abilities in the Global South to reimagine the work in Disability Studies, DisCrit, and the work of global institutions, such as the CRPD. We focus on the violence experienced by dis/abled people at the nexus of race and ability that is fluid across the globe. We conclude our analysis by proposing a more humane and liberatory, Global South-informed DisCrit.

Background and conceptual underpinnings of the UNCRPD

In this section, we begin by reviewing the history of the CRPD as well as its purpose and the underlying ideologies that it advances. We then describe some of the articles of the convention, specifically Article 24 as it relates to inclusive education in the global context. We conclude by summarizing critiques of the CRPD, specifically Article 24.

During the 2001 UN General Assembly, the Mexican delegation proposed to develop an international convention to protect the rights of persons with dis/abilities. The proposal led to the establishment of an Ad Hoc Committee to develop a comprehensive convention on the rights of all people with dis/abilities. The CRPD arose as a result of this Ad Hoc Committee's efforts to develop a text which would ensure that dis/abled people will enjoy the rights conferred on them through previous UN treaties (Lord 2009; Schulze 2009; Walker 2014). Thus, the purpose of the committee was not to pen down new human rights, but to: a) describe the obligations to countries of protecting the rights of people with dis/abilities in previous international treaties and b) develop a text which would ensure equal and effective enjoyment of existing human rights by all people with dis/abilities (Loper 2010).

The UNCRPD adopts a broad categorization of dis/ability through a social model lens. First coined by Oliver in 1981, advocates of the social model view disability as a 'social phenomenon' located within the 'social world' and not inside the human body, senses, and mind (Connor and Gabel 2010; Ferguson and Nusbaum 2012). In the preamble (e) of the CRPD, disability is defined as:

> An evolving concept and that [dis/ability] results from the interaction between persons with impairments and attitudinal and environmental barriers that hinders their full and effective participation in society on an equal basis with others. (United Nations 2006, 1)

This definition of dis/ability contrasts with the traditional, medical model of disability which identifies disability as residing solely within the human body and views people with disabilities as needing medical assistance to 'correct' their bodies and/or behaviors. Instead, the convention identifies people with dis/abilities as competent, active, autonomous members of society (United Nations, n.d.).

Following the definition of disability, the text of the convention begins with preambles containing the human rights provisions of the Charter of the United Nations. Some of these provisions include: a) inherent dignity and worth of every person; b) entitlement to individual rights and freedom; c) anti-discrimination; and, d) universality to name a few. The preambles are then followed by 50 articles and 18 optional protocols of the convention that explain the basic principles of the rest of the treaty.

Article 24(1) establishes the provisions of education. It identifies that state parties shall guarantee inclusive education[4] at all levels and that it should be directed to:

(a) The full development of human potential and sense of dignity and self-worth, and the strengthening of respect for human rights, fundamental freedoms and human diversity;
(b) The development by persons with [dis/abilities] of their personality, talents and creativity, as well as their mental and physical abilities, to their fullest potential;
(c) Enabling persons with [dis/abilities] to participate effectively in a free society. (United Nations 2006, 16)

Following this, Article 24(2) states that in realizing these rights, state parties shall ensure that people with dis/abilities are not excluded from general education and should be provided reasonable accommodations to meet their individual educational needs. Article 24(3) of the convention states that state parties shall facilitate social development skills through 'Braille, alternative script, augmentative and alternative modes, means and formats of communication and orientation and mobility skills, facilitating peer support and mentoring ... [and] sign language and the promotion of the linguistic identity of the deaf community' (p. 17). Article 24(4) then ensures taking appropriate measures by 'employ[ing] teachers, including teachers with [dis/abilities], who are qualified in sign language and/or Braille, and to train professionals and staff who work at all levels of education' (p. 17). Finally, Article 24(5) ensures that people with dis/abilities can have access to 'tertiary education, vocational training, adult education and lifelong learning without discrimination and on an equal basis with others' (p. 18).

The CRPD's adoption by nation states is significant in promoting the awareness of rights of people with dis/abilities across the world. It's efforts to make disability rights a new global 'norm' is indeed commendable and the step has been perceived positively by many countries throughout the Global North and South. However, the text of the convention bears a deeper analysis about how it contains and promotes Eurocentric and Global North agendas through its various Articles. In the next section, we identify some of these critiques of the CRPD.

Summary of various critiques of the CRPD

Critiques of the CRPD can be broadly organized into three interrelated categories: a) the CRPD is a neoliberal project (understanding dis/ability through the ableist construct of productivity) (Jenks 2017; Stiker 2019); b) the roots of disability rights consciousness lie in the social model of disability and the text is greatly influenced by special education laws of the U.S. and U.K. (Heyer 2015); and, c) the CRPD fails to detect, capture, and recover the intersectional experiences of subaltern people with dis/abilities in the Global South, and/or those migrating or seeking refuge (Meekosha, 2011; Meekosha and Soldatic 2011; Migliarini 2017).

The CRPD as a neoliberal project

Human bodies within a neoliberal paradigm are viewed in terms of their productivity in society and hence connecting what bodies can and cannot do in exchange for their inclusion and participation in society (Hughes 2012). Neoliberalism further devalues contributions of the disabled body by placing a great emphasis on productivity (Jenks 2017). Economization of the human body is prevalent globally, wherein economic worth rationalizes certain individuals as more valuable than certain others (Brown 2015). The language of the CRPD relies on neoliberal rationality and economization of the individual, while overlooking the interpretations and individual experiences of dis/ability in many societies in the Global South and beyond (Gorman, 2010).

The CRPD text universalizes dis/ability knowledge imported from the Global North, which represents only a fraction of one billion people living with dis/abilities globally (Meekosha and Soldatic 2011). The text of the CRPD defines people with disabilities as 'those who have long-term physical, mental, intellectual, and sensory impairments which in interaction with various barriers may hinder their full and effective participation in society on an equal basis with others' (United Nations 2006; Article, 1). In contrast, many countries and peoples in the Global South define disability in historical, cultural, social, political, and economic terms (Cutajar & Adjoe, 2016; Jenks 2017; Johansson 2014).

In fact, a single country may have multiple cultures, such as India, that attach varying connotations to the notion of dis/ability. For example, the notion of Karma attached with disability identity is one of the many interpretations of disability in Hinduism (Ghai 2002). Karma theory explains that disability is associated with deep suffering, which primarily originated through Karma – an individual act – for which there will be corresponding Karmic compensation in this life or the next (life of rebirth). Similarly, some languages may lack the word disability, associate it with divine blessing, and/or do not view the dis/abled body from the lens of productivity (Rizvi 2017). We acknowledge that these understandings are not universal nor is any culture monolithic. However, diverse understandings of dis/ability are not readily present within the CRPD and a single definition fails to capture the diversity of cultural, religious, and historical contexts found throughout the Global South and North.

Global North legal influences

Scholars have critiqued the CRPD as highly influenced by U.S. civil rights discourses as well as educational laws including the ADA and IDEA (Ribet 2011; Walker 2014). The IDEA (1997) prohibits discrimination against students with dis/abilities. Under IDEA, school districts are obligated to provide free and appropriate public education (FAPE) at no cost to parents and/or families. The provision of equal educational opportunities for all students may be well-intended, but it also creates a culture of legal-compliance over other forms of enacting inclusion based on belonging, relationships, and systemic change efforts (Voulgarides 2018). Article 24(2) of the CRPD reflects similar language:

> Persons with disabilities are not excluded from the general education system on the basis of disability, and that children with disabilities are not excluded from free and compulsory primary education, or from secondary education, on the basis of disability [and] can access

an inclusive, quality and free primary education and secondary education on an equal basis with others in the communities in which they live. (United Nations 2006, 17).

Scholars have also identified inherent contradictions within Article 24. For example, the convention values full inclusion of students with disabilities within general education classrooms. However, 'inclusion' lacks explicit definition and leaves room for conflicting interpretations by nation states. While this may not be a point of contention for some (as it is important to understand inclusive education in cultural ways and available resources), leaving inclusive education to the interpretations of signatory countries may do more harm than good during implementation (Johansson 2014; Winzer and Mazurek 2019).

Attending to this argument within an Indian education context, Johansson (2014) stated that 'though inclusive education was rarely defined, it was given different meanings in the way that it was used [by the policy makers and school personnel]' (p. 1225). Drawing on current national policy documents and interview data from eleven private schools in Kolkata, she argued that, while the term inclusive education carried varied meanings across policy documents, it often led to exclusionary practices for students with certain types of dis/ability labels. The notion of the 'includable child' is frequently used to make decisions about students who fit and those who do not fit in inclusive schools and classrooms. Johansson further notes that this suitability depends greatly on the behavior of the child and the ability of the child to fit within existing programs.

The concept of inclusive education as students fitting into normative structures is common practice throughout the Global North and South (Florian 2014). Inclusive education has been used to refer to a range of educational configurations, leading to the creation of alternative systems to the mainstream education system or placing students in pre-existing schools and classrooms with already available (limited) resources. It has also been used to refer to the creation of remedial classes, transition classes, resource rooms, and/or special classes within supposedly inclusive schools (Muthukrishna and Engelbrecht 2018; Singal 2006). And, although the Least Restrictive Environment (LRE) within U.S. context does state that the student with a disability should be educated with their non-labeled peers to the maximum extent appropriate, much is left up to schools to interpret the phrase 'maximum extent appropriate,' which has led to continued and varied forms of segregation. Inclusion also plays out qualitatively differently for Black, Indigenous, and Youth of Color (BIYOC) than their white counterparts labeled with the same special education label due to issues of power, privilege, cultural hegemony and whiteness of U.S. special education systems (Annamma, Connor, and Ferri 2013).

Within the Southern African context, Muthukrishna and Engelbrecht (2018) conducted a systematic review on decolonizing inclusive education and explored tensions in implementing the policy in four African countries. The authors identified that inclusive education is a policy that, in practice, has been 'promoted in a technical, assimilationist manner, clearly influenced by dominant special education ideologies' (p. 5). The authors contend that traditional special education structures still prevail in the guise of 'inclusive education.' To address colonialism in this context, one needs to critically engage with Eurocentric, deficit-oriented labeling and categorization that leads to some students being placed into the separate schools. The problem of segregation is further entrenched by certain international donor organizations that invest in the education and development of students with certain dis/abilities only, overlooking all students with dis/abilities (Hummel et al., Muthukrishna & Engelbrecht, 2018).

What is more problematic is that much of the current practices of segregated schooling is supported by the CRPD legislation. Walker (2014) identifies that 'the absence of discrimination does not connote inclusivity' (p. 125). The CRPD states that all state parties shall provide reasonable accommodations for students' needs. The term 'reasonable accommodations' was first introduced by the ADA (1990) in relation to providing appropriate accommodations and modifications to individuals with dis/abilities without placing an 'undue hardship' or burden on employers, businesses, and hiring companies. Similarly, Article 2 of the CRPD defines reasonable accommodations as:

> necessary and appropriate modifications and adjustments not imposing a disproportionate or undue burden, where needed in a particular case, to ensure to persons with [dis/abilities] the enjoyment or exercise on an equal basis with others of all human rights and fundamental freedom. (CRPD, 2006, p. 4)

Under such provision, any school district (public or private) can get away with refusing admission to a student with a dis/ability in their school, further limiting equal educational opportunities for ALL students with dis/abilities (Johansson 2014). To this point, one must question the applicability of inclusive reform when schools are essentially given permission to exclude based on claims of the unreasonableness of accommodations or modifications (Donohue & Bornman, 2014).

Another related issue is the fact that the CRPD document only refers to certain dis/ability categories, providing no reference to individuals with intellectual disabilities or the psychological and emotional impact of dis/ability labels (Anastasiou and Kauffman 2019; Iqtadar, Hernández-Saca, and Ellison 2020; Walker 2014). Such absences leave the interpretation of accessibility needs of students with intellectual disabilities at the discretion of educational institutions in the state parties, again, dominated by the Global North special education and medical model hegemony.

Failure to recover intersectional experiences

Finally, few scholars have critically analyzed the text of the CRPD through the lens of intersectionality (De Beco 2020; Kayess, Sands, and Fisher 2014; Ribet 2011). Intersectionality refers to an individual's intersecting identities (specifically race and gender) as well as the process of subordination experienced at the intersection of discrimination and vulnerabilities (Crenshaw 1990). The text of the convention is least responsive to global intersectional dis/ability politics. In fact, in some ways it erases race-consciousness from international disability law (Ribet 2011). In the context of gender and dis/ability as identified in the convention, Ribet argues that, 'the concept of "disability intersectionality," to the extent that it exists at all in social and legal discourse, is generally articulated as a fairly monodimensional critique of identity essentialism' (p. 185). Although identifying the discrimination experienced by women and/or girls with dis/abilities in a global context is important, the text mostly relies on an additive conception of vulnerability and subordination. Such a dynamic of intersectional subordination warrants an in-depth analysis of how compounding vulnerability shapes and constitutes the experiences of women with disabilities in a global context, specifically the Global South.

Adding to Ribet's (2011) analysis through an intersectional lens, we extend the argument that the convention bears deeper analysis of intersectional disablement such as genocide, warfare, and mass human rights violations leading to intersectional oppression in the context of the Global South. We acknowledge that the CRPD is not a prescriptive text, however, being the only international convention regarding the rights of people with dis/abilities, we argue that the convention should complicate and engage the process of impairment and intersectional disablement globally, and specifically in the Global South.

In the next section, we engage in an intersectional analysis of the CRPD using a DisCrit framework to critically analyze how race and ability supremacy work together across the Globe to uphold notions of normalcy, and to engage in a Global South-informed DisCrit discussion. We argue that a DisCrit-informed analysis is important to account for constructions of dis/ability and race within geopolitical, global contexts.

UNCRPD and disability critical race studies

In this section, we offer an analysis of the UNCRPD grounded in a Disability Critical Race Studies (DisCrit) framework and Critical Disability Studies scholarship to explore how race and dis/ability work in tandem for historically marginalized, subaltern people with dis/abilities of the Global South in situations of war, poverty, and torture (Annamma, Connor, and Ferri 2013). We first begin by providing an explanation of the DisCrit framework. We then draw attention to two erasures in the UNCRPD: 1) the erasure of intersectional oppression through State violence in the Global South and North that subaltern people with dis/abilities experience on a daily basis; and 2) the lack of intersectional attention throughout Article 24, including race, ability, culture, language, immigrant and/or refugee status, and religious identities to name a few. We conclude our argument by naming how the UNCRPD erases individual voices and experiences of historically marginalized people.

Disability Critical race studies (DisCrit)

DisCrit is an emerging framework that explores how racism and ableism are interdependent and socially constructed. DisCrit aims to account for ways that multiply minoritized people and students experience intersecting oppressions, which have considerable consequences on their life chances and experiences (Annamma, Connor, and Ferri 2013; Crenshaw 1990; Hernández-Saca, Gutmann Kahn, and Cannon 2018; Iqtadar, Hernández-Saca, and Ellison 2020). DisCrit acknowledges the corporeality of human differences, while questioning the norms that create such differences. Thus, ability, race and/or other categories, such as gender, social class, caste, and tribal systems in some Global South countries, normalize the experiences of white able-bodied individuals over Black, Indigenous, and Youth of Color (BIYOC) and contribute to the reproduction of social hierarchies in society (Annamma, Connor, and Ferri 2013). Focusing on the experiences of those who are multiply-marginalized, DisCrit values multidimensional identities and privileges voices of people marginalized in society (DisCrit, tenet four).

In this conceptual paper, we specifically draw upon the seven tenets of DisCrit to identify how UNCRPD restricts and marginalizes the multidimensionally rich experiences of People of Color with dis/abilities within the Global South. We also highlight the ways in which DisCrit can be expanded to be more inclusive of the lived experiences of those living in the Global South and who are affected by the policies and practices of international organizations, working to advance and globalize the Eurocentric, individualistic ways of the Global North. While one might argue the positive impact of certain international policies, and we agree with such analysis to some extent, we ask for a critical stance of the interest convergence of the Global North through such organizations (Amin 2006).

Erasure of intersectional oppression

DisCrit centers the voices of marginalized people and underscores how race and ability superiority work together to uphold norms that further marginalize dis/abled people with multiple minority identities in society (DisCrit, Tenet one, two, and four). A close reading of the convention document reveals that the CRPD does not fully account for the intersectional oppression of people with dis/abilities. The text of the convention acknowledges that nation states shall consider preventing people with dis/abilities from: a) being subjected to torture and cruel treatment; b) being discriminated due to a dis/ability label for entering into a country; c) receiving gender and age-based violence and exploitation; d) segregation and abandonment within their communities; and, e) leading to further dis/abilities. However, the CRPD does not explicitly condemn or require nation states to refrain from intersectional oppression experienced through war, mass destruction, or globalization in Global South countries.

As Ribet (2011) has noted, by only including provisional measures after the impairment has occurred, the CRPD prevents further analysis of power relations within and between nation states that *cause* intersectional oppression and dis/ability. By extension, and from a DisCrit conscious lens, we argue that the convention has effectively erased the intersectional experiences of subaltern people/individuals with dis/abilities who are multiply oppressed within. For example, since 2010, the government of India has reportedly used pellet guns to blind young Muslim boys en masse in the Kashmir Valley (Nath 2019; Misri 2019; Perrigo, 2018). In the 2019 unconstitutional revoke of the special status of Kashmir by the Hindu nationalist Modi Government, mass shootings increased the number of disabilities (mainly blindness) and deaths in the valley. Many of these victims and their family members also experienced trauma and permanent psychological impact. We argue that by not including a clause within the CRPD text or clear directives to stop countries from engaging in such heinous acts of deliberate disablement, the convention inadvertently creates space for mass human rights violations of historically multiply-marginalized people to occur within and between nation states (De Sousa Santos, 2018).

From a DisCrit perspective, the voices of marginalized groups and individuals, such as the young Kashmiri boys, should be included and privileged on local and international platforms, to counter-narrate the official reports provided by the State, such as the Indian

Government. As an extension, and situating DisCrit within a global intersectional dis/ability politic, we advocate that DisCrit scholars engage in the emancipatory struggles of the dis/abled people, many of whom are multiply-marginalized within their communities, residing in the Global South.

Lack of intersectional attention in article 24

Article 24 of the CRPD also does not account for the intersectional experiences of students – including immigrants and/or refugees with dis/abilities, culturally and linguistically diverse students, as well as female students with dis/abilities (DisCrit, Tenets one and two). Through this silence, the convention complies with existing hegemonic structures of racist, sexist, and ableist, capitalist, neoliberal policies and practices, such as standardized assessment in schools, hyper-surveillance of students of color within special education, deficit views about immigrant and/or refugee students' racial and linguistic abilities, as well as human rights discourses steeped in ability supremacy through dictates or expectations of productivity.

From a DisCrit perspective, hegemonic power structures of ableism and whiteness – a position of white race privilege and structural advantage (Frankenberg 1993) – flow within global societies and educational settings to maintain unequal power relations and intersectional oppression for People of Color with dis/abilities (Crenshaw 1990). To understand this contention, and from a DisCrit lens, we now provide an example that focuses on the educational experiences of immigrant students who received dis/ability labels in their country of resettlement. We do this as we understand that with growing immigration in countries of the Global North (Peguero 2009), decoupling racism and ableism provide an important framework for understanding the educational experiences, stigmas and stereotypes, as well as the racial and dis/ability microaggressions faced by immigrant and/or refugee students labeled dis/abled (Annamma 2013; Bal 2009; Migliarini, Stinson, and D'Alessio 2019; Song 2018).

In the international context of Italy, Migliarini's (2017) research engaged with nine refugee service organizations in the city of Rome. Migliarini used a DisCrit framework to explore the intersections of race, students' migratory status, and dis/ability labels in relation to the educational experiences of asylum-seeking students. The findings from her study suggest that the bodies of migrant children coming from sub-Saharan West African countries to Southern Italy are considered '*risky bodies*,' whose presence must be 'controlled,' 'monitored,' and 'prevented' (if possible) in the national territory (p. 181). Italian professionals working with migrant children often viewed them from deficit ideologies based on their religious and racial identities. Further, Migliarini's findings point to the educational processes and discourses of Italy (implementing the Salamanca Statement[5]) positioning children as 'less "able" or different from a predetermined, standardized "norm"' (p. 127). Deficit views about migrant students' abilities – which are rooted in Eurocentric cultural and medical perspectives – subjectify asylum-seeking children as 'illiterate' due to their Muslim Sub-Saharan background and education (p. 130). Migliarini's findings also indicate that this presumed 'illiteracy' is measured by children's 'inability to speak European languages, such as French' (p. 15) and professionals' refusal to acknowledge how existing racism and ableism further reproduces white and ability supremacy in the Italian context.

Reading the CRPD from a race and dis/ability-conscious lens one finds that race is almost absent from the convention. Moreover, neither the Salamanca Statement nor the CRPD take into consideration the diverse and dense global experiences of victims of mass destruction, warfare, and torture as people who experience disablement. Within the convention, race appears only once and in the preamble. Our intentions are to disrupt this silence on race within international treaties and conventions, such as the CRPD, and make plain how racism and ableism work together for many people and students experiencing global racial and dis/ability subordination. We argue that international conventions, speaking on behalf of local subaltern people/individuals with disabilities, should include the voice of those most affected by the global intersectional dis/ability politics. On the contrary, and as previously questioned by some scholars, the CRPD text appears to be too greatly influenced by the Western civil rights discourses and disability education laws in the U.S. (Ribet 2011; Walker 2014). Western civil rights discourses, and even the social model of disability, do not appear to be complex enough frameworks for capturing and understanding the experiences, cultures, histories, and beliefs of people in the Global South. A critical read of the limitations of civil rights discourses and the social model of disability is necessary and warranted.

Our final critique of the CRPD is that it does not provide space for the individual voices of subaltern people/individuals with historically multiply-marginalized identities. For example, it does not complicate the gendered experiences of women with dis/abilities (Ribet 2011). Hammad and Singal (2015) case study explored the intersectional educational experiences of six women with dis/abilities in the Punjab province of Pakistan. While four of the six women experienced both mainstream and special education systems, all six suggested that there is no representation of people with dis/abilities in the school curriculum as well as in broader society. Their findings suggest that the lives of all the women were influenced by the education they received as well as the means present to achieve their educational goals, such as access to schools, teachers, and government policy. However, their capabilities and gendered specified roles were largely associated with how society viewed women with dis/abilities in Pakistani context. As a result, while their life choices were successful in certain areas of life, such as achieving high levels of education and/or work life, they were not accepted for other roles in society such as marriage. Thus, Hammad and Singal (2015) argued that their choices were indeed influenced by multiple factors, such as being a woman with dis/ability in a Pakistani society, others people's attitudes towards them, by how dis/ability is viewed, and how they themselves viewed their impairments in day-to-day life.

Reviewing the CRPD document, one quickly grasps that gender is barely acknowledged, and when it is, the focus is on an additive form of vulnerability, without any reference to the complexity of individual experiences or including individual voices (McCall 2005; Ribet 2011). Article 6 of the convention is the only place where the discussion of gender is compartmentalized. Part one of Article 6 reads: 'States Parties recognize that women and girls with disabilities are subject to multiple discrimination, and in this regard shall take measures to ensure the full and equal enjoyment by them of all human rights and fundamental freedoms' (p. 2). While important, the intersectional experiences of women and girls with dis/abilities should expand and their voices should be included to recognize the multiplicities of vulnerability (DisCrit, Tenet 4).

At this point we want to make it explicit that the experiences of young boys with dis/abilities also bear an analysis. In developing countries of the Global South such as Pakistan, child labor, specifically for young boys living in poverty is a harsh reality. While Pakistan has ratified most of the key international conventions of child labor, the lack of minimum employment age is a considerable factor that fails many young boys and girls while pushing them to child labor (United States Department of Labor's Bureau of International Labor Affairs 2013). To reiterate, the convention lacks any mention of the intersectional oppression that people with dis/abilities (such as gendered, social class, those living with lower caste, tribal system) experience in the Global South. Including gender as an additive form of vulnerability within the convention document does not do justice to the rich and diverse experiences and everyday life realities of people with dis/abilities. Further, it does not complicate how the interworkings of gender and dis/ability work differently for some people, such as those from working and/or middle class, and may privilege some over the others. It must include the voices of people with dis/abilities affected by such international treaties and conventions when making decisions and also to better understand the cultural, historical, social and political diversities in our world.

Conclusion

In this paper, we have engaged the text of the UNCRPD with a framework of DisCrit and Critical Disability Studies scholarship (Erevelles, 2011; Hall, 2019; Meekosha & Shuttleworth, 2009). We acknowledge that this conceptual paper is a beginning conversation to bring DisCrit and the UNCRPD together to analyze intersectional dis/ability experiences within the Global South as well as experiences of those migrating from the Global South to the Global North. Our intent is to engage a global and humane, emancipatory theoretical positioning of DisCrit through simultaneously, critically analyzing the role of the UNCRPD in Global South dis/ability politics and in the education of students with dis/abilities in the Global South. DisCrit is a valuable theoretical framework and methodological tool to analyze the global systems of intersectional dis/ability oppression as well as systems that are playing a role in maintaining existing global 'ability' and 'racial' hegemony by either directly being involved in it or by keeping silent in mass violations of 'human rights', such as in the case of shootings in the Kashmir Valley to mass blind young Muslim boys.

Building on DisCrit, we acknowledge that race and dis/ability are socially constructed categories (re)produced by hegemonic power structures[6] (Annamma, Connor, and Ferri 2013; Crenshaw 1990); hence, working in tandem. In this conceptual piece, we propose that the seven tenets of DisCrit must account for global intersectional dis/ability politics, by engaging in the systems of oppression in the Global South experienced by those who are most directly affected by the policies of Eurocentric ideals at epistemological, ontological, axiological, and etiological levels (De Sousa Santos, 2018). It is important to account for a more humane and liberatory understanding of intersectional dis/ability in local as well as global contexts. We understand that the local is never detached from the global and that intersectional dis/ability is a fluid concept for global dis/abled people. Since medicalized concepts and understandings of dis/ability are fluid across the globe, cultural differences intact, we call for a Global South informed DisCrit to better understand the experiences of Global dis/abled people with intersectional identities. Hence, we propose through our loving critique that future work within DisCrit theory and praxis account the following points for an emancipatory struggle of global intersectional dis/ability politics:

(1) Emphasize the social, global cultural, psychological, emotional, and material constructions of race and ability, which sets one outside of global ability supremacy and racial[7] 'norms;'
(2) Engage the global intersectional onset of dis/ability through war conditions, mass destruction, globalization, Global North interference and invasions in countries of the Global South for economic and political purposes;
(3) Center the voices of globally dis/abled multiply marginalized people, both in the Global South and those migrating from the Global South to the Global North; and,
(4) Call out the Global North interest convergence and resist its' neoliberal concepts which create a mythical divide of 'Global North/South' to understand human beings (through racial, dis/ability, tribal, social class, caste identities to name a few) that values the economization of human bodies and their productivity through local and global institutions and structures.
(5) Acknowledge, support, and align with all forms of global activism, resistance and justice movements in order to counter-narrate the silence, lack of representation and power within and between multiple levels of global and local civic society and institutions for critical revolutionary praxis.

In the context of the first point stated above, we acknowledge that the third tenet of DisCrit emphasizes "the social construction of race and ability and yet recognizes the material and psychological impacts of being labeled as raced or dis/abled, *which sets one outside of the western cultural norms*" (Annamma et al., p. 11, added emphasis). However, we push ourselves and DisCrit scholars to identify how disabled people in the Global South and/or those migrating to the Global North from the Global South – who are already stigmatized as being *outside of the western culture* – are impacted by how they are understood within the western culture. In other words, we question the existence of normalcy of western cultural norms globally through our framing of '*global ability supremacy and racial norms.*' While it is often assumed that colonialism has ended in much of the world, we understand that the Global North still exercises power on the Global South through globalization, global policies, and a Eurocentric gaze, as well as through international organizations such as Human Rights Watch, the UNCRPD, and World Health Organization to name a few (Amin 2006; Armstrong, Armstrong, and Spandagou 2011). Hence, in the spirit of loving critique (Paris and Alim 2014), we encourage a push for more scholarship of global intersectional dis/ability experiences and Global South dis/ability politics (Erevelles 2011; Meekosha and Shuttleworth 2009) within DisCrit scholarship.

Finally, and within the context of the UNCRPD, we acknowledge that the convention does include some reference to the intersectional experiences and provisions of education and life opportunities to females/girls with dis/abilities. However, the lived experiences of those living with multiple identities (such as people with dis/abilities and those with 'lower' caste or religious marginalized identities, young boys or girls, and/or immigrant and/or refugee status to name a few) are quite complex in the Global South.

For this reason, we engaged with DisCrit in this paper to call out the erasure of the: a) intersectional oppression that dis/abled people of Global South experience on a day-to-day basis and b) the intersectionally-rich experiences and voices of the subaltern people/individuals with dis/abilities within Article 24 of the document. We contend that the convention must acknowledge and include the voices and experiences of historically marginalized communities and people with dis/abilities in the Global South. In alignment with DisCrit's requirement of activism fo all forms of resistance (DisCrit Tenet 7), this acknowledgement and support can be done through engagement with grassroots organizers and activists' justice movements, greater representation from minority communities, and a shifting away from Global North texts, documents and ideologies. It is timely not only for a politics of recognition of Global South bodyminds, but also for countering the silence and lack of representation within Disability Studies (DS) and power at multiple levels of global and local civic society and institutions to disrupt Global North intersectional dis/ability hegemony.

Notes

1. We acknowledge that the Global South is not monolithic, neither are its morals and values. However, the collective nature of approaches and ways of living in many of the Global South countries historically contrast with individualistic approaches to various UN conventions.

2. In this paper, dis/ability means that both disabilities and abilities are socially, politically, emotionally, culturally and historically constructed in societies. Our use of the slash does not represent a binary between disability and ability to view people through a lens of productivity. Rather we use slash to disrupt how 'disability' is constructed, identified, controlled, intervened, fixed and maintained globally (Taylor, Ferguson, and Ferguson 1992) through systems such as special education, and national and international laws and policies, such as the UNCRPD. Furthermore, and complementary to DisCrit, we seek to understand the intersectional experiences of disability through the voices of people with disabilities at their nexus of multidimensional identities (DisCrit, Tenet 4). Given that DisCrit emphasizes the social construction of disability and ability (DisCrit, Tenet 3), we also use the slash to underscore the non-monolithic and context-specific nature of both disability and ability, as opposed to reinforcing a 'fixed' notion of being human (Wachsler 2012). When we do use the term 'disabilities' or 'disability', it is to acknowledge and contrast how the use of the slash, like person-first terminology, are generally used in the academy and by non-disabled people, and are not necessarily supported by dis/abled people themselves, who would rather 'say the word' as a term of identity, pride, and culture.

3. By a global intersectional dis/ability politic we refer to how dis/ability is created and experienced by Black, Indigenous and Youth of Color globally through war conditions, mass destruction, globalization, as well as Global North interference and invasions in countries of the Global South for economic and political purposes.

4. The concept of inclusive education broadly links to school improvement efforts, both structurally and ideologically. Structurally shifting away from the traditional and segregated special education settings and ideologically valuing human differences (Florian 2014).

5. The Salamanca Statement is a rights-based international policy of UNESCO (1994) on inclusive education for ALL students, especially emphasizing children with special needs (Migliarini, Stinson, and D'Alessio 2019).

6. Hegemonic power structures are dominant ways of being and doing within a society that favors some people by allowing them to exercise domination over those not favored through these social categories (Crenshaw 1990).

7. We understand that racism may be experienced differently in different parts of the world. For instance, people may experience racism through their 'lower' caste status or tribal affiliation in some Global South countries.

Disclosure statement

No potential conflict of interest was reported by the author(s).

ORCID

Shehreen Iqtadar ⓘ http://orcid.org/0000-0002-9125-1766
David I. Hernández-Saca ⓘ http://orcid.org/0000-0002-3070-4610
Bradley S. Ellison ⓘ http://orcid.org/0000-0003-3885-5525

References

Amin, S. 2006. "The Millennium Development Goals: A Critique from the South." *Monthly Review* 57 (10): 1. doi:10.14452/MR-057-10-2006-03_1.

Anastasiou, D., and J. M. Kauffman. 2019. *The Right to Education: Analysis of Article 24 of the UN CRPD*. Indianapolis, IN, United States: Council for Exceptional Children Convention. doi:10.13140/RG.2.2.10471.50080.

Annamma, S. 2013. "Undocumented and under Surveillance: A Case Study of an Undocumented Latina with A Disability in Juvenile Justice." *Journal of the Association of Mexican American Educators* 7 (3): 32–41.

Annamma, S. A., D. Connor, and B. Ferri. 2013. "Dis/ability Critical Race Studies (Discrit): Theorizing at the Intersections of Race and Dis/ability." *Race Ethnicity and Education* 16 (1): 1–31.

Armstrong, D., A. C. Armstrong, and I. Spandagou. 2011. "Inclusion: By Choice or by Chance?" *International Journal of Inclusive Education* 15 (1): 29–39. doi:10.1080/13603116.2010.496192.

Bal, A. 2009. "*Becoming Learners in U.S. Schools: A Sociocultural Study of Refugee Students' Evolving Identities1.*" Unpublished doctoral diss., Arizona State University.

Brown, W. 2015. *Undoing the Memos: Brown Neoliberalism's Stealth Revolution*. Cambridge, MA: MIT Press.

Connor, D. J., and S. L. Gabel. 2010. "Welcoming the Unwelcome: Disability as Diversity." In *Social Justice Pedagogy across the Curriculum*, edited by T. K. Chapman and N. Hobbel, 217–238, New York: Routledge.

Crenshaw, K. 1990. "Mapping the Margins: Intersectionality, Identity Politics, and Violence against Women of Color." *Stanford Law Review* 43: 1241.

Cutajar, J., and C. Adjoe. 2016. "Whose Knowledge, Whose Voice? Power, Agency and Resistance in Disability Studies for the Global South." In *Disability in the Global South*, edited by S. Grech and K. Soldatic, 503–516, Switzerland: Springer.

De Beco, G. 2020. "Intersectionality and Disability in International Human Rights Law." *The International Journal of Human Rights* 24 (5): 593–614. doi:10.1080/13642987.2019.1661241.

De Sousa Santos, B. 2018. *The End of the Cognitive Empire: The Coming of Age of Epistemologies of the South*. London: Duke University Press.

Donohue, D., and J. Bornman. 2014. "The Challenges of Realising Inclusive Education in South Africa." *South African Journal of Education* 34 (2). doi:10.15700/201412071114.

Erevelles, N. 2011. *Disability and Difference in Global Contexts: Enabling a Transformative Body Politic*. New York: Springer.

Ferguson, P. M., and E. Nusbaum. 2012. "Disability Studies: What Is It and What Difference Does It Make?" *Research and Practice for Persons with Severe Disabilities* 37 (2): 70–80. doi:10.1177/154079691203700202.

Florian, L. 2014. "What Counts as Evidence of Inclusive Education?" *European Journal of Special Needs Education* 29 (3): 286–294. doi:10.1080/08856257.2014.933551.

Frankenberg, R. 1993. "Growing up White: Feminism, Racism and the Social Geography of Childhood." *Feminist Review* 45 (1): 51–84. https://www.jstor.org/stable/1395347

Ghai, A. 2002. "Disabled Women: An Excluded Agenda of Indian Feminism." *Hypatia* 17 (3): 49–66. doi:10.1111/j.1527-2001.2002.tb00941.x.

Goodley, D., and K. Runswick-Cole. 2013. "The Body as Disability and Possability: Theorizing the 'Leaking, Lacking and Excessive' Bodies of Disabled Children." *Scandinavian Journal of Disability Research* 15 (1): 1–19. doi:10.1080/15017419.2011.640410.

Gorman, R. 2010. Empire of rights: The convergence of neoliberal governance, 'states of exception,' and the Disability Rights Movement. *Paper presented at Cripping Neoliberalism: Interdisciplinary Perspectives on Governing and Imagining Dis/Ability and Bodily Difference*, October 8, 2010. Prague: Charles University.

Hall, M. C. 2019. Winter 2019 Edition. "Critical Disability Theory.„ In *The Stanford Encyclopedia of Philosophy*, edited by E. N. Zalta, California: Stanford University. https://plato.stanford.edu/archives/win2019/entries/disability-critical/

Hammad, T., and N. Singal. 2015. "Education of Women with Disabilities in Pakistan: Enhanced Agency, Unfulfilled Aspirations." *International Journal of Inclusive Education* 19 (12): 1244–1264. doi:10.1080/13603116.2015.1043962.

Hernández-Saca, D. I., L. Gutmann Kahn, and M. A. Cannon. 2018. "Intersectionality Dis/ability Research: How Dis/ability Research in Education Engages Intersectionality to Uncover the Multidimensional Construction of Dis/abled Experiences." *Review of Research in Education* 42 (1): 286–311. doi:10.3102/0091732X18762439.

Heyer, K. C. 2015. *Rights Enabled: The Disability Revolution, from the U.S., To Germany and Japan, to the United Nations*. United States: University of Michigan Press.

Hughes, B. 2012. "Civilising Modernity and the Ontological Invalidation of Disabled People." In *Disability and Social Theory*, edited by D. Goodley, B. Hughes, & L. Davis, 17–32. New York: Palgrave Macmillan.

Iqtadar, S., D. I. Hernández-Saca, and S. Ellison. 2020. "If It Wasn't My Race, It Was Other Things like Being A Woman, or My Disability": A Qualitative Research Synthesis of Disability Research." *Disability Studies Quarterly* 40: 2. https://dsq-sds.org/article/view/6881/5571

Jenks, A. B. 2017. "Rights Enabled or Disabled? the UN CRPD and Fixing Meanings of Disability in the Global South." Unpublished doctoral diss., University of Delaware.

Johansson, S. T. 2014. "A Critical and Contextual Approach to Inclusive Education: Perspectives from an Indian Context." *International Journal of Inclusive Education* 18 (12): 1219–1236. doi:10.1080/13603116.2014.885594.

Kayess, R., T. Sands, and K. R. Fisher. 2014. "International Power and Local Action: Implications for the Intersectionality of the Rights of Women with Disability." *Australian Journal of Public Administration* 73 (3): 383–396. doi:10.1111/1467-8500.12092.

Loper, K. 2010. *Equality Law and Inclusion in Education: Recommendations for Legal Reform*. Centre for Comparative and Public Law. http://dx.doi.org/10.2139/ssrn.1712710

Lord, J. E. 2009. "The UN Disability Convention: Creating Opportunities for Participation." *Business Law Today*, 19, 23. https://heinonline.org/HOL/LandingPage?handle=hein.journals/busiltom19&div=65&id=&page=

McCall, L. 2005. "The Complexity of Intersectionality." *Signs: Journal of Women in Culture and Society* 30 (3): 1771–1800.

Meekosha, H. 2011. "Decolonising Disability: Thinking and Acting Globally." *Disability & Society* 26 (6): 667–682. doi:10.1080/09687599.2011.602860.

Meekosha, H., and K. Soldatic. 2011. "Human Rights and the Global South: The Case of Disability." *Third World Quarterly* 32 (8): 1383–1397. doi:10.1080/01436597.2011.614800.

Meekosha, H., and R. Shuttleworth. 2009. "What's so 'Critical' about Critical Disability Studies?" *Australian Journal of Human Rights* 15 (1): 47–75. doi:10.1080/1323238X.2009.11910861.

Migliarini, V. 2017. *"Intersectionality and the Education of Dis/abled Asylum-seeking and Refugee Children in Rome: Criticism and Discrepancies of "Integration-style Inclusion" Models."* Unpublished Doctoral diss., Roma Tre University.

Migliarini, V., C. Stinson, and S. D'Alessio. 2019. "'Senitizing'migrant Children in Inclusive Settings: Exploring the Impact of the Salamanca Statement Thinking in Italy and the United States." *International Journal of Inclusive Education* 23 (7–8): 754–767. doi:10.1080/13603116.2019.1622804.

Misri, D. 2019. "Showing Humanity: Violence and Visuality in Kashmir." *Cultural Studies* 33 (3): 527–549. doi:10.1080/09502386.2019.1585465.

Muthukrishna, N., and P. Engelbrecht. 2018. "Decolonising Inclusive Education in Lower Income, Southern African Educational Contexts." *South African Journal of Education* 38 (4). doi:10.15700/saje.v38n4a1701.

Mutua, M. 2002. *Human Rights: A Political and Cultural Critique.* Philadelphia, PA: University of Pennsylvania Press.

Nath, A. 2019. "Camera as Weapon: Ways of Seeing in Kashmir." *Studies in Documentary Film* 13 (3): 268–282. doi:10.1080/17503280.2019.1672922.

Paris, D., and H. S. Alim. 2014. "What are We Seeking to Sustain through Culturally Sustaining Pedagogy? A Loving Critique Forward." *Harvard Educational Review* 84 (1): 85–100. doi:10.17763/haer.84.1.982l873k2ht16m77.

Peguero, A. A. 2009. "Victimizing the Children of Immigrants: Latino and Asian American Student Victimization." *Youth & Society* 41 (2): 186–208. doi:10.1177/0044118X09333646.

Perrigo, B. 2018. "Faces in the Darkness: The Victims of 'Non-lethal' Weapons in Kashmir." *Time,* September. https://time.com/longform/pellet-gun-victims-kashmir/

Ribet, B. 2011. "Emergent Disability and the Limits of Equality: A Critical Reading of the UN Convention on the Rights of Persons with Disabilities." *Yale Human Rights & Development Law Journal* 14: 155.

Rizvi, S. 2017. "Exploring British Pakistani Mothers' Perception of Their Child with Disability: Insights from a UK Context." *Journal of Research in Special Educational Needs* 17 (2): 87–97. doi:10.1111/1471-3802.12111.

Schulze, M. 2009. *Understanding the UN Convention on the Rights of Persons with Disabilities.* New York: Handicap International.

Singal, N. 2006. "Inclusive Education in India: International Concept, National Interpretation." *International Journal of Disability, Development and Education* 53 (3): 351–369. doi:10.1080/10349120600847797.

Song, Y. 2018. *"Schooling at the Intersection of Refugee Identity and (Dis)ability: Implications from North Korean Students with Refugee Backgrounds."* Unpublished doctoral diss., Syracuse University.

Stiker, H. J. 2019. *A History of Disability.* United States: University of Michigan Press.

Taylor, S. J., D. Ferguson, and P. M. Ferguson. 1992. *Interpreting Disability: A Qualitative Reader.* New York: Teachers College Press.

United Nations. 2006. "General Assembly." Convention on the Rights of Persons with Disabilities and Optional Protocol. https://www.un.org/disabilities/documents/convention/convoptprot-e.pdf

United Nations. n.d. *"Convention on the Rights of Persons with Disabilities (CRPD)."* https://www.un.org/development/desa/disabilities/convention-on-the-rights-of-persons-with-disabilities.html

United States Department of Labor's Bureau of International Labor Affairs. 2013. "Findings on the Worst Forms of Child Labor, Pakistan Moderate Advancement." https://www.dol.gov/sites/dolgov/files/ILAB/child_labor_reports/tda2013/pakistan.pdf

Voulgarides, C. 2018. *Does Compliance Matter in Special Education?: IDEA and the Hidden Inequities of Practice.* New York: Teachers College Press.

Wachsler, S. 2012. "Languaging Disability: Where Do 'Ability' and 'Dis/ability' Fit In." *Ability Maine.* https://www.abilitymaine.org/ArticleArchive/%22Languaging-Disability%3A-Where-do-%27Ability%27-and-%27Dis%2FAbility%27-Fit-In%3F%22

Walker, K. 2014. "Comparing American Disability Laws to the Convention on the Rights of Persons with Disabilities with respect to Postsecondary Education for Persons with Intellectual Disabilities." *Northwestern University Journal of International Human Rights* 12: 1. http://scholarlycommons.law.northwestern.edu/njihr/vol12/iss1/5

Winzer, M., and K. Mazurek. 2019. "UN Convention on the Rights of Persons with Disabilities. A Critique of Article 24 of the CRPD: Precedents, Polarized Paradigms, Flawed Contingencies." *World Studies in Education* 20 (2): 5–22. doi:10.7459/wse/20.2.02.

Index

Note: *Italic* page numbers refer to figures and page numbers followed by "n" denote endnotes.

Ability Profiling and School Failure (Collins) 81
ableism 12, 42, 43; Black families 42–45, 47–53; Black girls to address 51–52; in parent involvement 45; and racism 1–3, 5, 6, 12–14, 21, 32, 36n3, 41, 43–45, 47, 48, 51–53, 58–60, 62, 66, 68, 69, 80, 81, 86, 87, 98, 108, 130, 132, 133
'Ableism is Trash' 35, 37n8
'Access is Love' 35, 37n9
acompañamiento 95, 100–102
action-aware theory 107
action for equity pledge 115–117, *116*, 119
Ad Hoc Committee 125
advocacy trainings 23–24
Aguilar, C. 92, 95, 101, 103
Alim, H. S. 84, 124
Althusser, L. 92
American sign language (ASL) 21
American with Disabilities Act (ADA) of 1990 93, 124, 127, 129
Annamma, S. A. 4, 12, 36n2, 36n3, 59–61, 65
Antiracism and Universal Design for Learning (Fritzgerald) 84
Applied Behavioral Analysis (ABA) 70n3
Artiles, Alfredo 2
associative/courtesy stigma 18
autism spectrum disorder (ASD) 13
autoethnography 4, 14, 15

Baber, Lorenzo 27
'baby penalty' 4, 30–31
Baglieri, S. 60
Being Lazy and Slowing Down 34
Berne, Patty 35
Biklen, D. 64
BIYOC *see* Black, Indigenous, and Youth of Color (BIYOC)
Black children 13, 43, 52, 53n1
Black Disabled Art History 101 (Moore) 62
Black families 4–5, 11, 13, 41, 45–46, 52–53; ableism 42–45, 47–53; data collection and

analysis 46; focus on black girls' support needs 50–51; parent involvement 43; repositioning black girls and 46–50; socialization 43, 51, 52; *see also* parent involvement
Black girls: Black families focus on support needs to 50–51; relocation problem 47–49; repositioning 46–47; respond to racism and ableism 51–52
Black, Indigenous, and people of color (BIPOC) 30, 69, 96
Black, Indigenous, and Youth of Color (BIYOC) 128, 130, 136n3
Black parent 4, 5, 14, 24, 43, 46, 49, 51
Black parent involvement 43–44, 47; *see also* parent involvement
Black students 42, 43, 48, 49, 53
Black woman 14, 15, 17, 24
Blake, J. 13
Bochner, A. 15
Boda, Phillip 5
Broderick, A. 2
Brown, Keah 35
Brown, Lydia X. Z. 35
Brown, N. 29
Brown vs. Board of Education of 1954 16

Carter-Long, Lawrence 36n2
citizenship 6, 91–104
Civil Rights Movement 16
'Collaborating with Families of Individuals with Exceptionalities' 79–81
collaborative context 111–112
collaborative network development process *110*, 110–111, 116, 118–119
collective care 34–35
college-going process 99–101
Collins, K. M.: *Ability Profiling and School Failure* 81
Collins, P. H. 2, 53n1
colonialism 8, 36, 128, 135
Common Core State Standards 62

communication 21, 22, 48–51, 53, 79, 126
community care 34, 95
complex support needs 63–65
Connor, D. J. 12, 36n2, 36n3, 65; *Urban Narratives* 23
Convention on the Rights of Persons with Disabilities (CRPD) 59, 123–124, 129, 131, 134; Article 2 of 129; Article 6 of 133; Article 24 of 124, 125, 128, 132–134; Article 24(1) of 126; Article 24(2) of 126, 127; Article 24(3) of 126; Article 24(4) of 126; Article 24(5) of 126; challenges of intersectionality 129–130; critiques of 126; Global North legal influences 127–129; history of 125; as neoliberal project 127
Cooper, Anna Julia 2
Cowley, D. M. 3, 6, 64
Crenshaw, Kimberlé 2, 12, 28
Critical Deaf Theory (DeafCrit) 8n1
critical inquiry 109–111
critical parent engagement 53
Critical Race Theory (CRT) 1, 2, 28–30, 58–59, 65–66, 92
Critical Race Theory in Education: Major Themes in Education (Dixson) 2
CRPD *see* Convention on the Rights of Persons with Disabilities (CRPD)
CRT *see* Critical Race Theory (CRT)
cultural competence 6, 109, 111, 114, 115
culturally responsive teaching 6, 109, 115
Cultural Reciprocity and Special Education (Kalyanpur and Harry) 81

Deferred Action for Childhood Arrivals (DACA) 102
deficit-based discourses 4, 5, 22, 44, 63, 66, 77, 78, 80, 128, 132
disability(ies) 13, 16, 20, 93–94, 97, 102, 136n2; ableism and 60, 61; across socio-cultural groups 58, 59, 69, 108, 109, 111, 119; gender and 133, 134; high school students 97–99; intersectional experiences of 63, 126, 129–133, 135, 136n2, 136n3; medical model of 125; and race 1, 2, 4, 6–8, 14, 59, 66, 80, 92, 93, 95, 130, 133, 134; rights of people with 126; and rurality 80; services in special education 102, 103; social model of 123, 125, 133; students with 59, 61–62, 91–97, 101, 103, 108, 117, 118, 128, 129; women with 133; young boys with 134
disability identity 43, 60, 69, 127
disability justice 34–35, 95
disability services 35, 91–93, 96, 97, 102, 104
disability studies 58–59
Disability Studies and Critical Race Theory (DisCrit) 1–6, 12–14, 24n2–25n4, 29, 35, 45, 59, 77, 92, 94, 95, 100, 102–104, 107, 124, 130,

136n2; action for equity pledge 115–116, *116*; collaborative context 111–112; collaborative network development process *110*, 110–111, 118–119; data analysis 112; within disciplinary teacher education 65–70; equity lab 116–118; framework 36n2, 64, 65, 69, 70n4, 130, 132; integration of 67–69; intersectionality and 28; intersectional oppression erasure 131–132; material manifestations of 115–118, *116*; methodology *110*, 110–112; ontological erasure in 63, 64, 70n4; participants/stakeholders 111; positionality 108–109; and rural teacher residency 78–79, 83, 84, 86–87; tenet five 21, 95, 100, 102, 103; tenet four 63; tenet one 45; tenet seven 109, 114–115; tenet six 66, 86; tenets of 29, 36n3, 45, 51, 131, 134; tenet three 109, 114; tenet two 109, 113; theoretical framework 109–110; trustworthiness 112–113; and UNCRPD 130–131; and universal design for learning 78–86; work with pre-service teachers 115
disability studies in education (DSE) 60
Disability Visibility (Wong) 62
dis/abled Black girls 47, 49–50, 53
disabled people of color 15, 60–62, 69, 70n2, 131, 132
dis/abled students 7, 44, 68, 95, 96, 102, 114
disciplinary teacher education 65–68
DisCrit *see* Disability Studies and Critical Race Theory (DisCrit)
DisCrit-informed curriculum, in teacher education 60–63
documentation/documentación 92, 93–94, 102, 104, 104n1
Doharty, N. 17
Dolmage, Jay 95
Down syndrome 12, 18–19, 22–24
DuBois, W. E. B. 2
Dudley-Marling, C. 23

education 7, 13, 29, 50, 52, 59, 79, 110, 117, 119, 124, 126–128, 133–135; among social justice traditions in 61, 70n4; for children 41–44, 47, 53; racism and ableism in 2; *see also individual entries*
educational justice 59, 61, 62, 70n4
Education for All Handicapped Children Act of 1975 (Public Law 94–142) 16, 124
educators 5, 6, 41, 61, 75, 87n2, 92, 103, 104, 109, 111, 114, 116, 117–120
Eichelberger, S. 58
Elder, B. 8, 61
Ellis, Carolyn 14, 15
Ellison, Bradley Scott 3, 6
Ellis-Robinson, Tammy 6, 7
Engelbrecht, P. 128
English Language (EL) 93–96

INDEX

entitlement 99, 102, 125–126
Epstein, R. 13
equity lab 116; educational practice 117; equity standards 117–118; identity and experience 117
equity literacy 109, 117
equity standards 117–118
Erevelles, N. 64

FAFSA *see* Free Application for Federal Student Aid (FAFSA)
fear 95–96
Ferri, B. A. 12, 36n2, 36n3, 65
Forber-Pratt, A. 3
Fornauf, Beth S. 5, 7, 81
Foucault, M. 95
Free Application for Federal Student Aid (FAFSA) 99, 100, 102
Fritzgerald, A. 85; *Antiracism and Universal Design for Learning* 84

Geertz, Eugenie 8n1
gender identities 5, 30, 45, 59, 76, 82
Giles, Mark 27
Gillborn, D. 1, 13, 49
Glennon, Theresa 2
Global North 3; dis/ability activism in 124, 127, 134–136; legal influences on CRPD 127–129; special education in 129
Global South 3; dis/abilities in 124–125, 127, 130, 131, 134–136; morals and values of 124, 136n1
Gloria Ladson-Billings 17
Goffman, Erving 18
Gonzalez, T. 13
Gurn, A. 23

Hammad, T. 133
Handy, T. 59, 61
Harvard Educational Review (HER) 84, 85
Hathaway, Donny 16
healthcare practitioners 24
hegemonic power structures 61, 67, 132, 134, 136n6
Henryism 33–37n7
Hernandez-Saca, David 3, 6
Heshusius, L. 65
Hess, R. 18
heterotopias of deviation 95, 103
higher education 6, 28, 32, 33, 35, 36, 91, 92, 96, 101, 102
high school students: acompañamiento 100–102; disability and migratory status 97–99; documentation/documentación 102; liminality with citizenship 99–100; practical implications 103; research implications 103
Hooks, B.: *Teaching to Transgress* 62
Ho, Sandy 35

Howard, T. C. 58
Huber, Pérez 28
Hudak, G. 22
Hughes, Sherick 15
human rights discourses 6, 7, 34, 123–126, 130–135

IDEA *see* Individuals with Disabilities in Education Act (IDEA)
IEPs *see* individualized education programs (IEPs)
Immigrations and Customs Enforcement (ICE) 93
imposter syndrome 4, 32
inclusive education 59, 61, 63, 64, 125, 126, 128, 136n4
individualized education programs (IEPs) 21, 43, 92, 95, 97–100, 103, 108
Individuals with Disabilities Education Act (IDEA 2004) 42, 102, 108, 124, 127
inequities 2, 5, 6, 8, 42, 44, 49, 62, 64, 67, 75, 76, 79, 81, 84–86, 93, 103, 107–109, 111, 115, 117–119
information sharing 111, 113, 116
institutionalization 18, 60, 109, 112
intellectual disability 65, 69, 70n1
intersectional dis/ability 5, 6, 125, 129, 130, 132–136, 136n3
intersectional identities 36, 36n1, 60, 64, 77, 82, 115, 117, 118, 120, 129, 134
intersectionality 12, 28, 60, 67, 82, 129; challenges of 129–130; and Dis/ability Critical Race Studies 28
intersectional oppression 131–132, 134, 136
Iqtadar, Shehreen 3, 6–8

Johansson, S. T. 128
Jordan, June 70

Karma theory 127
Kihn, P. 22
King Thorius, K. A. 84, 85
Kirshbaum, M. 44
Kliewer, C. 64
Kozleski, E. 18
K-12 systems 6, 102, 103
Kulkarni, Saili 5, 7

Ladson-Billings, G. 85
Latina 4, 12, 14, 29, 31, 36n1
Latino/a family 15–16
Latinx 28, 29, 31, 35, 36n1
learning disability (LD) 13
legislation 16, 93
Leigh, J. 29
Leonardo, Z. 2
Lewis, T. L. 44
liminality 99–100

lived experiences 4, 17, 28, 29, 33–35, 64, 68, 109, 112, 113, 131, 135
local community center 11
Lorde, Audre 2, 29; *Burst of Light* 34
Love, Hailey 4, 5, 7
loving critique 6, 84, 124, 135

Marchand, A. D. 53
marginalization 2, 4, 28, 42, 45, 63, 67, 69, 81, 108
marginalized identities 12–15, 135
Mascio, Bryan 5, 7
Mayuzumi, Kimine 34
Meeting Families Where They Are (Harry and Ocasio-Stoutenburg) 20
meritocracy 17, 95
microaggressions 4, 14, 18, 29, 32, 132
Migliarini, V. 8, 61, 132
migratory status, high school students 92–94, 97–99, 102, 103
Miller, A. L. 65
Milner, H. R., IV 58
Mingus, Mia 35
Molina, A. 18
Moore, L. 35; *Black Disabled Art History 101* 62
Morrison, D. 60
mother-scholar of color 27–37
Moutz et al. (2015) 33
Mueller, C. 3
multidimensional identities 2, 36n3, 69, 109, 113, 117, 131, 136n2
multiply-marginalized Black families 41, 44, 45, 51
Muthukrishna, N. 128

National Longitudinal Transition Study 96
neoliberalism 33, 127
neoliberal norms 35
neoliberal university 28, 31–34
New York City high school: liminal experiences with citizenship 99–100; multilingual with disabilities in 96–99
New York City Public Schools 17
Nishida, Akemi 34
non-Black constituency 17
normalcy 14, 22, 24, 29, 36n3, 45, 66, 78, 80, 86, 87, 95, 130, 135
Nusbaum, E. A. 5, 62, 63, 65, 70n4
NVIVO software 99
Nyegenye, Sylvia 4

Ocasio-Stoutenburg, Lydia 4, 7
Okello, W. K. 29
Oliver 125
Ong-Dean, C. 13
ontological erasure 63, 64, 70n4
Osei-Kofi, Nana 27

Padía, Lilly B. 5–7, 91, 98–100, 102
Padilla, A. 3
Pakistan women with dis/abilities in 133, 134
parent advocacy 15, 18
parent involvement: racism and ableism in 45; shift away from 44; traditional conceptualizations of 41–43
Paris, D. 124
participants/stakeholders 111
Patel, L. 96
Pennington, J. 15
Petersen, A. J. 64
Philip, T. M. 61
Piepzna-Samarasinha, Leah Lakshmi 35
Plyler v. Doe (1982) 93, 94
police brutality 20, 75, 92–93
positionality 108–109
preservice teachers 5, 6, 59, 75–79, 109–111, 115
proactive socialization 51–52
P-12 students 60–61

Race, Ethnicity, and Education (REE) 1, 2, 7, 8
race/racism 12, 29, 60, 75, 81, 85, 93, 95, 137n7; and ableism 1–3, 5, 6, 12–14, 21, 32, 36n3, 41, 43–45, 47, 48, 51–53, 58–60, 62, 66, 68, 69, 80, 81, 86, 87, 98, 108, 130, 132, 133; Black girls to address 51–52; and disability 1, 2, 4, 6–8, 14, 59, 66, 80, 92, 93, 95, 130, 133, 134; disability and 59; in parent involvement 45
racial injustice 20
racial microaggressions 4, 29, 32
reasonable accommodations 126, 129
REE *see* Race, Ethnicity, and Education (REE)
reverse-mainstream preschool classroom 21, 25n5
Ribet, B. 129–131
RTR *see* rural teacher residency (RTR)
rural education 76–77
rurality 76–77
rural teacher educators 5, 76, 77, 84
rural teacher residency (RTR) 78–79, 83, 84; 'Collaborating with Families of Individuals with Exceptionalities' 79–81; improvement of 86–87; summer institute 81–84

sacrificio 4, 7, 30–31, 33, 35, 36, 101
Salamanca Statement 133, 136n5
Sarkar, T. 3
school-sanctioned parent involvement 44
schools/schooling: deservingness in 94–96, 100, 101, 103; as ideological state apparatus 93–95; norms 86–87; system for disabled students 68
science education 5, 65–68
self-care 33–34
self-categorization theory 108
self-determination 58, 59, 108, 113, 118
Shahjahan, Riyad 27, 34

INDEX

Singal, N. 133
social construction: with material realities 45; of race and ability 2, 7, 24n2, 36, 45, 51, 66, 67, 87, 114, 135, 136
social identities 18, 24, 28
socialization 31, 43, 51, 52
social justice 35, 58, 62–64, 67, 68, 70, 82, 83, 111
socio-cultural groups 58, 59, 69, 108, 109, 111, 119
special education 23, 43, 44, 50, 52, 58–62, 70n1–3, 76, 79–81, 85, 101, 118, 126, 129, 136n2, 136n4; citizenship status in 91–104; disability services in 102, 103; and disability studies 60; disproportionality in 65, 108; in Global North 129; for high school students 93–96; in K-12 schools 91–92, 96, 102; pre-service teachers 107–111, 113–115; programming 5, 96; students of color in 59, 132; traditional 63, 128
special educators 92, 114, 118
stakeholders 6, 109, 111–114
'staying power' of labels 22
Steinborn, M. L. 62, 63, 65, 70n4
stereotype threat 4, 32
stigmatization 18, 24
Stovall, David O. 27
students: with complex support needs 5, 59–61, 63–65, 68, 69, 70n4; with disabilities 59, 61–62, 91–97, 101, 103, 108, 117, 118, 128; with low-incidence disabilities 63, 64, 70n1
support-centered *versus* disciplinary-centered approaches 5, 49–50
systematic instruction 61, 63, 70n3

Tatum, B. 17
Taylor, S. R. 34
teacher education 3, 5–7, 58–70, 75–80; disciplinary 65–70; DisCrit-informed curriculum in 60–63, 69; tendency of 59
teacher educators 5, 60, 62, 75–77, 84, 86–87, 108
teacher preparation 62, 78, 109, 112, 115
Teaching to Transgress (Hooks) 62
tenets, DisCrit 1–2, 29, 36n3, 45, 51, 109, 131, 134; five 21, 95, 100, 102, 103; four 63; one 45; seven 63, 109, 114–115; six 66, 86; three 87, 109, 114; two 63, 66, 109, 113
testimonio 4, 28, 29, 35
Thompson, Vilissa 35
Tolbert, S. 58

Torres, Lisette 4, 7; *Write Where It Hurts* 30
traditional parent involvement 41–43, 50
traditional special education 63, 128
transition planning 96, 97, 100, 103
Traxler, Rachel Elizabeth 5–7, 91, 98
Trent, J. W., Jr. 60
Trump, Donald 52
trustworthiness 112–113
Tuck, E. 104

UNCRPD *see* United Nations Convention on the Rights of Persons with Disabilities (UNCRPD)
UN declaration of Human Rights 123–124
Undocumented Critical Theory (UndocuCrit) 92, 100, 101, 103
undocumented students 7, 92–97, 100–103
UN General Assembly (2001) 125
United Nations Convention on the Rights of Persons with Disabilities (UNCRPD) 6–7, 123, 125–126, 134; and disability critical race studies 130–131; intersectional oppression erasure 131–132
United Nations (UN) treaty 123
United States: daycare in 31, 36n6; immigration policies 92; rurality and rural education in 5, 76–77; rural teacher residency in 78–83; school system 92, 94; teacher education in 75–76; undocumented communities in 96
United States Department of Education Teacher Quality Partnership Grant 87n2
universal design for learning (UDL) 5, 7–8, 35, 76–86
urban education 77
Urban Narratives (Connor) 23

Vargas, Dior 35
vizibilzation 63–65, 67, 70n4

Waitoller, F. R. 84, 85
Walker, K. 129
whiteness 2, 17, 24, 36n3, 59, 60, 66, 67, 76–78, 80, 81, 96, 128, 132
white supremacy 59, 75, 84, 92, 109
Wilt, Courtney 4
Wong, A. 35; *Disability Visibility* 62
Write Where It Hurts (Torres) 30

Yang, K. W. 104

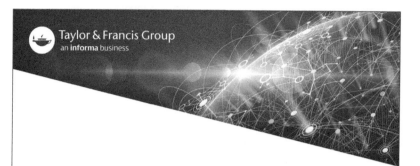